# Human Life in the Balance

# HUMAN LIFE
# IN THE BALANCE

## David C. Thomasma

Westminster/John Knox Press
Louisville, Kentucky

*To my family—*
*This book was written during times*
*that tested all our values*

Book design by Gene Harris

First edition

Published by Westminster/John Knox Press
Louisville, Kentucky

PRINTED IN THE UNITED STATES OF AMERICA

9   8   7   6   5   4   3   2   1

**Library of Congress Cataloging-in-Publication Data**

Thomasma, David C., 1939–
    Human life in the balance / David C. Thomasma. — 1st ed.
        p.    cm.
    ISBN 0-664-25059-9

    1. Life.   2. Creation.   3. Christian ethics.   I. Title
BT696.T46   1990
179′.7—dc20                                            89-16621

# Acknowledgments

Every author with a family feels compelled to thank them for their support. Mine was especially generous; not many families are as helpful to authors. I finished the manuscript in Florida at the winter home of my parents, Charles and Rosemary Thomasma, while my wife, Lyn, and my children, Piet and Lisa, suffered through some of the coldest weather Chicago has ever had. As my hometown tried to freeze all exposed flesh instantly, my mom and dad pampered me so that I could complete the book.

Other friends and colleagues also deserve my thanks. There are too many to thank all of them by name. I mention only those with whom I have discussed at length some of the ideas in this book: the late Bishop Carroll T. Dozier of Memphis; Professor Gerard A. Vanderhaar, S.T.D., and his wife, Janice, both of whom are active in peace work and are among my closest friends; Edmund D. Pellegrino, M.D., the John Carroll Professor of Medicine and Medical Humanities and Director of the Institute for the Advanced Study of Ethics at Georgetown University, with whom I have enjoyed a close friendship and have coauthored books; Glenn C. Graber, Ph.D., a friend and former colleague in medical ethics with whom I have also written books; Clyde and Sara Ebenreck, both Ph.D.'s, who have devoted their lives to human values and the care of the earth; Erich H. Loewy, M.D., and his wife, Bobbi, who is studying for her Ph.D. in philosophy and medical ethics, friends and colleagues alike and wonderfully gentle human beings; the Rev. Thomas and Alice McElhinney, who supported my efforts to publish this book; John Monagle, Ph.D., and his wife, Marjorie, whose love and support I have always counted on (it was John who suggested the book's title); and my Loyola colleagues, particularly Kenneth Micetich, M.D., the Rev. William Ellos, S.J., Ph.D., Patricia Marshall, Ph.D., and David Ozar, Ph.D. I thank all these friends for sharing their ideas with me and critiquing my own over the years. Of course I would like to thank Anthony Barbato, M.D., Provost of Loyola University Chicago Medical Center, for his support, and the Rev. Robert Harvanek, S.J., former chairman of the philosophy department, for reading an earlier version of this manuscript.

My editors at Westminster Press are to be lauded for their patience with me regarding this book. Keith Crim, Ph.D., and Janet Baker are particularly to be thanked. Their belief in its value meant a great deal to me during some difficult times.

Finally, my special gratitude to Karin Dean, administrative secretary, and Doris Kulpa, senior secretary of the Medical Humanities Program, who helped me assemble a book from a collage of ideas; Doris especially helped me with all the references. Joan Allman deserves thanks as well, for typing much of the manuscript under pressure as she simultaneously learned a new word-processing format.

*Chicago*                                                                              D.C.T.

# Contents

I set before you life or death. . . . Choose life.

Deuteronomy 30:19

Dr. Bruno Bettelheim reports the behavior of a nine-year-old autistic patient, a boy called Joey, who conceived that he was run by machines. "So controlling was this belief that Joey carried with him an elaborate life-support system made up of radio tubes, light bulbs, and a 'breathing machine.' At meals he ran imaginary wires from a wall socket to himself, so his food could be digested. His bed was rigged up with batteries, a loud-speaker, and other improvised equipment to keep him alive while he slept."

*But is this just the autistic fantasy of a pathetic little boy?* Is it not rather the state that the mass of mankind is fast approaching in actual life, without realizing how pathological it is to be cut off from their own resources for living, and to feel no tie with the outer world unless they are connected with the Power Complex and constantly receive information, direction, stimulation, and sedation from a central external source, via radio, discs, and television, with the minimal opportunity for reciprocal face-to-face contact?

—Lewis Mumford, *The Myth of the Machine*

# Introduction

In each of us, and in each of our political, social, and cultural institutions, lurks a monster. This Grendel, this monster that Beowulf fought, is our capacity to wound those we love, destroy our environment, and cannibalize our culture.[1]

Upon seeing the evil this monster is capable of, every age tends to regard itself as the worst.[2] Perhaps this is because the past is easier to romanticize than the present. Is our age any worse than other ages? Surely the fourteenth century, with its wars and plagues, uprisings and corrupt popes, mad leaders and unfair taxes, qualifies as one of the worst of times. Yet, as Barbara Tuchman suggests, the difference between that time and ours is one of degree, not of kind.[3] And ours is an age of a higher order.

Instead of plagues, we have the bomb. Mad leaders? Recall Hitler and Stalin. Wars? World Wars I and II, Korea, Vietnam, Iran/Iraq. Uprisings? This is the century of revolution; the America of 1776 and the France of 1789 pale in comparison. Our society is so violent the daily papers feature academics who specialize in analyzing violence and organized crime, as if the former were random and despicable and the latter were a stabilizing influence.[4]

Every age grapples with its own monster of destructiveness. But ours is on a different scale. The monster seems to have grown larger. Our century threatens to go backward—backward to a time when the concepts of equality and the dignity of the human person were less well developed. If we consider these concepts to be checks on the monster, stones rolled across his cave entrance, then we have every reason to be concerned now about protecting human life.

Without question, the greatest challenge facing us is the refinement of our traditional vision of the intrinsic value of human life. The challenge was bequeathed to us by the nineteenth century. During that time, enormous social and political changes occurred as a consequence of new technologies and industries based on them.

All reforms rested, however, on an appeal to the fundamental dignity of human beings. Despite the incredible fractures of rural life, society maintained its commitment to the value of human life, even though it often failed to manifest that commitment in its structures.

The twentieth century is another story. It is the first century in which massive destruction of cities and "innocent" citizens was authorized, sanctioned, and carried out. These actions were not just the desperate final agonies of warped dictatorships, they were also the actions of democracies dedicated to destroying the limitations on human dignity the dictatorships symbolized. Immense strides in technology were often accompanied by equally immense struggles to assert human rights, over and in the midst of that technology.

Thus the great issue of the twentieth century is the issue of the value of human life. Western society pays little explicit attention to the general issue, our politicians even less. We are so engaged in the skirmishes that it is difficult to step back and reflect on the larger engagement and its implications. But the issue will not go away. It will be bequeathed to the citizens of the world in the twenty-first century. We have only scratched the surface of implications of our technological revolution for the value of human life.

Yet it is an overwhelming political and social concern of citizens around the world. The perceived belligerent disregard for the value of human life by Western nations is the cause of public outcry in less-developed countries. It is the cause for violent revolutions, such as that in Iran, against the West and all it stands for. It is the cause for the gradual erosion of fundamental values in Western nations themselves. It is the fodder for extremist groups everywhere, who themselves violate the value of the lives of those who disagree with them. The reaction becomes the victim of the stand against which it reacts. Violent times seem to require violent solutions. There is little tolerance for differences. There is no unity in opposition.

Some important attention has been paid to particular instances of the clash between formerly cherished values about human life and new technologies. Most prominent is the field of medical ethics,[5] but business ethics and engineering ethics are not far behind. Consider the attention paid in the media, in academic institutions, and in the legislature to individual cases like *Baby Doe* and *Karen Ann Quinlan* and *Elizabeth Bouvia*. Educational programs have been instituted in universities and training courses. Societies have been formed to influence the legislature to create laws concerning the living will, so that individuals can exercise some control over the application of technology to their lives.[6] Additionally, public concern for the moral direction of technology has been a theme of twentieth-century literature and art. One thinks of Picasso's *Guernica* or Thomas Pynchon's

*Gravity's Rainbow*[7] or the writings of Hans Jonas and Martin Heidegger on the impact of technology on our culture and self-image.

Despite enormous concern about the value of specific human lives, the larger question itself is only now being addressed as a political and social problem, in the waning years of the twentieth century. In Sweden the Green party, a party that is focused on environmental issues, captured more seats than expected in an election in 1988, shortly after dying seals appeared on the coasts of countries near the North Sea and the Baltic Sea. Concern for dying dolphins along the American East Coast led to a study that blamed fish tainted by a poison called brevertoxin present in red algae. Greenpeace in the United States questioned the study.[8] It is hard to say what killed the seals near Sweden. Still later, politicians in the United States announced that the ultimate human values issue of the twenty-first century will be the greenhouse effect![9] One-issue coalitions and political action groups focus on the care of the elderly, the poor, the rights of women to have abortions, antiabortion amendments, and so on. Each of these concerns—real, valid, powerful, emotional concerns—is only a footnote to the larger question of human values and technology.

To that deeper question this book is devoted. It is not the first, nor will it be the last. The book grew out of a previously commissioned work that commemorated the tenth anniversary of the *Roe v. Wade* Supreme Court decision that permitted abortion until the third trimester. At that time I thought it appropriate to label this work an "Apology," using the term in the same sense as early Christian apologists who decided to construct a dialogue with Roman secular society, on issues that concerned them both, using reasonable arguments and persuasion as their tools.[10] It was roundly rejected by conservatives for not being the book they would write, one that would condemn modern society for permitting abortion and other violations of human rights. Pressure was brought to bear on the publisher, and the book was dropped because it seemed "soft" on too many pro-life issues. That increased my resolve to try again.

This new work is the result of that attempt. I hope it will contribute to a growing awareness of the fundamental values at risk in a modern technological society, and the need for political and social action on a united front, so that human beings themselves, while constructing a successful civilization, do not fall victim to it.

*Human Life in the Balance* is published at a time when our society is reexamining its commitments to the rights of women to decide about what happens to their own bodies because of concerns about the vulnerable forms of human life. Some hopeful signs also appear at this time among nations concerned to limit and reduce the awesome and negative effects of nuclear armaments. The book is intended to stimulate reflection on the life-destroying tendencies of our culture and to encourage a rededication to the dignity and value of human life.

I have written this book in the form of a defense of those values. While not identified with any pro-life movement, I am concerned, as are many reflective persons of all political and religious persuasions, that regard for the value of human life is in great jeopardy, both the unborn's and the mother's. Although not always affirmed in thought and deed, the value of human life is an important Judeo-Christian concept rooted in our social institutions and cultural heritage. If it is not constantly reaffirmed, it may well atrophy.

Why should this reaffirmation take the form of a defense? Several reasons suggested this approach. First, I wish to appeal to all human beings of goodwill, especially those who also have an open mind. While I am hopeful that many who already are committed to the ultimate value of human life will find much of value in this work, I also hope that persons who are puzzled about the great moral dilemmas of our time will find here an opportunity to reflect on their own ethical commitments. The book is intended equally for the dedicated and the distressed.[11] It is for those who have taken stands against war, against abortion, and against bigotry, and for those who are concerned, even alarmed, by the increasingly destructive blows inflicted on their fellow human beings by poverty, exploitation, arms races, genocide, infanticide, age discrimination, child abuse, and the neglect of the elderly.

A second reason is that the form is distinctly Christian. Early church fathers used it to confront the objections to Christianity first posed by pagans and, later, by heretics. Today we need defense of a Christian vision of life because our complex technological culture exalts relativism above that vision, at the expense of the dignity and value of each human life. Ambivalence and confusion result. Even as our political structures continue to accept without dispute the equality and value of every human life, the most extreme views about the value of human life are tolerated.

This approach also permits me to consider seriously the arguments of others, even those considered anathema by the mainstream, as Thomas Aquinas constructed his *Summa Contra Gentiles* as an explanation of Christian doctrine, which he clarified by contrasting it with opposing views.[12] Taking the arguments of others seriously, while being committed to a position oneself, is a rare virtue, one that seems to me to be lacking in the abortion debate particularly but also in other deeply divisive issues of our time. The abortion debate has been especially rancorous. It has been a history of politics without persuasion. Neither side has listened to the other, really listened to the other's concern for values that form the building blocks of the kind of society we want to make. As Larry Churchill and José Siman have argued, the abortion issue is fraught with misplaced arguments. The real issue in the debate is what kind of society we want to become.[13]

To help rectify the situation, this book will examine all the arguments for the concerns they reveal about the value of human life. No opinion offered in good faith will be dismissed with a mere rhetorical flourish or wave of the hand. The book will be ecumenical, irenic, and catholic—that is, universal—in its approach to the difficult disputes about the value of human life. The issues of abortion, euthanasia, infanticide, nuclear war, pollution, class struggles, and biological engineering should call forth from us our best side, our enthusiasm for life, not our monster of destructiveness.

A third reason why I took the approach of defending the value of human life is that, in its appeal to each reflective person, it does not argue from a revealed stance of a particular religion but rather from premises all might share. To convince someone of the truth of a point of view, one cannot start with essentially contested premises.

One reason why the positions of pro-lifers and pro-choicers cannot match is that they each start from assertions contested by the other. The pro-life position claims that a fetus is a human person, an innocent human life. But that is a point at issue. The pro-choice position claims that a woman's right to choose is more important than the life of a fetus. That is also a point at issue.

Thus I try to move beyond disputed claims to some cultural given with which many contesting parties might agree. The *method* of this work is theological; it argues from reasons of fittingness, not from rational proofs or scientific demonstrations. But the *content* is not theological. It does not derive its arguments from the teachings of one religion that are to be applied to some issue. Rather, it attempts to be persuasive by assembling a range of arguments and reflections that, cumulatively, would convince a reasonable, open-minded person. Thus Justin Martyr, a superb apologist and a father of the church, wrote his defense of Christianity to appeal to the Roman emperor and to philosophers. I write this book to appeal to reflective persons to consider the importance of creating a life-affirming society.

In so doing, I collect arguments from many disciplines. Most especially, the reader will find arguments from the history of religions, from philosophy, and from our political heritage. When discussing a theory of choice in the last chapter, I appeal to the Judeo-Christian heritage. That is as close to theology as the book comes.

Standing alone, none of the arguments in the book will be very convincing. But taken together, they summarize the fittingness of a dedication to the inherent value of human life. The point of view inimical to my thesis is that human life can be valued only externally. As such, it is subject to the whimsy of others.

I clearly take a stand for the value of human life. That is the final purpose of such a defense. Cardinal Newman employed this tactic in his *Apology*, explaining the course of his own life, the decisions he made and their motives and consequences.[14] Similarly, this book explains why it is important to make the decision to dedicate oneself to the value of human life and to accept its consequences. Accordingly, I will defend the thesis that in an age of madness it is best to act on the side of life.

But is our age so mad? Have you ever thought how apt the acronym for our defense policy is? Officially, our defense is based on "mutual assured destruction," or MAD. It is, indeed, mad.

Consider how each country in the world is forced to rely on the cool heads of the two superpowers, neither of which has been remarkable for its restraint in the past. As more countries build nuclear bombs as "deterrents," all of us will have more cool heads to worry about. Our MAD defense policy may be worth a chuckle at the bar, over a cold beer, but chuckling at this human foible is not enough.

The Rev. H. Lamar Gibble, an American Protestant clergyman, attending a conference on disarmament sponsored by the Russian Orthodox Church, is quoted as saying:

> Neither our system nor their system is demonic, but neither is angelic either. We've both been going down the same dead-end street. We've both been building terrible nuclear weapons. We've both been moving in an insane direction.[15]

Not only is MAD insane, it provokes the kind of twisted thinking that characterizes our century: Machines are more important than people. According to the SALT II proposals, it is more important to save bombs than lives. The neutron bomb has the wonderful advantage of destroying people but not buildings and material. Evacuation plans are proposed in which the survivors are to be selected to ensure a balanced labor force or for scientific and technical abilities. Citizens with low priority would be "the elderly, the infirm, the unskilled, the unessential." As Robert Kingsbury, a civil defense specialist who proposed this plan, said, "I fully accept the fact that the suggested plan is very unpalatable and truthfully rather sickening to think about, but I think it is realistic."[16]

It is interesting that what is "realistic" is an acceptance that scientific and technical skills, the very skills that helped create this madness in the first place, will be important for survival *after* a nuclear holocaust. Even more disconcerting is the frame of mind that accepts the nuclear destruction of human beings as inevitable. Our machines, and our bombs, are viewed as more important than our people.[17] This habit of mind, I suggest, is a vice, a vice born of the industrial age. It is no accident that the quotes I have cited on this topic all come from a single day's front section of the *Chicago Tribune*, my hometown newspaper. These and similar news accounts can be found in almost any large-circulation newspaper. Every day we read and digest and, eventually, swallow the idea that people are victims of their machines: that there is nothing we can do to reverse this process.[18] It is embedded in our thoughts and deeds. We chuckle when Shields and Yarnell mimic robots. That chuckle is laughter at our own slavery.

Of course, a policy of mutually assured destruction ensures twisted thinking. Robert Kingsbury actually assumes that there will be survivors of a nuclear war. But, as Physicians for Social Responsibility argues, physicians themselves must oppose nuclear weapons on the grounds of preventive medicine. Some people would survive the blasts but not the radiation effects. The ozone layer is significantly damaged by even a few mushroom clouds, such that the sun's rays would blind most creatures and burn vegetation. What difference, then, whether a scientist, a laborer, a housewife, an executive, or, heaven forbid, even a philosopher survives?

I have illustrated the madness of our age by citing just one feature of it, a policy of defense by assured destruction of the whole world. But proponents of this policy have no monopoly on the vice of twisted thinking. Did you ever wonder why many liberals who were so ferociously opposed to the Vietnam War are so blasé about abortions? Or why many of the persons opposed to abortions appear to be so conservative about defense issues? Against abortion but for war? For abortions but against war? On the face of it, it does not make much sense. Some philosophers are willing to face the consequences of their consistency, as if consistency were more important than human life. Thus, rather than question the truth of their thinking, if it leads them to support infanticide, they conclude that infanticide is morally permissible. For example, Victor Grassian says:

> The critics are right, however, that a consistent adherence to my mode of reasoning will have logical consequences which appear morally repugnant to some. For example, since I would consider late-term abortions morally permissible when a fetus is discovered to be severely deformed, and since I do not think that the act of birth should confer special rights to a fetus that it did not possess just prior to birth, I should, in all consistency, be willing to grant the moral permissibility of infanticide in certain circumstances. I am so willing.[19]

I once heard six philosophers argue with perfect logical consistency that future generations have no rights because they do not yet exist. These arguments were posed during an energy crisis. In that crisis, most citizens were making major choices about homes, work, driving habits, vacations, and the like on the basis of conservation. But what is conservation? It is, at least in part, an effort to ensure the quality of life of future generations. A newly married couple purchases insurance to protect children as yet unborn. A nation stockpiles energy resources against an uncertain future. Environmentalists guard our forests and waterways. As a people, we do, in fact, ascribe some rights to future generations. Thus the "logic" of the philosophers is not borne out by the way we actually live.

Another way that twisted thinking about the value of human life enters our culture is the ambivalence we have about capital punishment. Most criminologists admit that capital punishment does not deter violent crime, and many prisoners on death row have been victims of violently abusive families themselves. Most are sick. They surely deserve incarceration; but death? The Supreme Court is currently considering whether age mitigates crime, in an expected decision about juvenile killers and capital punishment.[20] This is important, since 29 persons on death row in 1989 were under eighteen when they committed murders. More important, what about the kinds of attitudes capital punishment produces in society itself? When Ted Bundy was to be executed in Florida on January 24, 1989, for his rape and murder of young women, a group of people took up vigil outside the prison. Some were university students who wanted to "catch" the execution before going to their morning classes; others were residents who for 11 years had wanted Bundy to die. They waved banners that said *Buckle up, Bundy, it's the law* and *Roast in peace.* When he died from having two thousand volts of electricity course through his body for one minute, they set off fireworks and cheered. This man was singularly evil, it seems, committing heinous crimes, but he did mention that most of the time he was drunk when he committed them.[21] Although no one would have sympathy with his deeds, one wonders whether this kind of retribution and the gleeful demonstrations of bystanders represent a society that cares about human life. For the challenge is not that we should sympathize with the victims and their families. Who would not? The challenge of being "for life" is being sympathetic to even the most vicious and downtrodden persons. Would that same crowd have been at Jesus' execution, blaming him for being the worst kind of criminal, a blasphemer, with banners waving, saying *He claimed to be the Messiah, but he cannot even save himself!* and *Bear down, Jesus, it's the law?*

These are reasons, then, why a defense of the value of human life is an appropriate way to greet the last decade of the twentieth century. Such a defense of the value of human life attempts to be reasonable; it takes the arguments of conflicting sides seriously; it uses a method of persuasion by arguments of fittingness; and it takes a stand that human life is more important than machines, than logical consistency, or than any other value.

To construct such value priorities requires a new vision and a new will about human life issues. It requires a change in Western values that uphold the subjugation and domination of our environment, downplaying the value of nonhuman living things. Worse, we are a throwaway society. We have little regard for long-term relations. One out of three marriages ends in divorce. Americans move frequently, exchanging houses, schools, neighborhoods, jobs, and friends like cards dealt in a bad hand of poker. Under the great seal of the United States, we might substitute the motto: Pitch, Toss, Trade!

These features are the dark side of an extraordinarily energetic and restless people. Add to these our penchant for rugged individualism and freedom, and, when faced with a choice between personal self-determination and the life of an unborn child, it is not surprising that the Supreme Court chose the former. We need much more emphasis on positive ways to relate to one another and to our environment.

The choice for human life requires a broadening of perspective, such that we care about all vulnerable human life, not just the unborn. Thus, lobbying and political action will have to encompass care for refugees, the aged, the poor, those oppressed, and those who are dying. As Joseph Cardinal Bernardin of Chicago points out often, religious bodies are not one-issue churches. The commitment to the value of life must extend from birth to death.

We must be able to present political solutions to difficult conflicts, such as an offer to care for, and adopt, all children born to persons who would have obtained an abortion, regardless of status or color.

I conclude the book with some moral principles that characterize persons who value human life. In so doing, I propose a theory of choice as a means for deciding issues in which major values about human life conflict. The theory of choice leads to an ethics of discretion, which closes the book. In short, limitations on the value of human life must come from one's voluntary acceptance or choice of those limitations, if external forces are not to override our own dignity.

In this introduction, I have posed the problem of twisted thinking that subjects the value of human life to other values. Sufficient evidence has been presented, I hope, to warrant agreement that we live in a mad world. Our monster is still at large. As the Nobel Prize–winning American author Saul Bellow says in *Henderson, the*

Rain King, "In an age of madness to expect to be untouched by madness is itself a form of madness."[22]

While we do well, then, to recognize the monsters of the age, that does not mean we have to be pessimists. There is some evidence that a conservative, rigid public policy era is now eroding. In fact, this book rests on the presupposition that we can, may, and must intervene to alter the future, to bring about individual happiness and harmonious social relationships. I have not been blessed with the eighty-one years and golden grace which suffused René Dubos's deathbed testament celebrating life with warmth and optimism. But I agree with this Pulitzer Prize–winning bacteriologist's assessment of our relationship to life. He was "more convinced than ever that life can be celebrated and enjoyed under the most trying and humble of circumstances." He thought we failed to take advantage of or fully comprehend our innate ability "to appreciate the simple wonders of life" because of the disenchantment and disarray of life in a complex technological age. "In human affairs," he said, "the *logical* future, determined by past and present conditions, is less important than the *willed* future, which is largely brought about by deliberate choices."[23]

These convictions, convictions born of years of study and writing, years of observations and reflections, led Dubos to state:

> A key to overcoming the passivity born of pessimism is to remember that the really important problems of our times are not technical. They originate in our thoughts, our uncertainties, or our poor judgment concerning parascientific values.[24]

Shortly after he wrote those words, he died. The fact that this testament appeared as an editorial in an airline magazine shows how much all of us hunger for some solution to our problems, some solution that generates a respect for human life.

This book is dedicated to strengthening our "poor judgment" about values, particularly the value of human life. I hope that readers will find it helpful in forming, or transforming, their own convictions.

# PART ONE

# The Challenge
# of Preserving the Value
# of Human Life

# 1

# The Meaning of
# "The Value of Human Life"

The person is the measure and criterion of goodness or fault in every human manifestation.

—Pope John Paul II

Words and ideas are important. But they can become confused. Sometimes a word carries an idea we do not intend. Sometimes our ideas cannot be communicated in tired phrases. At other times, our words carry emotional content that inhibits another person's ability to hear what we are saying.[1] Or, we may give an old word a new meaning to shoulder. This chapter is about the interplay of words and ideas. Without clarification of this interplay, a statement that one respects "the value of human life" will be virtually meaningless.

First, I will discuss words and ideas, then the importance of context in understanding words and ideas, and finally the meaning of the phrase "human life has value."

## Words and Ideas

For the most part, our words do a creditable job of carrying our ideas. Because of this first-rate job, we can be caught off guard when new ideas are given flesh in old words, new words are coined for old ideas, and old words are dumped into a brand-new basket. Some examples of this will help demonstrate the problem of talking about the value of human life.

One example of new ideas and old words is Franklin Roosevelt's effort, in his first presidential campaign, to describe his vision of a way out of the Depression. His new, and now contested, idea was to involve government more directly in the control of the economy, the conduct of corporations, the regulation of banking, the planning of crops, and the like. The vision was radical. It had been voiced previously only by socialists and communists. Yet Roosevelt's idea, unlike theirs, called for a partnership between government and industry rather than a wholesale takeover of industry by government. It was an idea later to be called the New Deal.

The words first used to describe this vision were "a concert of interests." Roosevelt used the term in an opening campaign speech. They were old words. The phrase could have been used to describe a concerto, from which a "concert" derives; they could have described a musical happening, a marriage, a form of American democracy. Roosevelt's talk, however, made the meaning clear. To his audience, the words sounded communistic. As a consequence, he never used them again.[2]

Other examples of old words for new ideas come from the ongoing diplomatic efforts to control arms. The acronyms SALT (Strategic Arms Limitation Treaty) and START (Strategic Arms Reduction Treaty) are part of our everyday language. Neither salt nor start, they symbolize, like a flag, enormously important human values on an international scale, values such as peace, freedom, harmony, lack of fear, self-determination, and respect for national boundaries. These old words portray the new ideas with a kind of efficient crispness we admire.

More complicated examples can be culled from debates about medical ethics issues. These are more complicated because they involve a twist from old, benign words to new, morally caustic ideas. Euthanasia and abortion are examples. "Euthanasia" originally meant a "good death."[3] Recently it has come to mean to kill someone or something in its own best interests. One euthanizes a dog "to put it out of its misery." In the Greek era, killing someone out of kindness was a virtue, as it was among Native Americans. The misery was not only physical.[4] It could also be psychological, such as suffering a loss of face. Today, however, the word has become emotionally laden and tied to burning ethical issues. For this reason, it is prefaced by "active" and "passive" to denote the sophisticated distinction between killing and letting die, between acting and refraining, between directly and indirectly killing a person.[5]

New medical technologies such as respirators and cardiac perfusion devices have created a brand-new problem:[6] We can often control when and by what means a person will die, even while death is imminent.[7] This creates an opportunity for a new kind of indignity, what Eric Cassell calls humiliation.[8] The indignity arises because others now have power, power provided by technology, over the most intimate of all of our acts, the act of dying. We ask what should be done when doctors "play God."[9]

Thus a new idea, that of controlling the time and means of death, was clothed in an old word, euthanasia, because we still want to be kind. If one does not clarify one's meaning, however, the use of the term can be confusing. To people who have not read the articles in newspapers and magazines, or watched the specials on television, talk about euthanasia of the old and sick can sound as though one proposes to put them away, like tired, worn-out pets.[10] Their reaction is instinctive. Horror.

Admittedly, the clarification of words is only the first step in trying to work out the serious and difficult moral problems regarding the value of life. They may never be worked out to our satisfaction. As Alasdair MacIntyre, a highly respected contemporary moral thinker, expresses this problem,

> It is an essential feature of contemporary moral debates that they are unsettleable and interminable. . . . Because no argument can be carried through to victorious conclusion, argument characteristically gives way to the mere and increasingly shrill battle of assertion with counter assertion.[11]

Despite this reservation, some progress is made among disputants merely by clarifying that about which they disagree. Often they find some common ground.

Examples of new words for old ideas also abound. Politicians are prone to use this ploy, trying to make it sound as though fresh and invigorating winds are sweeping through the White House or on Capitol Hill, when, in fact, business is being conducted as usual. Thus "communism" was a new word coined to express the ancient requirement of communal life—holding all property in common. Eastern religious monks practiced it. Jesus might have required it for discipleship. The early Christian church required it. American cults like the Shakers and the Oneida community practiced it. In coining the word, communists hoped to convey a new, secular meaning for an ancient religious idea.

The use of the old idea–new word ploy in politics can take the form of propaganda. George Orwell warned about the politicization of language in his *1984*[12] and in *Animal Farm*.[13] The latter, especially, is a satire about the follies of communism.

Thus one might call an attempt to line up the peasants a "five-year plan," making this attempt sound rational and innovative. "Redistribution of wealth" sounds interesting, while "robbing from the rich" denotes foul play. "Resettlement camps" sounds verminous, while "political education seminars" sounds just fine.

Communists and others given to dictatorial rule have no monopoly on manipulating language. During the war over the Falkland Islands, it struck me that English-language papers used the English names for the islands and the towns, subtly suggesting thereby that Argentina had no claim on the territory. Meanwhile, the Argentinians referred to the islands as the Malvinas and named the towns in Spanish.

Women, blacks, and Hispanics have experienced firsthand how language can be a powerful force in subduing whole groups of people. Most publishers now recognize the legitimacy of removing sexist and racist language from books and newspapers. Through the choice of words, also, the note of sanction can be eliminated from terms used in political disputes. For instance, the United States continues to wrestle with the issue of illegal aliens and refugees from Central America, primarily because they take away some of the lower-end jobs from the highest percentage of unemployed citizens. The latter would clearly seem to have a right to apply for these jobs ahead of illegal aliens. Therefore persons in favor of treating illegal aliens *as if* they were citizens prefer to use the phrase "undocumented workers" or some other creative term. This phrase suggests that all that is wrong is some bureaucratic foulup resulting in the workers' not getting the papers they needed. This is quite a different matter from entering a country illegally. By creating this new term, the aliens' advocates avoid the opprobrium built into the phrase "illegal alien," which darkly colors the issue of the workers' status.

The Supreme Court ruled on June 15, 1982, that the children of illegal aliens have a right to public education on the grounds that they should not be punished for the misdeeds of their parents.[14] This ruling, no doubt, formed the basis for future claims on food stamps, health care, and other goods as well as the subsequent legislation establishing the possibility of citizenship. The status of the workers no longer became illegal. It certainly removed the opprobrium of "alien." A new vocabulary of citizenship emerged.

Many of the disputes about the value of human life—disputes about the morality of abortion, the death penalty, war, conscription, euthanasia, and nontreatment of defective newborns—are riddled with emotionally charged language. They parallel the interplay of word and idea I have discussed so far. For example, attitudes and political camps are formed around words like "fetus" (pro-choice language), "unborn child" (pro-life language), "defective newborn" (pro-choice about treatment), "special newborns" (pro-treatment), "senior citizens" (pro-aging rights), and so on.

I suggest that the words in which we couch our discussion of moral issues respecting the value of human life become so rapidly politicized that it is all but impossible to have a rational discussion. Who in the world can be against choosing? Who wants to be labeled as being against life? Yet when a side is chosen, there is no retreat. Everything is either/or. Labels fly. Reason never gets off the ground.

As reader G. R. Paterson notes in a letter to the editor in the *Chicago Tribune*,

> Political manipulation of language interferes with clear thinking and should be resisted. Sound public policy is thwarted when issues are discussed in deliberately evasive and murky language and when things are not called by their true names.[15]

This politicization takes a perfectly good word, dribbles it down the court, and slam-dunks it in a totally new basket. Words are taken to stand for political positions rather than for ideas. The following are some examples:

For persons without a knowledge of the Nazi motives, the campaign for *Mutter und Kind* in pre-World War II Germany sounded a great deal like current religious and political concerns for the institution of the family. While "mother" and "child" are two of the most ancient words in any language, in the Nazi campaign they were used in a tricky way to suggest a form of patriotism. Even trickier, they actually were used to represent not the traditional values but something totally different—the purity of Aryan racial stock and its propagation. The program was actually one in which racially pure women were impregnated with the sperm of certified Aryan males so that a new race of superpersons would emerge.

A second example of using words to stand for something only remotely related to the concept is the transformation of the word "gay." Presumably through its connotations of debonair, with some sense of flair or abandon, it has been changed from a synonym for "happy" to a political moniker for the rights of homosexuals.

A third example of a politicized word or term is the code name used for the strike on June 7, 1982, by Israelis into Lebanon. The strike force consisted of sixty planes which bombed Beirut, hundreds of tanks, and twenty thousand men. The Israeli object was to capture Palestine Liberation Organization (PLO) strongholds in southern Lebanon and to wipe out the PLO entirely. The code name was "Peace for Galilee."[16] Peace? Hardly. With the strike, the Israelis violated a U.S.-negotiated cease-fire, invaded another country, jeopardized the uneasy peace then existing in the Mideast, alienated world opinion, turned sixty thousand residents into refugees, and created a climate for eventual retaliation by the PLO. Retaliation for attacks on Israeli border towns and an assault on an Israeli ambassador in England, supposedly by the PLO, was ostensibly the motive for the invasion in the first place. Funds were raised throughout the world for supporting this war under the name "Peace for Galilee Tax." Only after ten more cease-fire violations and the August encirclement and bombing of West Beirut, was the personal representative of the President to the Middle East at that time, Philip Habib, able to have the surviving PLO members dispersed to other Arab countries. This was not a "strike." It was a war. Years later the ramifications of the exercise of such power continue to haunt the peace process.

It would be hard to say who was right or wrong in this case. The animosity goes back to the biblical era. It is at least clear, however, that bombing and invasion are not acts of peace. Similarly, given the volatile Mideast environment, it is equally clear that initiating hostilities will not achieve an end to hostilities. Although peace is much more than a lack of hostilities, such a lack is an essential condition. The word "peace" itself has been violated in this usage.

I have offered some examples of the misuse of words in the major arenas of human life. We have seen that the interplay of word and idea can be tricky. Almost anyone can manipulate words for political aims. Several conclusions are possible from the reflections I have offered.

First, the same words may represent different ideas and persuasions. The person next to you at a rally, pro or con anything, may not actually stand for all the same things you do. For example, women were disappointed and angered when the men with whom they worked for civil rights for blacks did not recognize many of the same rights for women.

Second, in debates about the value of human life, one should be wary of the politicization of language. While it is laudable and necessary to stand up for your beliefs, it is neither laudable nor necessary to permit those beliefs to be manipulated by politicians for their own gain. Nor is it laudable or necessary to try to force these beliefs on others who do not share them.

Third, once a belief enters a political process, the idea behind the belief may be unutterably altered for the worse. Just because civil rights movements were able to achieve gains for those oppressed by prejudice in this country, it does not follow that a similar movement on behalf of the unborn or animals will achieve the same results. The religious and constitutional bases for civil rights were so clear, and the methods of nonviolent resistance so noble, that the movement, over time, took on an inexorable quality. With respect to the unborn and animals, the religious and constitutional questions are precisely what is at issue.

Fourth, because of the interplay of word and idea, then, it is better to debate and discuss issues thoroughly for twenty to fifty years before acting on them. This is not an excuse for inaction. Rather, it is meant to respect the dignity of people who disagree about an important issue relating to the value of human life. Opinions need to be heard. Ideas and words need to be sharpened. When the religious, philosophical, and legal values of a concept are contested, the forming of ad hoc political movements around the concept for and against will do nothing to clarify the matter. It will not achieve the desired objective, because persons who disagree want respect as well. To steamroll a large group, or even a minority, by passing laws forbidding or permitting this and that will actually destroy the climate of respect for human life that a nation must uphold. I suspect that pro-life, pro-choice, pro-ERA, and stop-ERA all fall into this category of jumping the gun on a contested issue. Persuasiveness can lie not only in words but in deeds. What conduct does respect for life or respect for choice lead to?

To carry this point one step farther: the civil rights movement acted against violations of a constitutionally recognized liberty whose origins also lay in our religious heritage—all persons are created equal. By contrast, pro-life crusades are acting against violations *of their own beliefs* without having successfully argued that these beliefs are guaranteed rights in the Constitution or commonly held in the Judeo-Christian heritage.

As a consequence of jumping the gun, issues become virtually unresolvable. The political process is used to test ideas before they have been clarified in philosophical, theological, legal, sociological, and psychological debates. Thus the Supreme Court ruling allowing states to draft laws permitting abortion during the first trimester explicitly cited the lack of agreement among theologians about the origin of life as a reason for its judgment. Over a decade after *Roe v. Wade,* more is known about the development of neurons in fetuses, and the possibility of pain, but no further progress has been made on the issue of the personhood of the fetus. Perhaps the "personhood" issue is not the real issue. The real issue is whether or not we wish to be a society that protects its most vulnerable citizens. And if so, what can we do about the rights of women to control their own bodies? Should they just be ignored?

The merits and the demerits of a position are often judged on the basis of the number of persons at rallies rather than on the truth of the matter. This number may reflect the organizing skills of a movement but may not (and probably does not) represent any clear-headed thinking about the matter at hand.

Finally, politicizing language guarantees that people will assemble around slogans that do not do justice to the cause, and that opponents will suffer an almost ridiculous abridgment of their ideas. People are not really antiabortion, they are for the value of developing human life. People are not really pro-choice as much as for the value of developing human life. People are not really antipeace, they are for the value of defending human life and its freedoms. People are not really antiwar, they are for the value of defending human life and its freedoms.

Without washing away the real disagreements among people, I do want to emphasize that disagreements are often misplaced. They may turn not only on fundamental values about human life but also on critical concepts like "potential" in the abortion debate, "defense" in the peace debate, "quality of life" in debates about treating the aged and dying with respect, and "equality" in the women's rights movement.

The ultimate reason that interplay of word and idea is so tricky, so subject to abuse, is that the context in which the words and ideas arise helps determine the meaning they will carry when heard by others. Major philosophers and the theologians in the twentieth century, thinkers as diverse as Ludwig Wittgenstein and Maurice Merleau-Ponty, have grappled with the role of context related to languages and ideas.[17] My exploration will focus on the way the context is a *belief* about the value of human life.

## Context

Interplay of word and idea is simultaneously rich and confusing because the exchange takes place in a *context*. This is especially true with respect to the words and ideas that swirl like dust in human life debates. Consider the terms in the chart below. They are selected from such debates to show the meanings one can attach to them, depending upon one's context.

|  | *Liberal* | *Conservative* | *Neutral* |
|---|---|---|---|
| **Body count** | An abhorrent reminder of the deadly disrespect war pays to human life. | A good mechanism for determining which side is winning a war. | A way of telling how many people came to a concert? |
| **Fetus** | An excellent, descriptive word used to describe a postembryo but prebirth state in the womb. The term is helpful because it does not "weigh" the fetus as equal in value to a fully grown human being. | An abhorrent and deadly term used to describe prebirth human life in order to rob it of its personal status and inherent worth. | A biological description of a stage in the development of the mammalian life cycle. |

| | Liberal | Conservative | Neutral |
|---|---|---|---|
| **Sexist** | A person, usually male, who refuses to recognize the equality of the sexes. | A term used to describe persons who hold dear traditional family structures and women's roles in society. | One who likes sex? |
| **Racist** | A person who is biased against the equal rights of all human beings, independent of race. | A potential hero who upholds the separation of races and their purity. | One who likes races? |
| **Euthanize** | To euthanize is to perform an ultimate act of kindness toward a human being, by not prolonging his or her death through medical or technological means. | A euphemistic term used in place of "kill"; part of a domino effect once abortion is permitted. | To put an animal out of its misery. |
| **Antinuclear** | A term used to describe high-minded people concerned about the future of the human race and the exploitation of the environment, who oppose nuclear power and/or nuclear war. | A term used to describe a bunch of softheads who resist the best means of energy and best deterrent for war. | A person who is against a basic building block of the atom? |
| **Pull the plug** | A courageous action taken so as not to prolong the act of dying. | The opposite of acting at all times to save human life. | What one does when one finishes a bath. |
| **Abortion** | An unfortunate but sometimes necessary activity to preserve one's freedom of choice and right to privacy. | An evil second to none, because it destroys the life of completely helpless unborn children. | A spontaneous miscarriage occurring with regularity in the natural process of gestation. |

| | Liberal | Conservative | Neutral |
|---|---|---|---|
| **Gay** | A popular term for an offbeat but ancient sexual preference. | A popular term for unhappy, psychologically warped individuals who love persons of their own sex. | Happy, cavalier. |

In charting the simplistic descriptions of terms based on one's context, I have actually also done violence to the categories of "liberal," "conservative," and "neutral." A chart is, after all, a characterization. Such a chart, however, does demonstrate the way in which context, one's life, one's acquaintances, one's influences, color the meanings of words. The words, and the ideas they represent, take on a volatile character because the color is an evaluation.

Put another way, each of the words represented in the chart is "heard" differently by different people. Each is a clue to the position the speaker is presumed to have taken, even if he or she has not actually taken any position. Imagine for a moment the person who sincerely wants to explore the abortion issue and who calls the creature in the womb a fetus. He or she would be judged by a pro-life audience as already positioned in the pro-choice camp. Imagine, too, a sincere individual speaking before the National Organization for Women who uses sexist references in his or her speech. Rotten tomatoes might fly.

How, then, do words and ideas carry valuative connotations? The neutral meanings of words are easy enough to discern. What is it that adds the "good" or "bad?" It is belief.

Because one person believes abortion is wrong, the neutral usage takes on negative coloring. Because another believes that war is wrong, the neutral term "body count" takes on gruesome meaning. The interpretation of words and ideas (in this case, a moral evaluation) stems from moral persuasions arrived at by individual persons.

Although rational arguments can be employed to *support* beliefs, they are almost always insufficient to counter beliefs. That is why arguing about human life issues is at once so important and so frustrating. In fact, beliefs rarely change. They are deeply rooted moral evaluations. Only new and disjunctive experiences can alter them, as, for example, when the devastation of battle, seen on the evening news, changed many Americans' beliefs about the Vietnam War. Stirring songs, martial airs, and patriotic flag-waving shimmered like a mirage when paraplegic and quadriplegic boys were carried off the airplanes. Yet twenty years later, politicians in the 1988 presidential campaign effectively used patriotism and flag-waving as symbols of loyalty to the United States.

Beliefs can be distinguished from knowledge, as Plato noted long ago. A belief is a product of persuasion, he argued in the *Gorgias*. But so, too, is knowledge. The reasoning that produces knowledge also produces truth, such that, within the limits of the discipline involved, knowledge is understood to mean truth. Belief, on the other hand, can be true or false. It is the kind of evidence produced in a law court, in which persuasion leads to a belief that a person is innocent beyond reasonable doubt, even though one does not "know" this in a factual, scientific, or demonstrable fashion. To say, then, that the value of human life is a belief is congruent to saying that it cannot be demonstrated scientifically. It is a first principle of ethics and politics, derived from metaphysical convictions about the nature of the person and society, from which other reasoning in these fields is derived. Thus Socrates asks Gorgias, a teacher of rhetoric:

SOCRATES: If anybody were to say to you, "Can there be both a false belief and a true, Gorgias?" you would, I think, say that there is.

GORGIAS: Yes.

SOCRATES: But can there be both a false and a true knowledge?

GORGIAS: By no means.

SOCRATES: Then it is obvious that knowledge and belief are not the same.

GORGIAS: You are right.[18]

It is important to note, however, that true beliefs are not to be taken lightly. They are arrived at after a great deal of reflection and are certainly not capricious. In fact, it may be true that authentic knowledge is rarely obtained and that, for most of our lives and in most of its situations, we operate on the basis of beliefs that we continually refine as new positions and new data become available to us. Hence Gorgias tries to show that rhetoric is more valuable than knowledge in persuading others by citing his visits with his brother, who was a physician:

GORGIAS: I have often, along with my brother and with other physicians, visited one of their patients who refused to drink his medicine or submit to the surgeon's knife or cautery, and when the doctor was unable to persuade them, I did so, by no other art but rhetoric.[19]

Plato's thinking on the question of true beliefs is also found in the *Theaetetus*, where Theaetetus proposes that knowledge is true belief. Socrates then answers:

SOCRATES:      You will find a whole profession to prove that true belief is not knowledge.

THEAETETUS: How so? What profession?

SOCRATES:      The profession of those paragons of intellect known as orators and lawyers. There you have men who use their skill to produce conviction, not by instruction, but by making people believe whatever they want them to believe.[20]

This discussion, including the example of courtroom behavior, leads Theaetetus to draw out the definition by stating that he learned that knowledge is true belief coupled with an account. Where no account could be given of a thing, there could be no knowledge.[21]

These references to Plato's thinking (and perhaps Socrates') on the nature of true beliefs and knowledge directly relate to the methodology of this chapter and of the whole book. My purpose is to provide an account that will help persuade those undecided or those who have decided for the wrong reasons that a commitment to the inherent value of all forms of human life (not just human persons) is required by our religious, philosophical, and political values. This account helps produce a belief. The belief is true, if you are persuaded by the evidence I produce. But it is not scientific knowledge. This means that those who do not agree with the conclusions of this book, for whatever reasons, are not lacking in data or in perspicacity but are lacking in the persuasion that those who do agree may acquire.

If what I have presented is true to any degree, then it is hardly likely that rational reflection alone will convince people who have taken a stand on the value of human life to alter their opinions, unless some inconsistency between belief and experience is bared.

I have suggested that the array of disputants around human life issues such as abortion, euthanasia, war, and racism tempts us to despair about ever reaching some consensus. I also have suggested, however, that many of the debates are misplaced because of fuzzy thinking, sloganism, politicization of language, and the like. The rest of the book will present a case that the value of human life ought to lie at the center of our moral concern for the twenty-first century. The case rests on the opinion that beneath the disparate positions taken on specific strategies to protect (or seemingly destroy) belief in the value of human life, there is a common territory of concern for this value.

Thus, despite the diatribes, people on opposite sides of volatile issues (nuclear power, equal rights for women, limited nuclear war, guns or butter, the status of minorities) may very possibly share a profound commitment to the value of human life. This shared commitment is lost in the inability really to hear what the other is saying.

The valuative tyranny of words and ideas has created a static-filled shield. No clear transmission of concerns can penetrate this interference.

Not everyone shares a commitment to the value of human life. But, on the possibility that more do share it than not and that more of us ought to share it if we do not, I now turn to a consideration of the meaning of the value of human life.

To argue that the value of human life must be protected carefully in the coming age, I must first describe what we might mean by it. That concern occupies the following section of the chapter.

### Value and Human Life

Many trends question the ultimate value of human life. Advancing technology, the ecological crisis, and the world political scene call into question our Western cultural assumptions of the value and worth of every human being. Virtually every European philosopher, and many distinguished American philosophers as well, since World War I, have seen that the question of human worth is at the heart of all cultural, social, political, and scientific crises. Most recently, Karol Wojtyla (now Pope John Paul II) has argued:

> Twenty years of discussion on the world outlook have made it clearer that it is not cosmology or philosophy of nature, but precisely philosophical anthropology and ethics which are at the center, contributing to the great and fundamental controversy on man.[22]

The moral response to the question of the value of human life in technological society has been succinctly stated by the American philosopher Hans Jonas:

> Care for the future of mankind is the overruling duty of collective human action in an age of a technical civilization that has become "almighty," if not in its productive then at least in its destructive potential.[23]

Given these insights, it is insufficient to discuss the serious debates about human life apart from assumptions about the value of life. Nonetheless, to say that human life has value sounds like a cliché. This is because the phrase is essentially a contested one. Most people agree that our moral, political, and religious systems require an assumption of the equal worth of every individual life. What this means, in practice, is contested to such an extent that the very meaning of the phrase depends on which ad hoc group is eager to claim the appellation "defender of the value of human life."

"The value of human life" is a contested phrase because the terms "value" and "human life" are metaphysically muddled. Few people have successfully defined either. Moreover, the assumption of individuals' equal value is just that, an assumption based on religious, philosophical, and political beliefs. It is a starting point, an ultimate principle. It can be defended. My defense in this book rests on considerations that merit attention in any discussion of human life issues. They might also apply in other contexts.

Just as the various terms, words, and ideas in the human life debates were explored in previous sections of this chapter, the word "value" and its meanings need some clarification. This is necessary before going on to the rest of the argument.

Values can be seen as weights assigned to things and to attitudes. The origin of the term "value" is economic, and it was used to indicate the relative cost of an item. Rapidly, however, it was extended to denote the quality of a product, a commitment to a thing, action, or person ("I value him highly") and a philosophical quality of moral principles (e.g., one value is respect for persons). When a term is stretched to this extent, it becomes harder to make concrete sense out of the phrase "the value of human life," and one is tempted to substitute the word "cost" for "value" in the phrase.

Some sense, however, can be made out of the phrase when it is seen apart from an economic meaning. A statement about the value of human life can be understood in a number of ways. It follows that what might be true in such a statement on one level may not be true on another. This is an important point, for if someone places a monetary value on human life, this monetary value may have no validity with respect to moral claims people may make on others' resources. One cannot "back into" the moral and metaphysical realm from the economic, for one then falls victim to the naturalistic fallacy—moving from a description of the way we act to the normative dimension of how we ought to act.

In addition to the point that different value languages are available and care must be taken when moving between them, another distinction can be drawn with respect to values: values can be extrinsic, intrinsic, or systemic.[24] Important for this discussion are the first two. To say that life has only a dollar cost is to place an extrinsic value on life. By contrast, to argue that human life has value is to claim that every human being is intrinsically valuable. Hence any slide from cost to value is a slide from extrinsic to intrinsic value and is thereby invalid.

Finally, whatever else one notes about the nature of values, it is important to keep in mind that they represent some comparison. They are weights in each of the languages employed. Thus, "the value of human life" as a religious expression means the relative intrinsic importance of human life when balanced against other lives or things in the universe, based on a myth of creative goodness in human nature. On the other hand, assigning an economic value to human life can only signify the relative extrinsic importance of one person's life compared with another's. I will argue that such an assignment is morally inadequate from three perspectives—religious, philosophical, and political.

## Conclusion

To say that human life has value is to believe that, in a population of things valued, human life must be considered to be important. But the claim is usually made more urgently than that. Sometimes we add the word "ultimate" to stress that human life in this population must bear the most weight. Because there may be some conditions under which preserving or respecting human life may not command our ultimate valuing, it is better to leave out the qualifier "ultimate." Instead, I would note that a belief in the value of human life usually includes the following connotations, listed by way of summarizing this chapter:

1. In comparison with other things and creatures in our known universe, human life is to be respected. If required by circumstances, human life is to be chosen over these other things and creatures. This is the reasoning behind "subduing all of creation." But our more recent awareness of the need for balance, ecological and otherwise, tempers the traditional meaning of subduing all things. Hence, the principle of the value of human life must be employed only under conditions we have not as yet entirely spelled out.

2. Externally speaking, our culture assigns more value to some human lives than to others. In this category, respect for human life may mean only economic status, standing in the community, the amount of insurance someone carries (in health care), a person's race. This is not the concept used in this work.

3. Intrinsically speaking, the value of human life means that each life bears inestimable worth regardless of externally applied criteria. The value cannot be measured by anything external, nor can it be so denied. This is the meaning to be applied to the phrase throughout the rest of the book, unless otherwise noted.

When we are forced to choose among lives—for example, in triage decisions during emergencies, in war, in weighting the lives of women and the unborn—we ought not to claim that one life has less intrinsic merit than another. Rather, we ought to own up to the terrible dilemma. We must act immorally. If our hand is forced to choose, we should not shirk from saying we had to sacrifice someone of inestimable worth, instead of hiding behind euphemisms and rationalizations. Perhaps this will help us establish greater respect for human lives in our public policy decisions.

# 2

# Pre-Persons and Post-Persons

"Look at us. We are the coming attractions!"
—Nat, in *I'm Not Rappaport* by Herb Gardner

Our society behaves in strange ways. On the one hand, every effort is made to foster the rights and values of human life. Millions of persons are trained in cardiopulmonary resuscitation to help rescue individuals who suddenly collapse. Up to $3 billion is spent each year in fertility research and treatment to help couples who cannot conceive have babies.[1] Large medical centers offer heart and heart-lung, kidney, heart-kidney, liver, bone barrow, and other transplants to prolong life. Chemotherapy and radiation are available to assist cancer patients. Kidney dialysis is available to all citizens as an entitlement of Social Security. Emergency rooms across the country stand ready to intervene and save lives. The list of support for the value of human life and its dignity is almost endless.

On the other hand, it often seems that we are not committed to the value of human life. Over one and one-half million fetuses are aborted each year. About forty million persons are uninsured or underinsured in the United States, making the available health care interventions adumbrated above inaccessible to them. The retarded are housed away from view. The marginally retarded and disabled and their families are helped through their growing years only with intense lobbying on behalf of "special" schools. After the school years, however, families must compete with one another for the few programs available to continue to support and stimulate such persons. Old persons are sometimes squirreled away in nursing homes and given inadequate stimulation. Their will to live suffers. The mentally ill and the homeless, with nowhere to go, line the sewer covers of our biggest and most impressive cities. The list of negatives seems also endless.

Is it a wonder, then, that we get mixed messages about duties to persons? Sometimes physicians, for example, throw up their hands in defeat. One exclaims, "I can't solve social and allocation problems at the bedside. If only the powers that be would make allocation decisions. I could live with them." But can health professionals live with this method of making health care decisions? And ought they?

Although we normally assume that there is a commitment in our society to equality of treatment, in fact our social behavior demonstrates a different ethic. Expectations about equality fall along a curve. This curve moves from what we could call duties to pre-persons, to fully functioning persons, and to post-persons. As the discussion will show, this language about persons is used ironically.

### Pre-Persons

In the category of pre-persons might fall embryos, fetuses up to the third trimester, anencephalics, defective newborns, the severely retarded, and other human beings who generally suffer, at the hands of fate and disease, a multitude of disorders from their earliest moments. These beings, in fact, are treated only as if they have a modicum of rights. Other than not making them suffer, we often behave toward them as if they have destroyed our faith in them, our faith that they will eventually become fully functioning persons. Since they will not, we accord them only peripheral or secondary rights. Their rights to life and life prolongation depend almost entirely on the wishes (and sometimes the whims) of persons who can make decisions about their care, about their nurture, and about their future.

Look at "test-tube babies," for example. It is clearly a wonderful use of modern medical technology to be able to assist persons who formerly could not have their own children. As one infertile person put it, "You grieve your infertility. You grieve for the child you're not going to have, who won't have your husband's eyes, your ears or your mother's nose."[2] Louise Brown of England was the world's first test-tube baby. In a laboratory dish her mother's egg was fertilized with the father's sperm, thus bypassing her mother's damaged Fallopian tubes. The fertilized egg was then implanted in the mother's uterus. As of this writing, many more babies—one even in China, where there is a terrible population problem—have been born this way. Unfortunately the technique is very expensive. In one year, 1987, Americans spent over $1 billion in infertility treatments, yet only about half of the involuntarily infertile couples were able to conceive a child.[3]

The techniques are also sophisticated. They require research on embryos, first sensationalized in this country at Vanderbilt in Nashville, Tennessee. In vitro (in test-tube) research was halted in the mid-1970s until the issue could be discussed and guidelines established. The technique also seemed to require that several embryos be created, the "spare" ones either dumped down the sink or, prior to that, subjected to biomedical research.[4]

British doctors criticized Robert Edwards, a test-tube baby pioneer researcher, for carrying out experiments on fourteen or fifteen "spare" living human embryos. The British Medical Association's ethics division noted:

> It is okay to take an ovum from a woman, fertilize it and put it back in the mother. But to take more than one ovum and experiment on it. . . . There is no consensus of opinion on whether that is human life, or, as Dr. Edwards says, can be treated as an experiment.[5]

Because the embryos are potential human beings, Dr. Walter Hedgecock, former British Medical Association officer, said, "It is really like pinning a baby down on a board and doing experiments on it."[6]

Concern over experimentation in this country produced national research guidelines. But it also produced laws such as an Illinois in vitro provision that virtually closed the door for a while on couples who wanted to take advantage of the new technique. Law cannot provide well for individual situations. The reason for the law, as described by State Rep. Harry Leinenweber (R, Joliet), was concern about attitudes toward life, including the language we use to describe it. In his words:

> We are concerned about what we feel are possibilities for abuse. And we are also very concerned about cavalier treatment of what we consider human life. If one thinks, however, that a "blob of tissues" instead of something special and deserving of protection has been created, then you don't have the same moral and ethical problem on your hands.[7]

At first, no clear moral policy emerged from any country on the moral uses of spare embryos that were produced in fertility efforts. Recall the sensational case in Australia of a couple whose spare embryos were stored, and then the couple died in an airplane accident. What to do about the spare embryos? Should they be implanted elsewhere? Are they the heirs of the million-dollar estate?[8] In Australia now, embryos have a right to be implanted after storage, whereas they do not have such a right in the United States.[9]

Especially troublesome would be the right of the embryo to protection under the law, when it enjoys no such right in abortion cases until after the third trimester.[10] This is of major importance today, since evidence exists that transplants from fetuses can assist persons who have Alzheimer's disease or Parkinson's disease. Does this now mean open season on fetuses? The research on embryos and fetuses continues. The Department of Health and Human Services established a blue-ribbon panel to advise it about continued research using aborted fetuses. In late 1988, the panel advised continued research, arguing that, although the ethical issues are still disturbing, the department was doing nothing illegal, since abortions are legal. Comments of researchers show the ambivalence in this issue: "I accepted these brains, of course. Where they came from and how they came to me was really none of my business." "Abortion is a tragedy, but as long as it occurs, I believe it is immoral to let tissue and materials go to waste if it can cure people who are suffering and dying."[11] These kinds of judgments are not far from the reasoning the Nazis employed about doing research on the remains of their prisoners. Father James Burtchaell of Notre Dame, a theologian member of the above mentioned panel, notes that the reasoning is based on the fallacy of the ends justifying the means and is concerned about the coercive elements in this research, since it may be a lucrative $6 billion industry if the hoped-for improvements in the health of others materializes. The fundamental objection is that the fetus cannot consent or assent to the research and that the surrogate decision maker, the mother who chooses abortion, by that very fact loses her right to act in the best interests of the fetus.[12]

Professor Kenneth Vaux of the University of Illinois wondered whether one might put fetal research and transplant issues in the context of an Old Testament or New Testament sacrifice, by which one lays down one's life for another. A gift, in other words. But as Patricia House observes, without consent one cannot be said to sacrifice one's life willingly. She also cites the Nazi experience as an explicit worry that to act without consent on another being is equivalent to an atrocity.[13] The role of choice is an essential component of the issues addressed in this book. I will have more to say about it in the final chapter.

In 1987, the Vatican warned in its *Instruction* on reproductive issues that the rights of embryos and the general vision of human life are in danger from highly technical manipulation of human life. In that document the Vatican suggested applying to the embryo all rights of a fully functioning human being, even though whether or not such early forms of human life are personal is subject to metaphysical indecision.[14] In general, the document was received with an open mind by most people but betrayed a deeply distrustful view of modern science. Vaux says it this way:

> [The *Instruction*] affirms a much-threatened normative value of the natural goodness and sacred mystery of birth. Regrettably, in its desire to preserve the deeply human nature of procreation, it plays down the

salutary potential of science to ameliorate incapacity in the same pro-
creative gift.[15]

As will be explored in subsequent chapters, shutting down technology and science is not only impossible, it is undesirable. Instead,
it should be directed to good human ends. The debate about "using" fetal tissue is different from employing science to assist persons
in reproducing, but both require very sophisticated and reverent
attitudes about the "normative values" of human reproduction.[16] It
is too early to curtail scientific efforts at this time. These efforts
should be closely watched and reviewed as they develop, but the
potential for good so far outweighs that of harm that they should
continue. The major harm in research on aborted fetuses, for example, is that individual women might be coerced into having abortions
"for the greater good of society." This would be unconscionable
from the point of view of respect for the value of human life. Similarly a woman might consider having an abortion before the third
trimester so that the fetal brain tissue might benefit her father during his slow decline from Parkinson's disease. Once again, treating
fetuses as objects for the good of others in this way violates their
own intrinsic value, as I will argue shortly.

A Protestant moral thinker, Henlee Barnette, argues that
churches ought to keep an open mind about surrogate parenting and
in vitro fertilization because science will progress at any rate and the
churches are capable of providing biblical guidelines for this research, based on love.[17] One can immediately discern the difference
between governmental guidelines and legislation, where there is no
common faith or metaphysics, and guidelines proposed by and for
faith communities regarding their own handling of the challenges
posed by modern technology.

This approach seems the best when dealing with disputed values
in society. Individual faith communities should be encouraged to
articulate their values, and an effort should be made to reach a public compromise when possible. When it is not possible, the state
must act for the common good. No one-issue campaign should be
allowed to impose its values on the rest of us, unless it can do so by
the persuasion and the use of the normal political channels available
to it. Pro-choice advocates seem miffed that pro-lifers try to amend
the Constitution or seek legislation and court decisions in their favor, yet this is the right of any citizen or body in the United States.
It is unfortunate, however, that more effort does not go into persuasion than coercion through law, as I will note in the final chapter.

Science and technology have had an enormous impact on health
care. And that impact has not always been positive. Many consider
the use of technological methods in medical care the very antithesis

of a humanized form of care. More specifically, concerns are constantly expressed that science and technology inure against compassion, that a health care system based on the newest discoveries, while perfectly designed to fight against disease, tends to reduce persons to objects. Modern medical care objectifies the body, treats it as a thing; thus, the concern continues, modern medical care conceals a dangerous ethics that encourages treating persons as things.[18] The vulnerabilities of incompetent embryos and fetuses are matched by those of the aged as well.

I can only mention here the projections about the future of research on embryos. Among others is that new life forms will be created, and there will be new symbiotic forms that combine living matter with machines.[19] These intelligences will be developed from our increasing efforts with genetics as well as with computers and robotics. The results will tax our current taxonomies about persons, beings, rights, and duties.

## Post-Persons

In the category of post-persons would fall the very old, those who have lost mobility and freedom in institutions, nursing homes, even in their own homes. Especially prone to being treated as post-persons are those who have become senile or suffer from Alzheimer's disease. These human beings were once persons. But in the eyes of society they seem to have suffered a loss of their rights because they no longer are capable of functioning within the realms of what we call "normal." Their interactions are those of extreme dependency, like the pre-persons. Such extreme dependency does not find favor in a society that equates personhood with autonomy, independence of action, and self-determination.

Josephine Brennan, the grandmother of an acquaintance of mine, was right. She was one of the "lucky" elderly who, despite the many indignities of advanced age, still retained her faculties and humor. She said, "Old age is not for sissies." She died six years after this statement, at age ninety-six. Her statement reflected the position of many elderly patients who find themselves fending off the blandishments of high technology medicine while still retaining their own sense of autonomy.[20] This balance is difficult for anyone to maintain. And it is more difficult still for those of advanced age who find themselves in institutions that almost naturally regard hospitalization and other medical interventions as a matter of course.

But many other persons of advanced age are not so fortunate. Among the indignities dealt them by the hand of fate are serious chronic and debilitating diseases that literally run them off the reservation where the rest of us live out our lives. As a result of these disorders they are cared for in long-term facilities. Their disorders often affect the mind and the spirit. Affliction leads to fear and bizarre behavior; the spirit is crushed, and a fragile, papier-mâché remnant of the former person lies in the bed.[21]

Such a fate befell Claire Conroy, who lay senile and debilitated in a nursing home, kept alive by means of a nasogastric feeding tube. The New Jersey Supreme Court, in its landmark decision in this case, supported the right of her nephew to speak for her values and to have the source of artificial feeding withdrawn.[22] The court also set up important procedures by which similar decisions would be made for other such persons in the state. In the main, the decision was a very good one. If she had been alive at the time of the decision, the court might have dealt with the situation differently. The decision, however, applied to a senile and debilitated person the moral rules that were normally applied to persons in a terminal condition. From one point of view, the decision could be seen as asserting that such a condition was equivalent to dying. Medical ethical and legal rules for removing medical interventions from dying patients were then applied to Claire Conroy's case.

Objections to the decision turn on the dispute about whether such a condition is, indeed, equivalent to dying. Behind this objection, too, is a major social question of our time: Why should such a being, such a state of life that holds no promise but only an ending, be the object of devotion and of the resources of families, caregivers, and society? One answer is found in a religious perspective on life. For example, in a recent visit to Austria that highlighted that country's terrible past record of anti-Semitism, Pope John Paul II recalled the routine atrocities committed by Austrian physicians: murders of handicapped, sick, and mentally retarded persons in society. He said:

> I call out to society from your midst: Human life should not be divided into that which is worth living and that which is not! Decades ago this division led to the worst forms of barbarism. All human life, whether born or unborn, whether fully developed or impeded in its development, every human life is endowed with a dignity before God which no one can desecrate.[23]

The basic reason for opposing treating the elderly differently from other citizens is one of social commitment. What sort of society ought we to be? Should we not treat all forms of human life equally? If we do not, will we not become as atrocious as the worst forms of political society that human history has ever witnessed?

Yet the Conroy case and the thousands of other cases that parallel it pose an opposite vision for society: Is it not better to consider a weakened and senile existence the same as dying or even identical to death itself? Why not relegate such elderly former persons to the status of post-persons? Why not assign them to the house of the dead? If we take as much care for their own wishes or those of surrogates,[24] we can avoid the excesses of Nazi society. Our rationing policy can then be seen to be rational and humane.

Some proposals to allocate health care on the basis of age seem to move the elderly into the house of the dead, precisely because they "cut off" the elderly from the modes of care we offer other persons in society. The National Center for Policy Analysis in Dallas issued a report that stressed how a nationalized health care plan would in all likelihood result in policies that would discriminate against older people.[25] Is there any possible alternative to these proposals? I will propose one in chapter 9. But the problems of our society in dealing with the aged need to be sketched at the outset.

### The Crisis

All the evidence points to a tremendous economic and political crisis in providing health care and long-term care for the elderly over the next fifty years.[26] In 1987 alone, about 6.7 million persons required some professional long-term care. Projections are that this number will grow to 9 million by 1990 and to 19 million by 2040.[27] But to consider the gerification of society, as it is called, as merely an economic and political challenge is to miss the essentially ethical dimension of the problem.[28] Gerification will produce far-reaching social changes that will disrupt cherished values of families and generations.[29] In particular, a bulge of increasingly dependent persons will appear near the end of the life cycle. The life cycle will continue to advance. It already approaches eighty years.

Rationing must be done, but how can it be done ethically? If we ration by age, serious difficulties arise for justice and for the nature of our society.[30] Among those difficulties are inequities of access,[31] a lack of respect for the aged in return for all they have done for the younger generations, the creation of institutional dumping grounds for elderly, unjust decision making for incompetent persons,[32] and cutting off care for many elderly persons who could profit from it and return to a normal life.[33]

### Ageist Social Policy

Three major proposals for an ageist social policy are currently being discussed. No doubt there will be others.

The hardest form of an ageist social policy is that presented by former Governor Richard Lamm of Colorado, who, though he denied saying it, reportedly claimed in an address in Denver in 1986 that old people have a duty to die and get out of the way. A year later, in a major policy speech to the Eddy Foundation in New York, "The Ten Commandments of an Aging Society," he argued that the young should not suffer because of health care we give to the elderly.[34] Actually all he had proposed was curtailing spending on the elderly on the basis of a utilitarian social policy.[35] The greatest good for the greatest number suggests that funds be left over for other social needs. Because of the increasing gerification of society, cutoffs must be made.

A less rigid proposal is that made by Daniel Callahan. His concerns are like those of Lamm. A rising share of the GNP devoted to health care will seriously shortchange other vital areas of national life. As he says about intergenerational justice: "We need to improve the quality of their [the ageds'] lives, not the quantity, and we need to assure intergenerational social justice, so that the medical needs of the young are not unfairly compromised by runaway spending on the old."[36]

The advances in modern medical technology should not serve as a recipe for both prolonging life and providing a better quality of life for the aged. Callahan therefore proposes that society should deny Medicare funding for extending the life span of the elderly. His proposal is based on the concept of a natural life span. The government would be required to help persons live out a natural life span, with attention to quality of life. After that point in life, perhaps at about age eighty, there would be no obligation to employ expensive medical technology at public expense. Instead, the elderly (all of us eventually) would be urged to think of death as an intimate part of life and of dying as a sort of service to the younger generation (in the sense that more would be left for them).[37] But if one is seventy-nine or eighty-five and develops cardiovascular disease, kidney failure, or an operable cancer, should this fact alone mean that public support for health care for that individual should be withdrawn?

The third view is that of Norman Daniels. Daniels argues that a prospective national policy, in which citizens decide ahead of time that certain technologies would be eliminated for all at a specified age, would be the only just method for allocating resources.[38] This is called a prudential account model, since each person, knowing ahead of time what to expect, would prudently plan for the future. Daniels' proposal is actually more complicated than this. A plan would be administered by prudent deliberators operating behind a veil that prevents them from knowing what age a person is now, the person about whom they allocate health care. They would allocate health care over a person's lifetime. There would be no discrimination on the basis of age per se, since all persons would be treated equally under this account, even though all might receive less as they age.[39]

The economic context should not so dominate social policy that the moral efforts of both patients and physicians to temper the process of aging and dying with important and fundamental human values is erased forever. In the end, ageism destroys the opportunity for such moral growth toward the end of life.

### People in the Middle

In the middle are the fully functioning persons. This category covers an enormous range of capabilities. These capabilities all include the measures of autonomy already noted. The edges of the category are constantly fluctuating. If a mildly retarded or disabled child cannot "function" up to a certain capacity, then we consider retiring him to an institution. We move such a person back to a pre-person status. If an elderly person gradually becomes confused and cannot take care of herself at home alone, we consider moving her into a nursing home. As she later gradually loses her self-determination and autonomy and becomes more passive, we move her gently but firmly into the category of post-persons. But most of the other people in the fully functioning category are a range of human beings who emerge normally from the womb and go about the business of developing and contributing to society. These are the middle persons. They enjoy many rights.

But they are also extremely vulnerable. As the population of the United States levels off,[40] and the number of persons over sixty-five increases, the people in the middle will increasingly be responsible for both the education and the nurture of the younger generation, all of the social services of society, and the care of almost one-third of the population over sixty-five years of age. I once saw a middle-aged woman in the hospital dragging along two very reluctant persons. The first was her son, who was resisting her with all his might. The other was her father, imitating the son's passive-aggressive behavior. The picture is a symbol of the days and hours to come for those in the middle.

If there is any human being who is the most vulnerable in society, it must be the adult woman. With the review of the right of privacy as applied to abortion, many women see themselves becoming increasingly vulnerable to the power of the state.[41] Kate Michelman at a Woman's Agenda Conference in Kansas City in January 1989 said, "This might prove to be the year women were put back in their place."[42] Women already experience a sense that they are made objects by males in society, reducing them to things.[43] Not only are their reproductive rights in jeopardy[44] but also they are the persons who must bear the burden of caring for the elderly, most often in their homes, and then, when they too become elderly, they are the ones for whom the "Federal Safety Net" most often fails. They sink into poverty. And they are not taken care of at home. The cover of *People* magazine for December 3, 1988, quotes a ninety-year-old mother: "How could my son do this to me?" Her son, Bob Goldie, says she was too frail: "I had no choice." She responded: "I hope I drop dead before I'm here one year."[45] This is how years of caring often end.

Yet they are not the only beings in the middle in jeopardy. One example of how technology causes a wealth of problems is that of serious disease. People who suffer from cancer can be blessed with highly advanced interventions. For example, there is Interleukin-2 therapy which takes one's white cells from the body, targets them as killer cells, and reintroduces them into the body; or one can have a cancer attacked by a limited-availability proton accelerator which concentrates the destroying beam on individual cancer cells.[46] At the same time, however, coverage for one's health and well-being is in danger of being cut by the government.[47] Further, the catastrophic disease insurance passed by Congress in 1988 was terribly inadequate. It was seen by most persons as badly burdensome to retirees.[48]

In addition, the increasingly entrepreneurial features of modern medicine in which paying patients are "skimmed" by for-profit hospitals and nonpaying patients are "dumped" to public facilities is touted as a "virtue" by some ethicists because it forces society to decide how it will allocate its funding.[49] This causes both patients and physicians to wonder whether physicians are still the patient's advocates?[50] A major change in the doctor-patient relationship has occurred, and that change may not always benefit the patient.[51]

And even if one can pay, entering into a clinical trial creates its own regions of hell, not only because of the uncertainty about possible outcomes but also because the physicians themselves are uncertain and cannot offer traditional reassurance support.[52] All of these features create the kinds of vulnerability that can be an opportunity both for virtue or for exploitation.

### Vulnerability

Pre-persons and post-persons are treated differently from fully functioning persons. Sometimes we can be proud that part of the difference is based on their vulnerability. Programs are established to assist defective newborns (such as Newborn Intensive Care Units), the retarded, the disabled, and other marginal people in society. There are counseling programs to help persons who care for these people. Organizations such as Alcoholics Anonymous, Overeaters Anonymous, and Gamblers Anonymous encourage self-reliance among those who have been disabled by disease. Also, hospitals have programs to foster prevention for persons who have suffered heart attacks. These are only a few examples.

Yet it seems odd that the mixed messages given health professionals by society include taking advantage of the vulnerability of these individuals. The more vulnerable they are, it sometimes appears, the less they enjoy the protection of "authentic" persons. This has always been one of the most telling objections to abortion. The more vulnerable fetus is subject to the decisions of others without its consent. Frozen embryos, "conceived" through the design of fully functioning persons, are left without wombs in uncertain pre-personal status. Are they to be implanted somewhere and given a chance to live, or are they to be destroyed? Deinstitutionalizing the mentally ill who could survive on medicines to control their disease seemed a wise and economically sound social objective. But without a place to go, these persons suffer the indignity of homelessness and are abused by other unfortunate people out on the street. Homosexuals are subjected to intense hatred and abuse as the "cause" and "carriers" of AIDS. Gay bashing has become a serious social problem itself. The poor are treated to programs, indeed, but the programs only reinforce the passivity and dependency they are designed to overcome. Hundreds of babies are now born with drug dependencies as well as with AIDS, innocently emerging out of the bodies of persons with incredible problems.[53]

In a truly life-affirming society, such vulnerability ought to evoke greater care for the disadvantaged, not less. We want to be such a society, but we fall short in many ways. Like any human concoction, society will always fall short of the ideal. Human beings are not perfect, and neither are our social institutions. Precisely for this reason, health professionals should not rely solely on society to establish treatment and care categories for its most vulnerable citizens.

## Conclusion

Society does not necessarily have the best interests of individuals in mind. Only a community committed to those best interests can enter the necessary dialogue about allocation of care with the noble aim of caring for individuals that society often disvalues. This noble aim must be nurtured by the millions of "normal" recipients of beneficence, the millions of us who are considered normal but who have benefited from the individually tailored compassion and care that our physicians and other health providers have offered us in the past.

If our social goals are set by utilitarian concerns of a technologically driven society alone, many persons will suffer at the edges of our categories of normality. They will be among our "throw away" people, to be discarded by the machinery of an industrialized and materialistic society. This is unacceptable not only to the inherent ethics of medicine but to all citizens for whom "the bell tolls." Each of us is diminished by tolerating discrimination against the most vulnerable, the poor, the homeless, the retarded, the disabled, the aged, in our civilization. We must open up the range of "normality" among us to embrace all our citizens, regardless of their health status or the condition of their life.

We turn now to the impact of technology on our perceptions of the value of human life. In Part Two I examine whether technology must be curtailed, controlled, or directed instead toward good human ends.

# PART TWO

# Human Life
# in a Technological Society

# 3

# The Value of Human Life
# in a Technological Age

We must learn to use the new instruments to our benefit, rather than
submit to exploitation by them.

—Amitai Etzioni

We, like Narcissus, are in love with our own image. Replicas of
various human capacities are imaged and arrayed around us. For
example, hoists, like arms, lift entire houses. Computers, like brains,
plan war strategies. Television cameras, like eyes, survey the world
around us. Pacemakers regulate heartbeats; dialysis machines replace human kidneys; the Jarvik-7 replaces a human heart. All
around us, machines imitate or simulate human function.

If machines are made to imitate persons, is it any wonder that
people sometimes imitate their machines?[1] Observe the raw power
of steelworkers, the cool, calculating computer expert, the astronaut
who looks and talks like an emotionless computer, the doctor who
communicates with the precision of a lab test.

This is said tongue in cheek, of course. Not every doctor communicates like a lab test; not every computer expert is calculating.
There is a danger, though, that we might come to think that human
reality is as easily manipulated, determined, and predictable as a
machine. When we do this, we divorce ourselves from the realm of
values—in particular, the value of human lives.

Healing the separation between values and assumptions made in
a technological society is the matter for this chapter and the final
chapter. The healing will force us to change the way we think and
behave. It will require nothing less than a new ethic for living. I
will discuss this ethic under three broad headings: Toward an Ethic
for Technological Society, below; Technological Progress and Human Values; and, finally, Technology and the New Moral Order. In
the final chapter, I will summarize the qualities of persons and
society that "err on the side of the value of human life."

## Toward an Ethic for Technological Society

"If a scientific civilization is to be a good civilization," Bertrand Russell wrote, "it is necessary that increase in knowledge be accompanied by an increase in wisdom. I mean by wisdom, a right conception of the ends of life. This is something of which science in itself does not provide."[2] If I could summarize the combined thinking of all cultures and religions about "a right conception of the ends of life," it is this: Each person and each culture is called to engage in a struggle, a committed and passionate struggle, for wisdom.

To elaborate on Russell's meaning of wisdom, I would add that wisdom means the union of some rational order in one's life and values with a discovered order in society and in the universe.

In this regard, Augustine reflects the usual Christian view. Rome had fallen, Augustine says, for want of order in the soul.[3] By their nature, persons seek order, not the unconscious order of swallows or bees, but an order that human intelligence understands. For persons, acts must have significance. People are dissatisfied unless they find "a disposition or arrangement of equal and unequal things in such a way as to allocate each to its own place." They must have purpose in their existence. Malcolm Muggeridge, in reviewing Professor Russell Kirk's *The Roots of American Order* (Malibu, Calif.: Pepperdine University Press, 1974), comments on this order:

> The truth is, of course, that any order achieved by human beings is valid only to the degree that it expresses the divine or transcendental order which pervades the universe. Men, that is to say, can only know order to the extent that they know God; on their own, they are as prone to chaos as the beasts in the jungle.[4]

In other words, an ethic implies a circular process wherein a personal life reflects "what is," and "what is" is appreciated in a personal life. An ethic is practical, cultural wisdom. Hence, an ethic for persons in a technological society, indeed, any ethic formulated in any cultural epoch, would have to include "union," the highest good of persons. This union synthesizes their potential with the possibility of its realization.

Of course, by "union" I do not necessarily mean "conformity." The existentialists have placed a giant question mark behind any attempt to establish conformity as a value in constructing an ethic. Precisely because a technological society fosters pluralism (even though it produces demeaning conformity), any ethic based on conformity to ultimate values is doomed to fail. Traditionally, a religious ethic does contain the element of conformity. Perhaps this is one of the reasons a religious worldview has been largely edged out by the technological.

Most ethical and moral attempts to orient our technological society to the needs and ends of human beings fail because they are naïve. They are naïve because they do not recognize the new environment in which we live, the real situation. I will first describe the problem; second, offer some definitions and assumptions; third, diagnose the situation we face as realistically as possible; and finally, offer some elements of an ethic for technological society.

## The Problem

In essence, any attempt to describe an ethic is an elaboration on Socrates' famous dictum: An "unexamined life is not worth living."[5] This theme is present throughout our civilization and is reflected in our day by two thinkers who otherwise diverge, Albert Camus and Bertrand Russell.

Camus observed in his first novel, "Like any work of art, life needs to be thought about."[6] And to cite Russell again, "Through the greatness of the universe which philosophy contemplates, the mind is also rendered great, and becomes capable of that union with the universe which constitutes its highest good."[7]

Like many of our contemporaries, I have become increasingly concerned about the future of our civilization. It seems to me that the promising child of science has grown into a terrible teenager. As parents of this monster, our task is both to recognize where we have failed and to guide technological society through a difficult adolescence. Adulthood will be reached when the fundamental needs and aspirations of human beings are met.

The stimulus for reflection on the value of human life in a technological age stems from two sources. The first is a book by Daniel Callahan, *The Tyranny of Survival,* in which he explicitly calls for an ethic for technological society. Callahan's thesis is that technology rapidly outruns our cultural wisdom about concrete ethical matters.[8] Not abandoning this point of view, Callahan later argued that the future of one form of ethics, medical ethics, will lie in the great public policy debates about the value of human life.[9] Shortly thereafter, he argued that the character of the modern era has changed to a great extent. Rather than experiencing ever greater wealth and economic growth, the West is faced with a stable, even stagnant, economic future. Because we will no longer be able to throw large sums of money at our moral and political problems, we all will be challenged instead to come up with more creative solutions. In particular, the ethics of self-determination, personal freedom, and personal development may have to be replaced by a more community-oriented ethic.[10] This view has been expanded in his *Setting Limits,* discussed in the last chapter of this book. Worth repeating here is the point that medical technology itself has so outpaced our ability to pay for it and to allocate it fairly that it is now time to curtail the very development of that technology.[11]

The second stimulus stems from the award-winning novel by Thomas Pynchon, *Gravity's Rainbow*. The novel is filled with paranoic wartime characters, postwar wanderings, and a search for a sexual-mystical rocket. The characters converge around a recognition of the true victor of World War II. Motorcycling past an intact factory, one principal character, a *Schwarzkommando*, ruminates:

> It means this War was never political at all, the politics was all theatre, all just to keep the people distracted . . . secretly, it was being dictated instead by the needs of technology . . . by a conspiracy between human beings and techniques, by something that needed the energy-burst of war. . . . The real crises were crises of allocation and priority, not among firms—it was only staged to look that way—but among the different Technologies, Plastics, Electronics, Aircraft, and their needs which are understood only by the ruling elite.[12]

Later, the principal Russian character, Tchitcherine, has his moment of recognition in the ruins of a battery:

> Is your IG to be *the very model of nations?* . . . "Say, there." It appears to be a very large white Finger, addressing him. . . . Right now, joints moving with soft, hydraulic sounds, the Finger is calling Tchitcherine's attention to—*A Rocket-cartel.* A structure cutting across every agency human and paper that ever touched it. Even to Russia . . . Russia bought from Krupp, didn't she, from Siemens, the I.G. . . . Oh, a State begins to take form in the stateless German night, a State that spans oceans and surface politics, sovereign as the International or the Church of Rome, and the Rocket is its soul. IG Raketen. [Author's emphasis.][13]

Still another recognition comes to the American character named Slothrop, again in the postwar period.

> Happyville. . . . The truth is that the War is keeping things alive. *Things.* The Ford is only one of them. The Germans-and-Japs story was only one, rather surrealistic version of the real War. The real War is always there. The dying tapers off now and then, but the War is still killing lots and lots of people. Only right now it is killing them in more subtle ways.[14]

I have spent time on Pynchon's insights, insights about international power, multinational corporations, loss of control, and depersonalization—in short, insights about the perceived evils of our technological civilization—because he writes powerfully about the real situation. Without this recognition, and a concomitant understanding of the power of technology over our lives, suggestions about an ethic will be utterly naïve.

Generally speaking, there is a lack of awareness regarding the vast technological tundra on which we play out our lives. There is little awareness of the nature of our present problem. It is not that we no longer speak clearly or have abandoned values or must search for security or re-create the past that is the ethical problem.

Rather, the problem is that we have lost control over technology. Put in a more challenging way, we no longer design technology to serve the fundamental needs and aspirations of persons. While human beings have been technological in the sense that they have always created tools, these tools, or "machines," were previously designed with the objective of fulfilling needs. Human needs dictated the design and control of the machine. This is no longer true. Today, technology itself often dictates the new design. Thus the standard accusation: technology has become dehumanized and dehumanizing. Writing about the increased costs of medical care, for example, John Mamana, a physician, states:

> Technology has become an autonomous force within the field of medicine. Technology requires its own labor force, its own economics (which is irrationally more rewarding to those who use it more), and its own moral code. Because of these factors, the institutional diffusion of new technologies proceeds with an energy of its own.[15]

I will discuss this point further in the next section of this chapter.

Derived from this problem is an important ethical question. How can one seek unity with "what is," the highest good of persons, if reality, or at least a large slice of reality, is a technological monster? Is the search for an ethic in an absurd situation itself absurd? Many would like to think so. To think this way, however, is to abrogate the very control over technology that is required to humanize it. In what follows, I make an effort to define an ethic for technological society instead. It is based on a measure of controlled hope rather than on dollops of despair.

## Some Definitions and Assumptions

Aware of the chaos and injustice in the present situation, how can one affirm values that will humanize technology? Some suggestions will follow. But first I will present assumptions and definitions.

I assume that humanity is inherently technological. We recognize dusty relics as the artifacts of some humanoid form of life because toolmaking is inherent in that life. In other words, technology is not just an extension of the senses. It is a very part of being human.

If this assumption is true, then technology itself is inescapable. The ethical problem is to orient technology to human ends. After all, a machine is any tool that harnesses the power of nature. Built into a machine is a created function that is at least in an intellectual union with nature. The maker of a machine understands nature, and he or she has a human end in mind in the design.

By "ethics" I mean practical, cultural wisdom as previously described. In a sense, I am describing a metaethic, a critique of culture itself. If it were easy to agree on the proper ends of human life, then part of the ethical problem would be solved. In the past we have seldom unanimously agreed on these ends. With the qualitatively new situation described, it becomes even more difficult. This point leads me to the next assumption.

Lewis Mumford and Lewis Yablonsky, among many distinguished others, have fully described the impact of modern technology on our own self-awareness.[16] Joshua Lederberg puts the point succinctly: "Dilemmas about new knowledge, especially about our own bodies, touch deep-rooted anxieties about man's perception of himself."[17]

Mumford argues that modern technology was conceived by warfare. Not surprisingly, then, it produces destructive ugliness, giantism, normlessness, infantilization, standardization, conformity, mass nonidentity, and a host of other undesirable features of contemporary life. Yablonsky, in turn, indicates the effects of these dehumanizing structures on our vision of ourselves. At the root of his point of view is that technology has created robotlike interactions among human beings. In a megamachine society, we have the death of the human, the death of compassion, and a world wired for death. Despite the centrality of the value of human life in our culture, then, technological advances have made this commitment to life virtually meaningless.

If technology is inescapable and if people have created a world wired for death, then modern technology produces instincts in us toward violence, not only toward one another but toward the proper ends of human life. Instead of our agreeing on the ends, modern technology is now dictating its *own* ends. And it does this, not as an outside force, but through the activities of "robopaths," a word Yablonsky coined for people who act like machines.

The machine has replaced human dialogue as the ground we till for practical wisdom. As such it has become our myth.

### Diagnosis of Myth

Instead of judging our acts by their human consequences, we tend to judge them on the basis of cost-benefit ratios, increased technological progress, and economic greed. I choose to accept Mumford's phrase by which to describe this process. Mankind seems dominated by a "myth of the Machine." Obviously, by "machine" here is meant something derogatory. Since this use contradicts my earlier benign use of the word, I will capitalize "machine" whenever the myth is discussed. Its meaning will become clear, I hope, as the argument develops.

In order to understand the importance of this new environment, I want to discuss briefly how this myth developed. By "myth" I mean any theoretical and practical system of meaning that embodies the values of a particular culture. In this sense, "myth" does not mean what is untrue, but what is most true, what is of absolute value for that culture.

It seems quite obvious that the myth by which humans have organized the energies of life for thousands, perhaps millions, of years is religion. Particular variants differ mainly in the absolutes deified. Whether it was nature (e.g., Babylonian religion), heroics (e.g., Nordic religion), society or the cosmos (Chinese and Greek), or even historical development (Hebrew), the myth deified absolutes that related to human conduct and the goals of human life.

In Western civilization, during the sixteenth century, cracks were introduced in this myth. The uneasy balance between faith and reason, church and state, religion and rising science inherited from the Middle Ages, began to go awry. One can only speculate on what might have happened had religion not reacted so defensively to new scientific discoveries. But it did, and so sounded the knell. Religion had to make way for Western technology. This replacement has now spread throughout the world.

In this regard, I cannot agree with Milton Singer, who argues that religion has not been "replaced" but has been "displaced." His analysis of sects, social movements, and civil religion does not convince me that religion will regain its former cultural synthetic power.[18] At best, religion will remain a somewhat effective "other view or force" adjacent to the Machine. As such a force, it can offer fundamental critiques of the pathways and progress of modern society, as indeed it now so often does.

I have proposed that technology is inherent to persons. How did it become a myth replacing religion in the West?

The following schema describes what happened:

| | |
|---|---|
| Step 1: Tools | Step 4: The Myth of the Machine |
| ↓ | ↑ |
| Step 2: Techniques | Step 3: Industrialized Technologies |

Steps 1 and 2 have been integral parts of the religious-myth synthesis. Humanity is toolmaking. This experience became part of cultural techniques. As the power to manipulate nature grew, it produced various technologies, systems of manipulation and design regarding stone, copper, iron, and so on. Dictated by the needs of warfare, these technologies began to be industrialized—step 3—at about the same time that science was cracking the religious myth (around the sixteenth century).

Significant portions of earlier religious beliefs were gradually edged out by science, in the realm of ideas, and by the dedication of human life to machines, in the moral, aesthetic sphere. The absolutes of religious dogma and morals were replaced by the absolutes of industrial technology. John Stuart Mill's ethics of utility is widely regarded as a morality for industrial growth because it promotes the greatest good for the greatest number of people.[19] Self-serving decisions made by large governments, corporations, and other institutions can be presented as being for the greater good. A popular bastardization of utilitarian ethics was the expression, "What's good for General Motors is good for the country." Later to be satirized as the General Bullmoose principle, this attitude has caused citizens of the United States untold grief during recessions.

As the power of religion waned, the synthetic organizing power of technology gradually grew into the Myth of the Machine (step 4). For those who remain religious today, a schizophrenia often develops between the myth of religion and the myth of the Machine, between church on Sunday and power politics the rest of the week. Later resistance to the process of mythologizing the Machine came from humanists, Romantic artists, and a few voices from the gears of this Machine (one of whom was Karl Marx, who so powerfully described the ultimate alienation of the worker from his or her work).[20]

But the process has been inexorable. Step 4 includes the interlocking of all technological systems, such that any jiggling of one will upset all the others. When the oil shortage of 1974 hit the United States, we quickly learned how oil affected all other aspects of life, from farm products to records, from travel to taxes. As the oil cartel overproduced oil during the late 1980s, relative calm appeared on the world markets, as inflation was kept in check. This calm contributed to the feeling of peace and prosperity that governed the presidency of Ronald Reagan. When one technological system in the economy suffers, whether it is oil or plastics, paper, steel, or autos, all other parts of the economic and social fabric also suffer. This happens not just within the borders of one nation. It is an international phenomenon. Step 4 was reached during World War II when the Machine churned out products to destroy the people of many nations, as Pynchon so chillingly observed.

Many organized religions today suffer from the reluctance to alienate, and therefore to change, the habits of the Machine in their practitioners. (Perhaps this is the reason why fundamentalist Christianity is so appealing to many American citizens; it rejects many technological assumptions of the modern age.)

For many, this process of not valuing religion was one of liberation from antiquated myths. But as our finest art, music, poetry, and sculpture often reflect, the dream of liberation has been transformed into a nightmare of oppression. The Machine levels. It destroys blatantly on the battlefield, more subtly in front of the television set. This is the war that always goes on, the war described by Pynchon.

## Elements of an Ethic for Technological Society

Although I have painted a somewhat depressing picture of the power of the Machine, I hope it is a balanced one. Human beings are not so stupid to trade off ancient oppressions for more modern ones. In fact, for each negative feature of the Machine, for each technology no longer under humanized design, we receive some new freedoms. For example, mass-produced cars, though they inhibit the values of dialogue, personal contact, and even the environment, also grant us new mobility and individual freedom to go where we want.

The question, however, is how to maintain human goals, the energy of life, the value of the distinctly human, in an increasingly technologized world. To answer this question, Callahan suggested a "reality principle." He proposed that an ethic for technological humanity should begin with a reality principle by which the community decides whether or not to develop a new technological device.[21]

Not "Can we develop this?" but "Ought we?" should be the starting point for an ethic in our day. Buckminster Fuller, in his many writings, seems to rest his optimism about technology on our ability to make this judgment.[22] Mumford should be read as a corrective to the over-optimism inspired by Fuller's attractive approach.

A new ethic would have to be dialectical rather than prescriptive. Other than in the area of justice, an ethic of obligation tends to destroy the very freedom needed to adapt to the constantly changing conditions brought on in a machine-dominated culture. More on this point will be presented in chapter 4, as I argue for an ethics of discretion.

The decision to create new technological advances must rest on a union with "what is." But if "what is" is "monstrous," where do we turn?

## Initial Outline of an Ethic

In his usual iconoclastic manner, Malcolm Muggeridge has written:

> An ethic cannot be constructed to the specification even of a Plato or Marcus Aurelius, let alone of some half-baked sociologist or elected legislator. It always makes me laugh when I read in the papers of how

one of our contemporary pundits has announced at a conference or scholastic get-together that we need a new set of values, a new ethic. Maybe we do, and maybe he and his colleagues can devise one to their, and even our, satisfaction. But how do they propose to put it into effect and ensure that it is observed? That's the difficult part.[23]

Although Muggeridge is surely wrong in thinking that some authority must ensure that an ethic be observed, he is correct in noting that a new ethic does not appear promptly from a few voices raised in its favor. An ethic is a practical cultural wisdom that emerges from a whole host of factors, only one of which is dialogue and discussion. In fact, it is a choice based on belief, as has already been argued.

Muggeridge is not the only thinker who pines for an age of centrally enforced morality based on a shared and unified (usually Christian) vision as the basis of culture. Another is a superb, contemporary ethicist, Alasdair MacIntyre. MacIntyre argues that the search for the foundations of ethics is frustrating. It is frustrating because there is no shared vision to undergird the strength of ethical principles. Once this vision was lost, the principles, often competing with one another, were left dangling without sufficient justification.[24] MacIntyre argues that in a postindustrial, postenlightenment society there exist no common values upon which to develop an overarching ethic.[25]

But if a shared vision about the value of human lives is possible, as I will suggest in chapter 4, then, at the very least, a choice to protect human life can lie at the heart of attempts to direct technology to human ends, the "proper ends of a good human life" called for by Bertrand Russell. A shared vision may not guarantee unity around ethical principles, but it may establish a kind of moral turf upon which we agree to work out enormously important public policy issues. Examples of these issues will be given in the next chapter, because they are required by a sophisticated understanding of how a society might "direct" its technology rather than stifle it.

A strong objection can be made to my assertion that humankind is now controlled by the myth of the Machine. The objection would state that technology is not manipulating people in society. People are actually manipulating one another and themselves. To expand on a theme of the National Rifle Association, bombs don't kill people, people do. People have not lost control of technology but instead have sold themselves to the gods of convenience and comfort. The objection might continue: We are not parents of the technological monster, we *are* the monster. Thus there is no qualitatively new environment as described in the preceding section of this chapter (i.e., no leap to a new order of dependency on machines). The "right thing to do" is no more difficult now than it has been in the past.

Although this objection has the merit of imputing responsibility for morality to human beings, a point with which I agree, it fails to grapple with the technological nature of persons. In fact, the objection is almost always raised in its more religious garb. In this clothing it has a strong form and a weak form. The weak form is a sort of Calvinistic mistrust of the works of persons, including the societies and technologies they build, as found in the writings of Jacques Ellul.[26] In its stronger version, the objection appears in every fundamentalist condemnation of the humanities, humanism, and modern culture. The term "secular humanism" often embraces for fundamentalists all that is evil in modern society. I once attended a meeting of the Tennessee Committee for the Humanities (of which I was a member) in Nashville, Tennessee. After the meeting, during which we were totally occupied with meshing the humanities with the adult, out-of-school public, I flipped on the television set in the motel room. A prominent fundamentalist preacher was addressing a huge crowd in a coliseum in Detroit. I entered at his sentence that roundly condemned sending "our children off to college," where their minds were destroyed by "contact with Marx, Engels, Hegel," and "all those other secular humanists." There went all our work, I thought!

Paul Tillich, a Protestant theologian, once wrote that the protests of protestantism had all been met by Catholic internal reforms, such that there was nothing left to protest.[27] He was wrong. The above objection is a powerful protest to the rather optimistic (by comparison) view of human nature and God's grace adopted by a Catholic vision of the redemption. Catholic countries have spawned many of the movements that stress the inherent beauty and nobility of humanity. The Renaissance is only one example. The "protestant" objection to technology, as we might call it, represents a profound rejection of any ethic based on the value of human life, if this value is not directly derived from God's salvation of the human creature. In this view, it would be impossible to form coalitions to resolve public policy issues about the dignity of human life with those who either do not believe in God or who do not need God to derive their beliefs about the dignity of human life. Unfortunately the protestant objection[28] neglects an essential piece of human nature in its stress on the majesty of God. God's majesty is not destroyed by admitting that human beings are inherently technical and have the capacity to understand and manipulate the world.

Attempts to "cope" with the Machine we find today are necessary and sincere historical processes. But in the end they remain half-hearted, impoverished approaches to a complex situation, a situation of loss of control. Such attempts have been popularized by Eastern religious movements, by junking the system and moving to the Arizona desert, by returning to Jesus as the "one way," by nostalgia, and so on. Though necessary critiques of the Machine, these movements can be palliative measures only. They do not, it seems, really recognize the power of the Machine over our lives. This power stems, in part, from the fact that we are inherently technological beings. Most of us will not sacrifice the goods and freedoms that technology brings. Who really wants to give up the ability to listen to the great music of the past, watch televised world news coverage, or enjoy a longer life?

Put another way, the union with "what is" should not be a search for security, for it will be a false security. The oiled gears of the Machine can lull us into thinking that, because our egos are stronger as a result of T.A., Erhard Seminars Training (est), Systematic Assertiveness Training, and whatnot, our individual freedom is enhanced. In a Machine culture, this is patently not so. The demeaning structure remains unchanged.

By contrast, a technological ethics requires a realistic affirmation of the future as the source for discovery of "what is." "What can be" is really intrinsic to what is. Rather than an effort to find some pieces of the past that fit our present puzzle, the future human good, the unification and diversity of the world, should be used as the basis upon which we make ethical decisions. The point needs elaboration.

The first component of this view is that civilization must unite and inspire. Otherwise it is not a civilization. It can unite and inspire only if it rests on a synthesis of knowledge and strength. The knowledge involved must come from intellectual tools we are only beginning to develop, tools that help us analyze the future with less guesswork. The strength of a civilization arises from a passion for independence and justice. Since we live in a world not enormously blessed with civilized virtues, such as respect for independence and justice, these virtues must be grounded in hope. Albert Camus expressed it better than I: "A craving for freedom and independence is generated only in a man still living on hope."[29]

The second component in humanizing technology is a coordinated allocation of time. Much human energy is spent in trying to overcome the past rather than in attending to the future. This seems true in one's personal life as well as in our cultural life. I am suggesting that past revision is not as necessary as we think. I am not arguing that relevant works of the past are not helpful. In fact, the more they spoke to and of their age, the more they have to offer now. Perhaps this is because they tapped the perennial struggles in human civilization. In our task, though, the future must occupy us far more than the past.

The third component of the decision to create or not to create new technologies must be a corrective to the instinct for violence and death caused in us by the Machine. In place of this instinct we can do no better than choose the value of human life. Considering the robotlike responses induced in us by the Machine, and for the reasons presented in previous chapters, it appears to be the best possible choice.

If an instinct for life affirmation were adopted by scientists, economists, technicians, medical practitioners, preachers, and government officials, we then could begin scrutinizing the quality of life and the goals of society.

As yet, I do not think we are trustworthy on this score. It makes little sense to speak of "the quality of life" if we do not in our cultural ethic recognize the dignity of life itself. Note how the warming trend between the superpowers that took place with the assumption of power by Gorbachev was still laced with distrust for years. When Gorbachev spoke before the United Nations and announced a unilateral reduction in weapons and army units, a sense of exhilaration among world citizens that the cold war was declining was tempered by the extreme caution of politicians, ever ready on the basis of past perceptions to exercise a social paranoia, looking for hidden motives as the basis of mistrust. Some commentators tried to diminish the "humanism" of Gorbachev's initiative by pointing out that the economy in the Soviet Union was so bad he had no other choice.[30]

For those ready to move to "the quality of life" as a moral absolute, nothing contradicts the insight of Thomas Aquinas on the necessary conditions for human well-being: health, sufficient means to live a virtuous life, and friendship, that is, strong bonds in a community.[31] If these were to be taken as the basis of human goals for technology, they could function as goals within our grasp. These are certainly some of the fundamental needs and aspirations of human beings.

### Conclusion

One final note before we turn to more specific considerations. The elements I have described do not offer concrete answers about what to do. Instead, they are intended to provide the basis of that cultural wisdom we lack. Again, Aquinas once wrote that all the arts and sciences work for the happiness of persons.[32] Clearly his observation was written in a happier age. The proposal for an ethic for technological society can be summarized as an affirmation of life and the future based on a recognition that human persons are inherently technological. Therefore the proposal leans heavily on design orientation toward the future good of the human community rather than on expunging the past. It is necessary to avoid the impending cultural collapse many artists and thinkers discern.

Surely there are many other approaches to the task of maturing an adolescent technology. My approach rests on a belief expressed by Camus, who said: "Art," and by context science, "was not invented to bring evil into the world."[33]

# 4

# Technological Progress
# and Human Values

Once, indeed, scientists decided to exclude theology, politics, ethics, and current events from the sphere of their discussions, they were welcomed by the heads of state. In return—and this remains one of the black marks against strict scientific orthodoxy with its deliberate indifference to moral and political concerns—scientists habitually remained silent about public affairs and were outwardly if not ostentatiously "loyal." Thus their mental isolation made them predestined cogs in the new megamachine.
—Lewis Mumford, *The Myth of the Machine*

Now that the problem of controlling our technology is more clearly delineated, it is possible to look carefully at the ways in which values are involved in the creation of technologies. This will help us better understand the meaning of technological progress. In particular I will argue that a good technology is one designed out of recognition of the fundamental needs and aspirations of humankind. The needs are not found in science but in life itself. Further, the proper approach to technology is not to curtail it but to direct it. A lack of direction is precisely a failure of a common will. This failure in turn is based on a lost vision about the value of human life.

### Assumptions

In order to circumscribe the problem of technological progress manageably, I will briefly describe assumptions I make about the nature of civilization, cultural wisdom, and the role of values.

Stated succinctly, a civilization is a synthesis of institutionalized forms of living. Examples of these forms run from modes of dress and behavior, art and music, political systems, and family structure, to the design of our buildings, cities, and flags. Such a synthesis has survival value. The synthesis that is civilization teaches us how to cope with constantly shifting relationships. As such, it has at least two functions. The first is to provide cultural wisdom regarding repetitions. Having learned how to cope with certain conditions, we acquire a pattern of responses to similar ones. The pattern then frees us to cope with new conditions as they arise. It would not do if each of us had to rethink the meaning of a stop sign at every corner.

The second survival value of a civilization stems from its function of relating thoughts and actions to myths of meaning constructed over the centuries. This is such a truism that many critics of our civilization predict its end by analyzing the feelings of anxiety and meaninglessness in contemporary art and music.

If an essential element is missing, namely, how to relate thought to action in an ethical way, then the synthetic force of a civilization crumbles. Without the effects of this survival value, we become prone to violence, unhappiness, and instability. Our society more and more takes on the character of that depicted in Anthony Burgess' A Clockwork Orange.[1] Human energies are necessarily focused on a search for meaning rather than on external creations. If this occurs for extended lengths of time, we become citizens of a chaotic new dark age.

The synthetic functions of patterning and meaning offered by civilization lead to a second assumption. A civilization embodies practical cultural wisdom. By cultural wisdom I mean a collective memory of past human contributions. It collects past theories and practices, science and art, religion and morality, law and politics, and so on. Cultural wisdom has a purpose. That purpose is precipitation. Cultural wisdom precipitates past successful ventures from all human attempts to solve problems. These successful ventures somehow are seen to have met the fundamental needs and aspirations of human beings. In sum, if civilization can be viewed as a model for behavior modification, cultural wisdom voices the proper ends of human life necessary for the goals of that modification. More precisely, then, cultural wisdom is a form of judgment, a judgment about the ends of human life. This judgment can be either theoretical (related to knowledge) or practical (related to action).

When I stated that our civilization lacked cultural wisdom, I prefaced the phrase with the word "practical." By practical cultural wisdom, I mean that realm of praxis in our collective heritage.[2] This realm can be further described as the moral realm, the arena of human life wherein thought is applied to action.[3] In this realm, science is applied and becomes technology. Also in this realm, various liberal arts disciplines are applied and become the humanities. In general, the moral realm would include both art and ethics. Both are interrelated in that they both express human values. I therefore consider technology one of the arts expressing human values.

A summary of what has been said so far will lead to my third and final assumption. The "right conception of the ends of life," to use Bertrand Russell's phrase, is the cultural wisdom lacking now in our civilization. Such a conception rests on values. Although values are found at the root of knowledge and actions, deciding what are the ends of a *good* human life is a judgment in the moral realm. The ethical issues of our time are found in this realm.

The moral realm is the locus of application of knowledge. To be more specific, disciplines such as engineering, medicine, ethics, politics, economics, art, law, and so on, apply their theories. The values inherent in these disciplines may or may not mesh with perceived values in the day-to-day world. My third assumption touches on the role of values in this realm.

Practitioners of disciplines applying knowledge to human problems are now embroiled in the major question posed today. The question of industrialized society in the past has been: Can we create a new technology? This question has now been superseded by another: Ought we to create a new technology? Professor Hallett D. Smith of the California Institute of Technology was quoted twenty years ago as saying:

> It is only too obvious that a scientist is going to be asked over and over again *"Should* we do this?"* [not only] *"Can* we do it?"*; and this question *"Should* we do it?"* demands what we call "value judgment."[4]

It is a postindustrial question, more concerned with the quality of life than with the quantity of new products.

Asking whether we ought to create a new technology often appears to scientists to destroy the unprejudiced search for truth. Under the influence of Sidney Hook, the "humanist Manifesto II" states:

> Technology is a vital key to human progress and development. We deplore any neo-romantic efforts to condemn indiscriminately all technology and science or to counsel retreat from its further extension and use for the good of humankind. We would resist any moves to censor basic scientific research on moral, political, or social grounds.[5]

To many persons this statement, particularly the notion that scientific research should not be checked on "moral, political, or social grounds," betrays dismal ignorance of the kind of distinction drawn by Russell.[6] Science does not necessarily include the correct conception of the ends of human life, as the nuclear arms and the ecology crisis dangerously attest. Some control or direction is appropriate. Neither persons nor technology is evil. But neither is so good as to require no supervision. This represents a fundamental failure of humanists to acknowledge the power of evil in the course of human affairs. Thus Joan Beck articulates the steps necessary to make sure that sufficient planning takes place in case the "greenhouse effect" does indeed occur, each step requiring the kind of sophisticated and complex cooperation about the future quality of human life that is the topic of the next chapter.[7]

At any rate, the clash between technological progress and human values is not really a dispute between truth seekers and reprehensible bigots. Rather, it represents the apogee of our cultural crisis: a crisis in uncooperative and competitive overspecialization. Our ignorance of other disciplines and alternative value systems can no longer be excused. Reintegration of disciplines at every turn is necessary, as Van Rensselaer Potter suggested in his *Bioethics*.[8] In fact, interdisciplinary education is no longer an option. The future of our civilization depends on it.

### Technological Progress

"Technological progress" has various meanings that alter the nature of possible value clashes. Technology embodies values in different ways, depending on the source of judgments applying knowledge to action. The charge often is made that technology has led to the domination of human values by mechanical ones. For example, as I mentioned in chapter 3, Lewis Yablonsky suggests that mechanical values dominate all interpersonal interactions, such that we begin to act as machines rather than as persons.[9] I hope to show how this charge can be variously understood.

Simply put, a machine or a technology is a complex combination of artificial design using the perception of natural laws for the solution of human problems. As a consequence, technologies are explicitly rooted in judgments about the goals and ends of a good human life. Technology is value-laden.

We are now sophisticated enough to recognize that every new technology carries with it a new set of problems. Introduction of throwaway plastic products causes problems of litter and garbage disposal. Medical advances prolong life and lead to problems of population control and definitions of death. A patient who has successfully undergone a heart-lung transplant, but must now remain on a respirator, may judge that this sort of life is not worth living. It is equivalent to death. The person may request that the respirator be turned off. Technologies should therefore be viewed as value tradeoffs between the enormity of the problem they attempt to solve and their power to create new problems.

The scientific application judgments involved in technology can be suggested by the technology itself or by external factors. The source of this judgment leads to different kinds of value clashes.

1. When the technology itself suggests its own progress, the impact on human values depends on the adequacy of the original technology in meeting human needs. For example, it is a human value to be able to stop an automobile. The drum brake suggests a disc brake, a noticeable improvement on large cars. If the original purpose of the design is kept in mind, and the human needs have not changed significantly, this kind of progress would seldom conflict with human values.

In other words, internal design changes, or progressions, are actually attempts to respond to the technology itself, which embodies human values. If the original technology no longer meets human needs—for example, a manual coffee grinder—improving the quality of its gear ratio will not enhance its usefulness.

2. The second meaning of technological progress is more problematical. When design alteration, or "progress," is suggested by external factors, human values are in danger of being submerged by mechanical, economic, political, or technocratic ones. Resentment of technology then occurs. This is tantamount to saying that technological progress dictated by factors other than internal ones may not be "progress" at all. At least such progress needs our scrutiny.

Technology will mesh with human values insofar as its design conforms to actual human needs. I will try to build a case in the next section for the enduring nature of these needs, needs that are seldom subject to faddish fluctuations in market conditions. If what I am saying is true, then a civilization that offers patterns and meaning for enduring values would not so easily be disrupted by technological progress attuned to these values.

In short, technology has a moral dimension. The perception of human needs and values demands another sort of perspective than that offered by science. In fact, the humanities offer just such a perception. It therefore seems necessary to include the humanities and their insights in all phases of the technological process. In this way, technologies would be designed that more aptly fit human needs.

External factors can override design in several ways. I will focus on three. Since design, embodying human values, is disrupted, so are the values upon which it is based. Since these values originally responded to human problems, the "improved" technology is then placed at odds with the perceived and accepted ends of a good human life. Further, I will concentrate my remarks on the *bad* features of three types of design override: external misperception of human needs; external market pressures; and new scientific discoveries in another area of research.

## Design Overrides

The first of the three design overrides is that the value of a technology can clash with other human values if human needs are misperceived. Is feminine hygiene spray a technological progression? Was it based on a need? Or rather was it dictated in part by a view that men and women feared odors of promiscuity? The dangers of skin reactions far outweigh the spray's doubtful usefulness. Here a misperception of a need overrode good design.

The Edsel was a car designed on gimmickry. It bombed. Apparently someone misperceived a fad for a need. Glitter and chrome gas eaters were formerly popular. They seemed to touch an authentic human need. Recent events prove they did not. We paid for our misperception in jobless autoworkers, an energy crisis, and a severely depressed Midwestern economy.

Long-term misperceptions are difficult to detect. What is popular is not necessarily that which touches authentic human needs. The rapid-transit systems we obviously need remain underdeveloped because we have misperceived needs of freedom and mobility in too atomistic a fashion. Individual cars appeared to be a real human need because they were popular.

A second design override comes from external market conditions. Under the pressures of a growth economy, not only human values but also science itself is subverted to the goals of a corporation. The latter sometimes inadequately reflect the authentic needs of the human race. In health care, hospitals are closing in the inner city because the state and health insurance cannot reimburse at anything near the cost of care, yet in order to survive, other hospitals are purchasing highly expensive retail space to attract paying patients. The needs of society for decent health care for all suffer immensely from "market condition" planning.[10]

Sometimes products are designed and then markets are created for them by advertising, advertising that only remotely resembles a true perception of needs. Do we really need more false eyelashes, bigger private homes, electric plastic-wrap machines for the kitchen, electric brushes, and so on? The values they represent, if any, are mostly narcissistic. People using these products begin to be dominated by them, become neurotic without them. They lose an easy ability to relate to other human beings because of their dependency upon machines. Eventually they feel dehumanized and strike out at technology itself.

The ultimate stupidity of expending our creative energies on this approach to "technological progress" is now visible to the layperson. We were once encouraged to buy a new car to stimulate the economy. The car used more fuel, which in turn drove up the price of imported oil, depleting the money remaining at home and causing inflated prices in all goods and services. This in turn contributed to an enormous imbalance in trade that caused the nation to lose jobs and drove up inflation and the national debt. One became doubly stupid: new car payments and higher costs for essentials. Small wonder that people today are more cautious about purchasing this kind of technological progress!

But external market conditions are not only a sample of stupidity. They can become dangerous as controls over technology. In the first place, they eventually lead to consumer caution about buying products and even consumer resentment, as I have noted. Second, they contribute to a dehumanized self-image of the workers. Karl Marx, in this regard, illustrated how external market conditions can cause unrest and even revolution.

Marx's theory stated that in a capitalist society the worker is alienated from his or her work by the forces of the free market. The worker's value as a person tends to be judged in economic terms by the amount paid for the work. If the free market demands that a car be sold through advertising its sex potential rather than its workmanship, it will not be perceived as having authentic value in difficult times. Its value will fluctuate, and with it, the worker's self-esteem. The self-perception of the worker as object controlled by external, extrinsic forces results. Eventually this dehumanized process will lead the worker to revolt.[11]

Finally, as a third design override, new scientific discoveries can be and have been applied in other areas than those intended. Instantaneous communication technologies are valuable. But when applied to electronic eavesdropping on individual human beings, they destroy the right of privacy necessary to live a decent, free, human life. If one grants that defoliants are helpful for clearing land, one need not grant that they helped the economy and the ecology of Vietnam or the health of those who came in contact with one defoliant, Agent Orange. If a new drug is discovered, it is not necessarily for the good of a drug-saturated society to market it. If one grants that splitting the atom was a great advance, one need not rejoice in the fact that individual terrorists and the syndicate can now make the bomb. An MIT student in 1975 figured out from available literature how to make the atomic bomb. He was a twenty-year-old undergraduate.[12]

In summary, good technology would be human design relying on scientific knowledge and the perception of enduring values. Technology can be attuned to human values if and only if it meets authentic human needs. These are difficult to perceive. At least we know that human needs cannot be monolithically deduced from science, technocracy, profit and loss economic theory, and/or any re-

ductionist view of persons. Rather, they can be perceived only
through an intense interdisciplinary, open-ended study of enduring
contributions to our civilization. And they must be studied from the
perspective of the future of the entire human race.

The crisis of our civilization is poignantly highlighted by the fact
that we have become immune to human needs by the very technologized society designed originally to support these needs. After all,
gadgets are easier to relate to than human beings.

## Values

I have stated that values are found at the root of judgments. The
enduring nature of values upon which a good technology must be
based ought to be underlined. I will do this by examining values in
science itself.

Before we examine levels of clashes between technology and human values, then, we must take a stand on an assertion made earlier,
that is, values are found in the theoretical as well as the practical,
moral realm. Is this tantamount to asserting that all sciences are
value-laden?

While the methodology of science abstracts from values in an effort to be clear, objective, and certain, the nature of the scientific
search for truth is based on a value system or "myth," as I have been
using that term. This myth includes at least three value judgments:
first, that problems are best solved by analysis; second, that analysis
is best accomplished by breaking down the problem into discrete
units (as does the atomic theory, e.g.); third, that truth is objective,
and asymptotically (continuously more nearly) approaches mathe-
matical certitude.

In other words, science-as-method may not be value-laden;
science-as-myth definitely is. This is especially true when science
becomes the very meaning of life (as it does for scientific humanists)
or when it is applied as technology. Differences in values can occur,
therefore, in the realm of scientific myth itself, in the use of science
in a technology, or in the application of a technology to human
needs.

The enduring nature of values can be recognized by their resistance to change. Within the realm of scientific myth itself, the ideas
of Werner Heisenberg, Albert Einstein, and General Systems Theory all call into question the three value judgments of analysis, component parts, and certitude, mentioned earlier. The latter have
become entrenched in scientific thought and in society at large.
They are not easily replaced by new value judgments: that problems
are best solved by synthesis (Systems Theory); that component parts
are not isolated but relate to one another in relative ways (Systems

Theory and Relativity Theory); and that we may not be able to be certain about ultimate physical processes (Heisenberg's Uncertainty Principle).

More recently in science, there is a perception that the universe is not as orderly as we have assumed since the Age of Reason. This is called the "Theory of Chaos."[13] The theory is that everything cannot be explained simply by noting things to the next decimal point or measuring and breaking the phenomenon down into component parts. Existing theories may explain how nature works in limited circumstances but cannot explain any phenomenon or entity completely. Chaos theory recognizes that change is inherent in nature's dynamic systems. True complexity touches on the edges of mystery.

In addition, judgments made in applying science to human problems touch on values inherited from the scientific myth. These values often clash with more human ones. By way of example, a surgeon may apply his science and technology diligently in amputating a leg. If the scientific value judgment that component parts can be treated as isolated units governs his practice, he will consider his task accomplished as soon as the leg is cut off. The amputee must fend for himself in a struggle to reintegrate his life around a lost limb. If he commits suicide because he cannot cope, what human need has been met by the surgeon's task?[14]

Looking again at the meaning of "values," they can be distinguished from beliefs and attitudes. A belief is a personal commitment to a thought or action wherein there is insufficient evidence. An attitude is a personal commitment with sufficient evidence. A value, on the other hand, is a weighting of the relative importance of an object, person, or idea. It is a concept in the mind of individuals about their experience. As such it prepares us for the future, for interpreting the experiences to come. Hence, a value may be thought of as a personal *future* orientation regarding a structure of life by which it is meaningful to think in a certain way. Analogously, the word "value" is predicated on groups of people or even entire civilizations. A value adds a temporal dimension to beliefs and attitudes. It is a commitment to the purpose or ends of a human life. When beliefs and attitudes change, they change because a person "values" something not expressed in either. I am suggesting that that "something" valued is a future orientation.

A belief that God created the world becomes a value for a person when that person stakes his or her future on it. Similarly, an attitude that women are as accomplished at decision making as men becomes a value when a person plans the future of his or her company around this attitude. I can draw this out even more explicitly. Staking one's life involves making judgments. Our attitudes and beliefs, as well as our knowledge, enter the judgment process. But the meaning of the judgment is future-oriented, otherwise we would not bother to make it. Expectations about the future give meaning to the past and the present.

For this reason, humanized technology must pay attention to the future needs of the human race. These needs will not occur automatically. A technology that does pay attention to these needs will do so because we have humanized it by controlling its direction.

Examples of enduring human values, then, can be culled from the energies that people and cultures expended on certain tasks. Among these values I would list sufficient nourishment, interpersonal communication, health, celebration, control of the environment, friendship, personal and sexual fulfillment, freedom of expression and creativity, harmony with others and with nature, living a virtuous life, and finding answers. Today our challenge is to meet these values on a worldwide scale. Buckminster Fuller argues that we have the technological means to meet these kinds of needs. We simply have not raised them to the level of political and social values.[15]

## Value Clashes

Applying knowledge to human needs necessarily involves a balance between the values upon which that knowledge is gained and the values upon which solutions to human problems rest. To strike that balance is difficult. Possessing guidelines for striking the balance of values would be to have at our disposal practical cultural wisdom. One component of practical cultural wisdom is the ability to distinguish various levels of value clashes so that the source can be clearly identified. Seven levels of value clashes can be discerned.

The first is differing values within the scientific myth itself. Insofar as the myth governs our perception of the world or our technological progress, the differing values become life threatening. I have already cited Einstein, Heisenberg, and General Systems Theory in this regard. Can relativity be expanded to include ethical principles? Is there no absolute right or wrong? If the nature of the universe is indeterminate, does that mean that there is no objective truth? Does it also mean that what is true is only commensurate with what is powerful?

The second level of value clashes occurs between two alternative myths. One is familiar with the seemingly endless science versus religion debate. Both are myths of ultimate meaning, and neither frequently respects the insights of the other. The struggle between the myths has often resulted in personal, social, and political trauma. The devastating Wars of the Roses is an old example. The Iran-Iraq war and the struggle in Afghanistan are present-day examples of conflicts between modern industrial states, representing the myth of progress, and science and antediluvian states, representing myths of religious loyalties. Russian soldiers retreating from Afghanistan during the 1989 negotiated settlement said, "We live in the 20th Century and they live in the 14th."[16]

The third level of differing values occurs when the design of a technology itself offers an opportunity for progress. I have already discussed how a drum brake might suggest a disc brake. This of course is an example of technological progress at its best. Suppose we take medical technology which prolongs human life, however. This technology was designed around an authentic human need. If life is beautiful, why not enjoy a longer one? The prolongation-of-life technology (including cardiopulmonary resuscitation techniques, transplant and bypass technologies, chemotherapeutic and antibiotic interventions, and even fluids and nutrition delivered medically) has produced two problems. One is an increasing older population; the other is the question about a person's right to die. Medical technology suggested another improvement: birth prevention devices, of which the pill and abortion are but two examples. To many, however, the introduction of these "improvements" represents an assault on the very reverence for life around which the prolongation technology was built.

The fourth level of value clashes occurs when a technology no longer meets human needs. No amount of improvement of the technology can salvage it. Enormous upheaval will have to occur to replace the "road" technology, built around private autos, with another means of transportation. It will probably take the form of video telephones, satellites, and computer communication. With these services in hand, why would it be necessary to commute to a centralized office, when one could work just as efficiently from one's home or apartment?

The fifth level of value clashes occurs when technology is designed around misperceived human needs. High-rise buildings neglect the need for personal living space. One can detect that from the upper-class proliferation of "second homes" in the country. Mass communication neglects the need for participation; thus the "staged for TV" demonstrations in our recent past. Vibrators and Mickey Mouse prophylactics neglect the need for sexual fulfillment, though they appear to many to offer it. They are only examples of the proliferation of exotic devices.

The sixth level of value clashes arises from external market conditions. A good case could be made that in addition to life-preserving values, respirators were produced because they brought a profit. Their use raises questions about the nature of a human person, the right to life, and the right to die with decency.[17] We ought to ask whether their use actually touches an authentic human need for the quality of life or whether as technology progresses it creates more problems than it solves. A good example of how this question applies to the clinical setting is the use of respirators on adults suffering from leukemia. Even if the leukemia is in remission, when these persons contract pneumocystis carinii pneumonia and are put on a respirator, they seldom if ever are able to survive without this machine. In other words, the decision to help them during the pneumonia becomes a decision to depend upon a machine for the rest of their life.

And the final level occurs when scientific research is applied to an unintended or unexamined area. Research on aborted fetuses will lead to eventual growth in artificial wombs or being transplanted in carriers. Is this really a desirable development? Have the long-term effects been thoroughly studied? Current research on the brain tissue of fetuses suggests that transplanting that tissue to persons suffering from Alzheimer's and other degenerative brain diseases (such as Parkinson's) will help them recover. Is it now to be open season on fetuses? Are fetuses to be viewed as a collection of harvestable organs?[18] I have already mentioned the possibility of the A-bomb being made by terrorists. Of even more concern is the possibility of terrorists making and using chemical weapons. But what of research on genetics being used to create a master race? Or research on artificial limbs leading to totally artificial human beings? Or research on bacteria leading to resistant strains?

## Directing Technology

In none of the cases am I arguing that scientific research or technological progress should be curtailed. Instead, my suggestion is that we spend more energy on it. But with this qualification: that we spend an equivalent amount of cultural energy on discerning the authentic, enduring human values to be designed into our technology. This will be a noisy and often frustrating process. Better to have it before than after the consequences. In this way, we will create a scientific civilization organized around a correct conception of a good human life.

Technology can incorporate the proper ends of a good human life. Its interlocking nature need not be destroyed; rather, it can be channeled. Through a process of public policy in which we err always on the side of the value of human life, if that can be said to be an error, technological progress can be a moral enterprise. It can represent the creative achievement of persons working for life-enhancing ends.

The reality principle to be used would be a community decision to develop new devices, to deploy them, and to determine in which contexts they apply. Explicit discussion of the role of values in each technological effort, and that value's suitability for the future, will occur.

It is a matter of great pride that we have begun just such an explicit discussion program, particularly with respect to the values of human life in medical, civil, and military technological advances. In each of these there is a broad spectrum of opinion leading to hearty public debate. Greater public participation in the continuous discussion is still required. I now consider this new moral order.

## Technology and the New Moral Order

In a powerful BBC interview shown in the United States shortly after he defected, Alexander Solzhenitsyn shared his perceptions of the major problem facing all human beings and particularly those of us in Western civilization. In this interview, characterized by Michael Charlton of the BBC staff as "a blow to the solar plexus," Solzhenitsyn said he failed to understand how "one can lose one's spiritual strength, one's will power; and possessing freedom, not be able to value it, not be willing to make sacrifices for it."

In his criticism of the West, Solzhenitsyn said, "The question is not how the Soviet Union will find a way out of totalitarianism, but how the West will be able to avoid the same fate." Confronted with the agonizing choice between cooperation with the oppression of others and self and the exercise of one's freedom, the Russian Nobel Prize winner articulated his and his followers' credo: "Better to be dead than a scoundrel."[19]

Obviously death is less to be preferred. But gaining control over structures of oppression, whether they be familial, economic, political, or personal, is extremely difficult. "Gaining control" is precisely the fundamental ethical call of our age.

To what extent has technology contributed to this moral issue? To what extent could technology contribute to eradication of international and personal oppression? Can technology contribute to a creation of a new world order, or does it by its very nature lead to totalitarianism? In terms of human personal and political freedom, is technology amoral, moral, or antimoral?

A lifelong student of technology and society, Hans Jonas has pointed out a tremendous challenge for our time to provide adequately for the future and to protect the rights of future generations. This is what technology has bequeathed us: choice, greater choices than ever before, a new freedom to design civilization and life itself.[20]

I would stress the urgency of the question of technology. An exploration of the positive and negative features of technology is essential to the survival of humankind. Such exploration is not an academic exercise. The answer to questions about moral good or evil brought on by technology will have a profound effect on the suitability of technological, versus human, solutions to our vast, global problems. Should we just throw up our hands and repeat Martin Heidegger's words at the end of his life that "only a God can save us"?[21] Or should we address the value dimensions of technology while it is being developed—a more difficult, indeed a more human, task?[22]

Neglect of the moral realm in applying technological solutions ignores an entire component of human nature. And just as the poor in India overturned trucks that were bringing birth control devices to their villages, so too will enormous masses of people overturn and reject technological solutions to human problems if these are not attentive to human values at the same time. Problems will not only remain unsolved, they will erupt into the destruction of all remnants of a civilized human life. It is my belief that current interest in medical, legal, engineering, and business ethics represents a footnote to the larger problem of the role of technology in a decent human civilization. The contribution in this section is an assessment of the arguments about the moral implications of technology. I will first discuss the views of those who see technology as antimoral; then, of those who view it as amoral; and, finally, as those who view technology as a moral enterprise. I should be counted among those in the last category. Sufficient arguments will be presented, however, to rule out technological solutions to difficult moral dilemmas. These must be resolved through an ethic of dialogue, the theme of the final chapter.

## Technology as Antimoral

There are any number of critics who claim that technology is antimoral. In other words, they believe technology to be the most pervasive evil of our civilization. Among major critics whose opinions have been well developed and received, are Jacques Ellul, Lewis Mumford, René Dubos, Wilhelm Reich, and Theodore Roszak. Ellul is a theologian-philosopher; Mumford was originally a supporter of technological improvement; Dubos was a biologist; and the last two are academics supporting a counterculture. Despite their beautiful prose and articulate positions, not one of the thinkers cited has proposed an alternative to the supposed evils of a technological society. Mumford and Dubos both advocate some unspecific return to nature, and Reich's celebration of a "new consciousness" is well known, but neither proposal can realistically alter the image of persons and society in our day.[23]

Samuel Florman, in his "In Praise of Technology,"[24] offered the following list of common dyspeptic points made by the antitechnologists. I add my own comments as well:

1. Technology is a thing or force escaping human control and spoiling our life.
2. Technology forces persons to do tedious and degrading work.
3. Technology forces persons to consume things they do not need.
4. Technology creates an elite class of technocrats and so disenfranchises the masses.
5. Technology cripples persons by cutting them off from the natural world of evolution, threatening survival mechanisms.
6. Technology provides technical diversions that divert humans from existential concerns.
7. Technology tends to extend visual perception, for example, through television, ultrasound, computerized axial tomography (CAT scan), and so on. In doing this, however, it separates vision from other sensing, such as feeling. In a way, it contributes to a Cartesian form of human extension, stressing the cognitive over the emotive.

These are only summary points, each with a certain measure of validity. Mumford offers no fewer than twenty-seven evil effects of technology, including giantism (love of quantity) and infantilization of persons (overdependence).[25]

What I take to be valid about these critiques is an aesthetic criticism of mass culture that has been a consistent feature of modern thought. But do these criticisms justify the charge that technology is evil in itself? I think not. The presuppositions of the critics of technology reveal some questionable assumptions, sufficient to weaken their thesis.

The first assumption is that human nature, our "true nature," is not technological but biological. This view is questionable only because of its exclusion of technology. Human beings are obviously biological entities. But they also have always made tools to control their environment. In fact, this is how anthropologists identify shards of ancient bones as humanoid, by also identifying primitive stone tools used to kill or carve prey.

A second claim is that technology escapes human control. Consequently there is a tendency to view it as a thing "out there," impinging on the value of human life. Actually, technology is an activity of persons, at least partially responding to the desires of persons. Human beings have always been on the move. An automobile responds to that need. In the form of a vast, interlocking system, technology is indeed in danger of escaping our control. But that is, as I have argued, the nub of the ethical issue. There would be no ethical issues if we had no chance of control. Everything would be determined.

A third claim is that technology is evil. Actually, persons make choices to depend upon or design techniques. The evil lies in sophisticated misdirectings of human values designed in or used to override technologies, as shown in Section One ("Design Overrides") of this chapter.

A fourth assumption is that technology somehow forces human beings to submit to its blandishments. This view is also tied to a romantic vision of a simpler life "down on the farm." Rather than forcing us to use it, technology forces us to make more *choices* about using it. In the past, people died. Just like that. Now we have a huge range of technical options available to prolong life, from anticlotting drugs to cardiac perfusion devices, from intravenous feeding to electroshock therapy for the heart, from respirators to nasogastric tubes, from neurosurgery to effective antibiotics.[26] The force created by these techniques lies in requiring us to make highly sophisticated, case-by-case legal and moral judgments about their use, from the standpoint of the inherent value of human life and the purposes of that life.[27]

A final major claim is that technology combines rationality and control, thereby creating a machinelike technocracy with its own values. In this way, as Ellul argues, a new kind of totalitarianism is created.[28] This is a very important point, vis-à-vis the comments of Solzhenitsyn. If technology creates a cadre of technocrats, it is not necessarily the case that this cadre is inimical to human ends, particularly if it promotes the value of human life. In every advance of civilization there is a risk. Technology may indeed overwhelm us. But this is not necessary. If the value of human life is respected, technocrats may really fulfill the noble aims of a decent human society.

An example of the risks that new technology can pose to any human value position is posed by what abortionists call accidental "live births." On May 4 and May 5, 1982, two fetuses miraculously survived second trimester abortion procedures performed at the University of Wisconsin Medical Center. One baby was twenty weeks old, and the other was twenty-four weeks old. Even though they were both rushed to intensive care, they died within twenty-seven hours after being "born." In the light of the thesis I have developed, the comments of Anne Gaylor, president of the Protect Abortion Rights and the Women's Medical Fund, did not properly respect the value of human life: "Those fetuses were going nowhere. Their births can't begin to negate the terrible need for legal late abortions." The Secretary of Health and Human Services said he was going to investigate the case to see whether the infants' civil rights were violated. A leading authority on abortions, Dr. Thomas Kerenyi, says of accidental live births, "It's like landing a jet plane. You're supposed to throw everything into reverse, and do the exact opposite of what you were doing. It's schizoid, but if you don't do it (help the baby to stay alive), you're easily open to accusations that you're playing God, a new Hitler, deciding who will survive and who won't."[29]

There are many who would have little sympathy for the doctors who are present and active at abortion proceedings. But let us assume, for the moment, that the legal ability is also moral. The doctors who are concerned about the issue of accidental live births are, *at least*, concerned in a human way about the responsible use of all abortion technology. As such, they are not the technocrats Ellul describes—not yet, at least.

But consider the desire to solve this moral, this agonizing human problem by better technology. At this point, the danger of a technocracy does emerge. Sure enough, in the same article discussing the human dilemma of live births, physicians are quoted as saying:

> Ultrasound is in much greater use now. It is much more accurate and should do away, to a large extent, with the problem of underestimation of fetal age, which was the biggest contributing factor to live born fetuses.[30]

The use of a decent human technology, ultrasound, to eliminate a moral problem is an example of a misuse of technology. It would lead to the kind of machinelike repetitive action in abortion that would dull the dim but still present moral challenge of the enterprise. It would be better, from the point of view of ethics, not from the point of view of law (which requires specificity of viability based on age), that the technology not be employed to "resolve" this dilemma.

Another example of our society dealing with the moral challenge of abortion came when the National Institutes of Health assembled a panel to consider the morality and legality of using aborted fetuses for research. It had temporarily been stopped. The panel of experts gave its considered opinion after a short period of time. Although concern was expressed for the morality of the research, a majority opinion of 28 to 3, with one abstention, held that since abortion is legal, nothing illegal was being done. The benefits were great enough to override any moral qualms. The panel recommended recommencing this research.[31]

I conclude this section by drawing a simple but obvious distinction. Critics of technology are correct in identifying evil *effects* of technology. But they are incorrect in attributing these to technology itself rather than to the human community that fails to deal with technology in an ethical manner. Fuller made this point often in his lectures and talks. The distinction I make follows from an old scholastically identified fallacy: *post hoc, propter hoc*. Critics fail to distinguish effect from cause. In any case, they cannot argue logically that technology is antimoral.

But those who praise technology also fail to see the extent to which our technology has become an ethical embarrassment. Daniel Callahan's call for a point beyond which we would not develop a technology is an important corrective to overoptimism.[32] Too often technological advances lack public accountability—precisely the reason, for example, for the development of the Department of Health and Human Services guidelines on medical research.

## Technology as Amoral

A fairly strong case could be made for technology as being morally neutral, acquiring its ethical applicability from the ends to which it is put.

Thus, Victor Marchetti and John Marks in their *The CIA and the Cult of Intelligence* describe, in horror, the defects of the intelligence system as a result of a kind of professional amorality, another wrinkle of the age-old ethical problem of ends and means. They describe amorality thus: "Righteous goals can be achieved through the use of unprincipled and normally unacceptable means."[33]

The very structure of ideology leads to the notion that means are morally neutral. Ruling groups can become so interest-bound to a certain situation that they fail to see the facts that underlie their domination. Implicit in ideology is a collective unconsciousness that obscures the real condition of society both to those who are masters and to those who are slaves. Thereby it stabilizes the situation.

This amoral view of means, however, fails to take the objections of antitechnologists such as Mumford into account. There is certainly some moral value implied in any technique that creates a change in the image of persons and society.

In fact, my definition of technology highlights the moral values in the very design of machines. This point leads to the next argument, however.

## Technology as a Moral Enterprise

My argument that technology is a moral enterprise is essential to the conclusions I will draw about enduring human values and the hope of a new world order based on a belief in the inherent value of human life. The argument is built on the following steps:

1. Human beings are not only biological but also technological. To separate technology from its nature as a human activity is artificially to divorce us from our own powers. In effect, it also divorces us from the proper measures of responsibility for our own actions.

2. As an essentially human activity, technology is an application of our knowledge in the moral realm. This point was developed earlier in this chapter.

3. Technology is subject to certain design overrides, also discussed previously in this chapter. Just as the good effects of ultrasound in diagnostic procedures can be subverted for morally contested applications, so too all technologies, most of which are designed to fulfill the proper ends of good human life, can be misused to impede those ends by destroying the value of human life.

4. The ethical problem is, therefore, not to belittle technology but to gain control over the purely technocratic decisions to use what is essentially a moral human activity for questionable ends. If we do not gain that control, then the totalitarianism that Solzhenitsyn warned about will come to pass. In this view, technology is not value-less. "Gaining control" also requires, in addition to the power to have that control, the use of a cultural wisdom about appropriate applications of technology that science, medicine, and engineering cannot alone supply us.[34]

5. Gaining control also means that we recognize what is the case. As developed in chapter 3, we must be able to perceive that we depend upon technology to live. It enters our self-definition in a major way. The popular film *E.T.* could lead a viewer to surmise that the adults would eventually surround the house where Elliott was hiding the extraterrestrial and bring to bear on E.T. all the technology at their disposal. To be an adult is to employ incredibly complicated machines. One of the moral touchstones of this movie was the innocence of children in objecting to this almost violent application of technology.

6. Freedom in a new world order is not freedom to do what one pleases. It cannot be a kind of romantic individualism, although we will pine for the days of the rugged individual—the sheriff in *High Noon* or Han Solo ("Solo" = "alone") in *Star Wars*. Instead, it should be seen as a freedom to take responsibility for what we have created.

It can be objected that liberty is an essential component of the inherent value of human life, as it was regarded in our heritage, which will be examined in Part Three of this book. Does not the view that responsible freedom is required by our technology somehow truncate this liberty? Actually, human beings experience three kinds of liberty, all of which are important. The individualism of the eighteenth and nineteenth centuries has tended to focus on autonomous freedom of choice. But if my description of technological society is correct, then our dependence on the Machine limits those choices and thereby seems to limit our freedom. Beyond choice, however, there are two other kinds of freedom.

Willed or not, we do live in a technological age. If we do not choose it, we may still head for the caves or the remote islands. Most of us like living with modern conveniences. Hence our freedom to choose is defined by the options open to us to use technologies. A second freedom is even more important. It is the freedom to commit ourselves to that which we have chosen. A spouse does that after marriage, which severely limits choices of available mates! A third liberty is the freedom to create new choices through the use of technology. These new possibilities then force us to reexamine our cherished values, to rethink assumptions about human life and its proper ends. All of these experiences are liberating: choice, commitment, creativity. They are rewarding, too, if well managed.

7. Finally, in a new world order, rule by technocracy is not historically inevitable. Ellul is wrong in assuming that technical and rational control necessarily transcribes into totalitarianism. The reasons have been developed already but are summarized as follows:

Technology cannot assess its own ethical values. This is a responsibility of the community.

Assessment of values requires public and objective criteria that must be developed through respectful discussion on an international scale.

Denial of human responsibility for the moral design and application of technology misrepresents the nature of human freedom. It leads, ironically, to pessimistic acceptance of a technical ideology. In this sense, any slave to technology is enslaved by his or her choice of slavery.

The public discussion of the proper ends of a good human life, toward which to aim technology, can profit immensely from a consideration of our heritage regarding the inherent value of human life. It is not impossible to conceive of swords being hammered into plowshares, of nuclear technology being used as a safe form of power, of space technology being used to provide modular housing for all, and so on.

Public discussion calls attention to our perceptions and their relation to the truth. Just as the assumptions about defense led to nuclear arms buildups, a public examination of the human need for security also leads now to demands for disarmament. Both 1982 Nobel Peace Prize winners, Alva Myrdal and Alfonso Garcia Robles, have been active for more than twenty years in calling for this disarmament. For them, it is disarm or die. The security we value is no longer there.

An international commitment to the inherent value of human life would establish a basic belief about technology and its applications without in any way closing off political and ethical debate. But at least we would know that we would not be destroyed by our own hand, that we would not be ground up in the gears we ourselves created.

## Conclusion

I had hoped to end in a paean of praise for future possibilities. Instead, I can only say that technology raises international moral policy issues. These issues cannot be resolved by privatized, ethical principles but demand international discussion by all. Simultaneously with raising such issues, technology forces us to (1) deal with issues out of self-interest at the very least and (2) offer technical solutions. Whether these solutions are suitable for four billion people is the terrifying ethical crunch. I have suggested they are not. More human ones are needed.

Technology is a moral enterprise that necessitates, at the very least, out of survival instincts, a global responsibility for a possible new international community of human beings. The possible frightens us. But when has the possible ever been without its risks?

The question was well stated by Solzhenitsyn. Can we escape totalitarianism? Technology is our chance. For in the end the problem of technology is a problem about the value of human life. It offers us the chance to be enormously resourceful. Can we be? We have always taken a new path or faced stagnation. I think we can have a new will for a new world.

# PART THREE

# Our Heritage Involving the Value of Human Life

# 5

# Our Religious Heritage

The humanizing and spiritualizing process of the world and of humanity does not take place in the last resort according to high-handed human plans, but is directed by the imperceptible but firm hand of God.

—Edward Schillebeeckx

In the midst of the war between Israel and the PLO in 1982, West Beirut was surrounded by Israeli troops. One of the most poignant moments in that siege occurred when Mother Teresa of Calcutta was evacuating severely retarded and handicapped children from a mental hospital in the Sabra camp—a guerrilla stronghold devastated by Israeli shells and bombs. As she talked to reporters, she lovingly held one of the children. And then she sadly remarked: "That war is evil, it must be said. I don't understand it. They are all children of God. Why do they do it? I don't understand."[1]

Nothing could more directly speak of the primacy of human values in our religious heritage than the lined, compassionate face of Mother Teresa protecting the brain-damaged child in her arms. With the broken bricks and rubble of war scattered in the background, she was compelled to assert that all are "children of God."

This belief in the inherent and equal value of all human beings under God is not an arbitrary hypothesis. Rather, it is a belief that can be traced through the world religions and the Judeo-Christian heritage. It directly transcribes into a moral system, the essence of which is respect for the value of each person. Thus the Rev. James Schall can assert that "the essence of civilization, of morality, of dignity is this: All life, Down syndrome or whatever, is worth living."[2] By showing the reasonableness of this view, I will also be arguing, by contrast, that any moral judgment that ignores such respect for the inherent value of each human life must be extensively and adequately defended. The burden of proof, if those are the right words, ought to lie on those who argue that there is no specific "inherent value" of human life.[3] In other words, I will be tracing what is called a normative basis for our ethical decisions, which basis is established on a belief.

This belief is a reasonable goal for "directing" our technology to good human ends. As such, then, Part Three of the book attempts to establish the protection of the value of human life as an appropriate and obtainable goal for our moral policies in the twenty-first century.

Because not everyone agrees with the belief that all human beings are children of God, chapters 6 and 7 show how the belief in the inherent equal value of human beings operates in the philosophical and political realms as well. The sections of this chapter are devoted to the religious basis of the belief: (1) The Moral Force of Religion; (2) The Value of Human Life in the Old Testament; (3) The Value of Human Life in the Christian Tradition; and (4) Conclusion.

## The Moral Force of Religion

A word about method is appropriate here. Recall that in the Introduction I noted that arguments of fittingness are the method of a defense of the value of human life. Even though a defense like this one does rely on religion and theological arguments as well, the premises from which it makes its arguments are not so much revealed principles as they are the ideas and practices of human beings in history. Remember that the reason for this method is to stimulate reflection in all persons of good will, not only those who share the same faith.

Thus Professor Frank Reynolds of the University of Chicago notes that

> this history of religions is perceived as a very general field that encompasses the whole range of disciplines that pursue the study of religion and religions in ways that strive to be "objective." From this point of view, the sole defining characteristic which identifies the field is its emphasis on generating theories and interpretations of religious data that are at the same time non-confessional and non-reductive.[4]

Such an approach may appear sterile to those already convinced by their faith that all human life has absolute value. In return for this failing, however, a broader appeal can be made, even to those for whom religion is only one of many strange manifestations of the human spirit. Here I can only sketch, largely from Western religious tradition, ideas about the value of the human person.

Nowhere is it inscribed infallibly that all persons are created equal, that they have equal intrinsic value regardless of their station or standing in life. Here and there the idea shines through the murk of human conduct, as in the Declaration of Independence. But to become the powerful force for cultural and political life that it can be, each generation must take the idea to heart. The idea must be put into practice, just as acts of love make one's belief in God real. As Michael Schmaus said, "Deeds of love make God credible."[5] Similarly, only actions will make credible a belief in the intrinsic value of human life.

Each generation must fashion from a belief in the intrinsic value of human life, like artist's clay, a new form. One of the historically consistent ways of inheriting, forming, and bequeathing the value of human life is through religion. As Hans Urs von Balthasar noted:

> A present experience is true and valuable only insofar as it is bound up with a certain vision and interpretation of the past and future, with a projection of our ruling ideal. . . . The Bible is filled with such projections towards its own historic past. Without them it would not possess a truth that was fully human.[6]

The value that inheres in the dignity of human life embraces everyone, not just those we regard as fully functioning persons. For a Christian the incarnation of the Son of God revealed possibilities of human nature such that the more one becomes like the love of God, the more truly human one becomes.[7] While a secular view might focus on rationality or free will as the marks of human dignity, individuals who are incapable of demonstrating rationality—such as the profoundly retarded, the debilitated aged, and even those born without higher cortical function—may, in a biblical view, still have dignity and worth as human beings.[8]

It is important to note that what people believe is often lost in practice. Karl Rahner, the Jesuit theologian, comments that there is a kind of moral atheism through which people may profess a belief in God but deny that belief with their actions.[9] Similarly, great world religions have sometimes been guilty of practices that give a lie to their beliefs, practices such as condemnation and torture of those who did not adhere to the tenets of the official religion; smashing the babies of enemies against a rock; capital punishment; and the institution of slavery. From the perspective of western religion, for example, the tradition of suttee (burning a widow on her husband's funeral pyre) in Hinduism seems to deny a fundamental belief in the dignity of each human person.

In the Judeo-Christian heritage, these lapses were doubly tragic. The faithful not only failed to demonstrate that God is love but they also failed to comprehend the point of the Adam and Eve story. They did not see that God had "permitted" (if one may so speak) fratricide, genocide, hatred, and mistrust among human beings for the sake of securing human choices, no matter how drastic the consequences.

The fact that religions as organizations and individual persons fail to live up to their beliefs does not detract from their validity. The recognition of failure is also a recognition of the validity of the criterion by which we judge an action evil. It is easy to get caught up in the moral persuasions of the moment, losing touch, as the witch-hunters did of old, with the authenticity of both human and divine experience.

Moral practice should always mirror dogma,[10] but in reality the practice may not mirror the dogma. Western religious tradition insists on the historicity of divine revelation, that is, the necessarily "situated" understanding of God's revelation in a social, living, historical situation.[11] Individuals and communities have constantly struggled to bring practice and theory into conformity with each other. As they do, only a gradual awareness of the rightness and wrongness of positions and actions can be acquired (just as Americans gradually became aware of the evils of slavery). Eventually persuasion and political action points the way to bring a practice in line with the teaching. On the other hand, the dogma itself may not be sufficiently understood or articulated. It may be in need of reform and growth itself, precisely because the practice does mirror the dogma and is found increasingly unacceptable. The "dogma" itself is historically situated. It is clothed in human experience. The practice of suttee may, in fact, be a historical expression of a teaching in Hinduism that no longer could remain immune to criticism.

Belief in the value of human life did not emerge, full-grown, with the first humans to practice religion. Religion as a system of beliefs and actions based on transcendent principles of worship and righteous conduct, either ritualistic or moral, takes centuries to develop.[12]

If a religion is to be meaningful as a social institution, its myth, rituals, and prescribed conduct must all reflect a symbol of social reality.[13] Constant change in real life will require constant change in precepts and principles.

There are three basic dogmas in all religions now extant, from which we can extrapolate the ideas of earlier religions. The first had to do with the nature of the supernatural. The supernatural is more "real" to primitive beliefs than it is to those in advanced religions.[14] The impersonal powers of nature permeate everything. In many religions there are personified supernatural powers hovering near every sacred tree, near every corn plant, near every stream. In general, the powers are believed to have an interest in human well-being or in the survival of the social unit.[15]

This perceived "interest" of the supernatural being in the natural contains a hint of the belief in the value of human life. One might conjecture that, because there is such an interest, the gods are somehow "attracted" to human life by a quality in that life, not just because they like to meddle. Of course, such reflection does not begin to occur until the advanced stages of social life, until a priestly caste emerges and takes time to reflect on dogma and its mythic underpinnings. As R. R. Marett's famous aphorism has it, "Primitive religion is danced out, not thought out."[16]

Another relevant feature of dogmas about the supernatural deals with the dead. In some religions the dead are seen as having departed human society. In others they are seen as still being part of society. In the former view, a cult of the dead arises, either to make the dead happy in their new life or to keep the dead from returning to disturb the living. In either case, reflections on this cult could easily lead to a postulate that some kind of "soul" lives on after death.[17] This postulate, in turn, fosters the idea that the gods might be interested in the quality of human life.

While some groups, such as Australian Aborigines and Blackfoot Indians, appeased the souls of the dead,[18] other groups saw the dead as cherished members of society. This was especially true in Japan, China, and Africa, where one's personal status in life was immortalized through ancestor veneration.[19] Despite entirely different social customs and rituals, one may still imagine the occurrence of a strong bond between the idea of a soul and the idea of supernatural interest in the affairs of society, as the religions became more advanced.[20]

The second fundamental dogma of all religions has to do with the nature of the physical world. In primitive religions, the world was often seen as a creation, but real interest lay in its sustenance. How was it maintained? In fact, the creation myths themselves, even very elaborate ones, were designed to explain how the world and society came to be the way they are now.[21] Little ritualistic or cultic significance is attached to creation. Rather, maintaining the order of the world and society is what is important. In a word, human survival, rather than theories about the origin and design of the universe, ranks first.

In many dogmas, though, cosmic order and social order are inexorably intertwined. This feature complements the idea of a supernatural interest in the affairs of human beings and the idea of a soul (or some other "divine" presence in human persons).

If society is disrupted, some great catastrophe can be predicted. And vice versa.[22] If one were a primitive living near Mount Saint Helens, one would explain the eruption as a failure to appease the gods or the spirit of the mountain (*The New Yorker*, in 1987 and 1988, carried a wonderful series of cartoons with "primitive" explanations of this sort with a volcano erupting in the background). More advanced religions would have cited rules of conduct so that the eruption could be viewed as a punishment from God for listening to satanic rock music or having too many topless bars in the State of Washington or having godless politicians. Whatever the specific cause of the disruption, the supernatural and natural orders are seen as resonating in harmony or disharmony, like adjacent guitar strings.[23]

Reflection will reveal that the primitive perception of a link between the divine, the natural, and the social provided the mulch for later beliefs about the inherent dignity of human persons. The ritual sacrifices of virgins, temple prostitution, war making, magical explanations for events, the caste system, and strange religious healings would make it hard for modern people to recognize any coherence among primeval religions and between them and modern religions, were it not for reflections on dogmas and myths that came later.

The last of the three basic religious dogmas is respect for the nature of human beings and their society. This dogma spells out the purpose of life. Two myths of human origin have prevailed. The first, that persons came into being either through divine intervention or natural development (e.g., from trees), is familiar to Moslems, Christians, and Jews because they all share this idea with many African religions. This view tends to stress human separation from the divine, though the chasm may be bridged by the theory of soul or godly character in humans.[24] The second myth is one that proposes a divine origin for human beings. In very primitive, kinship-based societies, the bonds of togetherness would be strengthened by belief in a common descent from the gods. Clearly, the dignity and worth of individuals who directly participate in a unified descent from their god are inestimable.[25] That is why kinship piety and group solidarity are so strongly intermixed with the survival of the tribe. This myth required respect for members of one's own group, including prohibitions against killing and the like. But members of other tribes did not deserve the same respect.

The concepts of the soul and personal immortality have important social consequences. Individual conduct, in advanced religions, greatly affects the supernatural outcome of a person.[26] Although this is not the case in primitive religions, there is still an ethical system operating in them. This system deals with the individual as part of a social unit rather than as a single person. Supernatural punishments are meted out to individuals, families, and even whole tribes, during this life rather than in the next. Thus, as Annemarie De Waal Malefijt argues, Max Weber's distinction between magical and ethical religions fails.[27] All religions prescribe conduct and offer theories of reward and punishment. The latter, however, are not limited to those religions which believe in an immortal soul, nor are all religions that embody such a concept equally interested in the moral nature of the afterlife.

The Delaware Indians, or Lenape, prayed every year at New Year's:

> Man has a spirit, and the body seems to be a coat for that spirit. That is why people should take care of their spirits, so as to reach Heaven and be admitted to the Creator's dwelling. . . . Do not think of evil; strive always to think of the good which He has given us.[28]

This sunny affirmation of each person under God led to explicit ethical duties. The afterlife is pictured much like the images offered by those who have been resuscitated.[29] It is a place of brightness. All spirits will be the same age and in good health, not crippled or old. All families will be together. "That is the reason that people are told to always help the cripples or the blind. Whatever you do for anybody will bring you credit hereafter," continues the prayer.[30] Clearly, each person shares the equal dignity of being created and having a spirit.

The idea of the dignity of human life is also embodied in the sacredness of life itself. The notion, in turn, stems from reverence for the creator. Aborigines in Australia turn back from civilization to participate in their ancient rites of initiation in order to affirm this cohesiveness of nature and tribe, past, present, and future. The marriage rite of the indigenous Ngaju Dayak of South Borneo actually represents to them the creator reentering life itself, beginning a new existence with the young couple. The Indians of the Labrador Peninsula believe that animals and people had the same spirit and that the bones of those animals had to be respected like human bones.[31] The central Algonquin also shared this belief in a soul for every living creature. Consequently, one bore much responsibility for hunting and killing animals, or in some religions, like Zoroastrianism in Persia, for even tilling the soil, for that was viewed as sacred too.[32]

To summarize, then, respect for the value of human life originated in tribal religions that coupled dogmas of creation, the supernatural, and a divine component in humans, animals, and life itself. This respect broadened slowly over the centuries, as social life embraced more and more tribes. As the social network increased in complexity, and reflections on myths, dogmas, and rituals were collected, a more nearly all-encompassing vision of the value of human life occurred. Rarely did this extend beyond one's own nationality.

This brief sketch of world religions cannot do justice to their rich variety or to the many disputes over interpretations of customs and beliefs. It does make clear, however, that reverence for human life is not just a phenomenon of modern religious systems. Further, the sketch provides some background for the thought experiment on the Old Testament, which follows.

### The Value of Human Life in the Old Testament

Ancient Western civilization is largely based on ideas developed by Greek philosophers and Jewish religious leaders. For this reason, I will now focus on the Judeo-Christian heritage regarding the value of human life, leaving the philosophical sketch for chapter 6.

Pretend for the moment that you are a scholar, seated in a large library. Collected for your use are the many traditions, stories, and writings of the Jewish people. You have been able to assemble these in chronological order, as they first developed, rather than in the library order in which they are assembled in the Bible. As H. H. Rowley indicates, the process of development of the "canon" of the Old Testament was almost imperceptible:

> Like the growth of a tree, which passes imperceptibly from the stage of a sapling that might be transplanted, to the stage where it is impossible to remove it, save by felling, canonicity grew imperceptibly.[33]

Modern scholars try to reconstruct the original historical sequence from a few pivotal stages of development based on the growth of the Hebrew Bible, as reflected in the three major divisions, the Torah, the Prophets, and the Writings.[34] Your chronology would be based on hypotheses from theories of hermeneutics, form criticism, literary criticism, and the like.[35] You develop a thought experiment in which you trace the idea of human worth until the time of Christ. You base your experiment on the best thinking of scripture scholars about the development of traditions and texts in the Bible.[36] You also detect parallels with world religions and their development (partially considered already in the previous section of the chapter).[37] You write:

The Jewish faith began in the mountains of northern Mesopotamia centuries ago. There, tribes of nomadic shepherds wandered the hillsides. Each tribe had its own household gods. For unexplained reasons, this group of Aramaic people began wandering over Persia (modern Iran), Palestine, modern Jordan, the Arabian Peninsula, and into Egypt about three thousand years before Christ. One tribe was headed by Abraham (Abram). In addition to their own gods, tribes also had their own fireside stories and worship rituals revolving around a god that went with them on their travels. Most other people had place gods. Evidence exists, for example, that early Jerusalem had its own god to which Abraham set up a monument (a pile of arranged stones—a pillar).[38] Unlike settled people, the nomads had gods that went with them from place to place.

The myths and dogmas of Abraham's descendants were parallel to their Aramaic brothers. The book of Genesis tells of some of these. They hold that man came from the soil, made by God. Women came from the side of man to be a companion, but had less dignity than man. Many African tribes have the same myth. Disorder and sin entered the world through a snake and the first woman. This story also explained why some related Aramaic tribes were close friends and how alliances were formed through pacts or covenants between tribes.[39]

From this early history, three major themes emerge. First, the tribal god establishes covenants with the tribe. These agreements make the tribe a close-knit, kinship piety sort of group; they also give human beings a sense of being both honored and honorable. Second, while no myth yet exists to explain the status of other persons, presumably foreigners, respect is shown to the gods of foreigners, especially place gods, by honoring them as one honored the people whom the god represented. Third, a god who is not tied to place and who makes covenants leaves room for later reflection about a personal god, indeed, about personal worth.[40]

In the next thousand years, some Aramaeans settled in Egypt and later were made slaves. The sharing of tribal customs, gods, and the experience of slavery in an advanced society all led to a more universal set of ideas about god and salvation. The Egyptians themselves considered and rejected the possibility of one supreme god. Revisions in the Abraham story also were made, and tales were told about a Jew who, like Joseph, "made it" in Egyptian society. Moses, raised in this society along with many other Jews, came to a syncretic belief in a supreme god. In fact, during his exile in the Arabian peninsula, he learned of a place god of the Aramaeans there, his father-in-law's god, called El Shaddai, the god of the mountains. Stories of this god, who revealed truths on mountains, are mixed with the tribal god who makes pacts.[41]

The ten commandments, the burning bush, the smashing of idols, the gradual realization by the Aramaean tribes that their one god was more powerful than all the gods of Egypt, and the later revelations to the early prophets, were all based on widely shared experiences about tribal gods.[42]

Set free from Egypt, the tribes began to infiltrate Palestine. They also began to realize that covenants with a supreme God who travels in a living pillar of fire obligated them to new ethical and ritualistic duties.

The failure of individuals was still seen as a communal failure. Thus the whole clan of Dathan was "punished" by God (perhaps in a landslide) for his unfaithfulness. The doctrinal groundwork was laid, however, for seeing the Jewish God in a new light and for seeing human beings in a new light as well.[43]

During the settlement of modern Palestine and Lebanon, tribes were assimilated into the Phoenician and other Indo-European cultures there. A few hung on to the tradition of salvation by a powerful, personal God. Many Jews, however, began to worship the fertility gods and goddesses, a continuation of the respect of earlier ages for place gods. Thus the problem of sacrifice of the firstborn is reflected in Judges and in the Genesis story of Abraham and Isaac. The Jewish God abhorred human sacrifice, a great advance in religious consciousness. The conflict between such abhorrence and the need for sacrifice was resolved by substituting animals.[44]

Similarly, Judah, the Southern Kingdom, objected to, and was later separated from, the Northern Kingdom and its religious practices. Amos called women who worshiped up north the "cows of Bashan" because in their wealth they neglected to take care of the widows and orphans.

As the Jews settled in and chose to be ruled by kings, as their neighbors were, traditional tribal values, covenantal duties, and the duty of respect for all persons in the tribe clashed with the class society that evolved. Israel's unique answer to this syncretic problem was the prophetic tradition, shared in its vigor only with Zoroastrianism in Persia and Buddhism in India, both of which flourished about the same time.[45]

Slightly prior to this time, around 800 B.C., the idea of individual salvation as part of a national pact with God was firmly established. "I will adopt you as my own people, and I will be your God." One had to love one's neighbor as oneself, because all were saved equally by God from slavery and sin, but one did not have to extend this love to those who were enemies. Against them one could wage a holy war.

During the centuries after David and Solomon, as the fortunes of Judah (south) and Israel (north) had waned, and Jerusalem itself fell to the Babylonians, the Jews examined their new circumstances and looked to a dismal future. As a psalmist laments after being captured and sent to Babylon: "How could we sing one of Yahweh's hymns in a pagan country?" (Psalm 137:4). Out of this experience, they realized around 500 B.C. that their saving God was everywhere. This realization appears in Second Isaiah and in many psalms written about that time. The fact that God's power extended beyond the borders of Judah, and that one could worship God in any country, was important to the concept of individual value.[46]

This faith in adversity became the very hallmark of the Jews throughout the world. It was coupled with an awareness that Yahweh was God over all. If so, he also must have created the universe, meaning that other gods had no power at all. And if so, each individual had the life of God created in him or in her. It was not far from this view to one in which every person, though not Jewish and therefore not saved by God, was at least regarded as a creature of God.[47]

During the reconstruction period and thereafter, in which Jerusalem was rebuilt by a remnant, a more universal vision of the goodness of all creation, the unity and majesty of God (Psalm 24), and the nature of God's salvation was joined with Persian, Greek, and, later, Roman ideas about human nature. In particular, the wisdom literature incorporates the notion of a people's salvation in terms of individual, personal salvation. The prayers, psalms, and aphorisms of this period all attest to an advanced perception of the value of each human being as created, and the value of each Jew as saved by God, where "saved" means "called to be a special witness to God's power."[48]

Having completed the thought experiment, let us consider what have we learned. First, when the history in the Old Testament is extracted from its biblical setting, as best as we can do so, we can see how circumstances, a vision of God, a difficult history, and a heritage of reflection gradually led to an awareness of God as an individual, personal creator. It is important to remember that human beings tend to worship what is most powerful. Many Jews did not abandon their God when nations that worshiped other gods defeated them in battle. By not abandoning their God, they taught all peoples something about God and about humanity. God was not a place god. People were dignified even in defeat. A difficult history, if sustained in faith, increased the perception not only of the power of God (that God demonstrates power through the weakness of people) but also of the power of individual persons (that sustained a faith in their own dignity in times of crisis).[49]

The second thing we learn from the thought experiment is this. As God is perceived, so is human society perceived. Some African tribes saw God and creation as spherical. They tilled their fields in circles, and they created spherical homes and circular villages. The Masai in Kenya still build in circles this way.[50] So, too, do the Jews establish their society on the vision of God. As the picture of God grows more dignified, all-encompassing, and more personal, so does the perception of human life. It moves from communal sharing to individuality, from the chosenness of the group, to the tribe, to the nation, to a remnant, to the poor of Yahweh, and, finally, to individual persons. One can trace this progression in the different traditions that contributed to the making of the Old Testament books. This is called salvation history.[51]

After the rebuilding of the temple, a school of theology was probably formed around the brilliant teachings of a prophet referred to by scholars as Second Isaiah, whose writings are found in Isaiah, chapters 40–55. Second Isaiah described a new exodus from Babylon back to Jerusalem. He also predicted that the Messiah would have to be a suffering servant. Jesus' own ministry was based on this view, and the prophecies in the Book of Isaiah are often cited in the Gospel as being fulfilled by events in Jesus' life.

The personal vision of God's saving activity, so important to the theory of the inherent value of human life, is given a definitive stamp by Second Isaiah. Thus a thanksgiving psalm influenced by his school (Psalm 116) describes how God has treated a person and his soul kindly, has rescued that person from death. In Isa. 50:4–9, the third chant of the Suffering Servant, there is a graphic description of how God will rescue a person (for Christians, the Messiah) from insults, from false witnesses, from weary lack of faith. Thus the vision of God is intimately tied to personal as well as communal freedom.[52]

Of course, much more could be said about the growth of religious awareness of the value of human life. And much more could be said about Judaic traditions on this point. But the central picture emerges: Old Testament anthropology is a study of the people of God. The ancient Semitic myth of creation is a story of how all persons (*adam* means "of the earth") sin and how this sin introduced progressively more disastrous evil into the world. Thus the breath of God (Genesis 2) points to the inherent dignity of the human race. But this is lost sight of through a lack of solidarity between Adam and Eve, through violence in human relations, through brothers who become enemies (Genesis 4), through wars, through nations that do not understand one another (Gen. 11:1–9), and through the disruption of death (Gen. 3:19).[53]

The stage is then set for God's remedial action, promised in Genesis by covenant and carried out in Jewish history.[54] The remedial action requires a people called and set apart to witness to the way God "hoped" things would turn out. The people of God experience the ups and downs of any people. Through their faith they constantly reinterpret their experience, combining the place God and personal God attributes. Second Isaiah (Isa. 49:15) envisioned the tenderness of God: "Does a woman forget her baby at the breast . . . ? Yet even if these forget, I will never forget you." The dignity of the person, then, lies in the special attention of being summoned by God to stand as his witness in the human community.[55]

## The Value of Human Life in the Christian Tradition

At the dawn of the Christian era, neither Jews nor anyone else, except perhaps some freethinking Romans, were prepared to claim that all human beings are children of God. Rather, the most evident human community was formed by the political structure of the Roman Empire, its underlying Stoic philosophy, and the laws that applied to persons of different races and beliefs. We will discuss the latter in chapter 6.

At this point, it is important to see how Jesus' vision of a religious life rested on the central idea of the inherent worth of every person. This vision was expanded by disciples and apostles, such as Paul, throughout an empire moderately receptive to a universal religion, just as it had been to other syncretic religions, such as the cult of Mithras, the bull. In other words, people who were accustomed to thinking in categories beyond national boundaries longed for an all-encompassing religion. Christianity provided a powerful form for that vision.

Jesus apparently did not arrive at an affirmation of the inherent dignity of all persons through any one philosophy. In fact, he found existing philosophy, as lived out by the Sadducees (who had adopted much of Greco-Roman philosophy) rather repulsive. Instead, he drew on a fusion of love of God and love of neighbor. This fusion represented a new reign of God in the hearts of human beings (Mark 1:15). His vision called for a change of heart, a *metanoia*, in order to "do good to those who hate you." Clearly, a person can choose love of an enemy over revenge only when that "enemy" is seen as a child of God or, in modern terms, as inherently valuable. The prophetic vision of keeping the covenant by taking care of widows and orphans, of preaching the news of God's salvation to the poor and downtrodden, and of opening the ears of the deaf and helping the dumb speak—all are works of faith in this new vision of human worth (Luke 4:18; Matt. 11:5; Isa. 61:1–2).

This insistence on faith not only in God but also in the value of other persons, even those not valued by society, those in fact thought repulsive by society (tax collectors, the Romans, heretics like the woman at the well, lepers, and prostitutes), provides the basis for the great dramatic moments of Jesus' ministry. Faith in the value of human persons was at the center of Paul's insistence on a new life-style (Rom. 6:1–4), on John's repetitive injunctions to love all humankind (1 John 4:7–21), and James's linking of faith and good works (James 2:14–18). As John put it bluntly, "Anyone who says, 'I love God,' and hates his brother, is a liar" (1 John 4:20).

Notice that all the outcast people of Jewish society were welcomed by Jesus. These people were the lepers (Luke 5:12), the poor, the beggars, the prostitutes, the possessed (Matt. 8:29), the widows (Luke 4:25), the diseased (Matt. 8:16), the sinners and the tax collectors (Mark 2:15–17), the Samaritans, and a Roman officer. What an assembly of ne'er-do-wells and undesirables! Jesus used the presence of these persons as opportunities to teach the real priorities of authentic religion: The Sabbath is made for man, not man for the Sabbath. He said to the Pharisees: "I put it to you: is it against the law on the sabbath to do good, or to do evil; to save life, or to destroy it?" (Luke 6:9–10). He then cured a man with a withered hand, after which the Pharisees became furious and plotted to kill him. In the Gospel of John, Jesus says something even more provocative to answer pharisaical objections to his cures on the Sabbath: "My Father goes on working, and so do I" (John 5:17). He kept repeating the statement of Hosea (6:6), "What I want is mercy, not sacrifice," as his reason for flouting the religious institutions of the time (Matt. 9:13; 12:7). He claimed that the Pharisees, by their tradition, made "God's word null and void" (Matt. 15:6–7), and he again cited Isaiah: "This people honours me only with lip-service, while their hearts are far from me. The worship they offer me is worthless; the doctrines they teach are only human regulations" (Matt. 15:8–9; Isa. 29:13).

The occasions for Jesus' anger and his responses about the Sabbath are all ones in which the observation of rules was put ahead of compassion or love of one's neighbor (and therefore of God). A sick person seeks help; or Jesus' disciples pick corn on the Sabbath; or they eat without washing their hands; or a woman chats with him at a well. It is not hard to imagine the religious authorities' violent anger, finally expressed in Jesus' crucifixion. It is not hard to see that Jesus did intend to introduce a fresh vision of genuine religion. Nor is it hard to detect the very core of that fresh vision—active mercy, compassion, and love for everyone, especially for those who seem, extrinsically, to be worthless, such as the handicapped children, almost without value or hope in a senseless war, helped by Mother Teresa.

What is not entirely clear is Jesus' own view of the extent of his mission. When a non-Jewish Canaanite woman pleaded for help for her sick daughter, Jesus refused until the disciples begged him to help her because she was making a pest of herself. Jesus' refusal was stated thus: "I was sent only to the lost sheep of the House of Israel" (Matt. 15:24). But he is led to remark to her: "Woman, you have great faith. Let your wish be granted" (Matt. 15:28). We also have his prediction of the call of the Gentiles to the kingdom (Luke 13:22–30; Matt. 19:30; Mark 10:31). Perhaps it was the centurion who asked for Jesus' help and prompted him to say, "I tell you, not even in Israel have I found faith like this" (Luke 7:9), who helped expand Jesus' vision of who would deserve a place in the kingdom.

In Jesus' vision belief in God requires belief in the inherent dignity of all persons. They are to be valued even above one's own religious traditions because they belong to the kingdom of God. The Sabbath is made for them.

The apostles and disciples recognized this well, as the citations of

Paul, John, and James attest. Each explains the value of persons differently. Paul bases it on the redemption by Christ—that all persons sinned in Adam, but now all have been redeemed in Christ (Rom. 5:12–21). John focuses on God's love of all persons, so that one's neighbor is everyone in the world, not just a member of the tribe or city or country.

It should not be forgotten that the reason for the gradual acceptance of Christianity in the Roman Empire had little to do with dogmatic concerns, for dogma had not been that well developed; rather, it was the *practice* of active love that gained adherents. Active love for all persons, works of compassion, and nonviolence toward enemies, once explained to Roman citizens in terms of their own philosophy, captured their imagination even as the political fortunes of the empire waned.

There is something fierce and forceful about a religious vision of the greatness of God and the consequent greatness of human beings. Americans could detect this fierceness of vision in the civil rights movement. To diminish any person is to diminish God himself. The reason nonviolent resistance to injustice works is that it affirms the inherent human dignity of the oppressor as well as the oppressed.[56] Nonviolence provides an avenue for that person to respond out of the highest human capacities rather than the basest ones.

The history of Western civilization, like the history of Israel, has not been one of unswerving devotion to Jesus' vision. Nor has the history of the Christian religion been characterized by continuous affirmation of the inherent dignity of all persons. The most obvious examples of failure include the crusades, the Inquisition, witch-hunts, the murders of supposed heretics, the murders of Anabaptists by the Lutheran Reformers, frequent wars (often, as in the Wars of the Roses, for ostensible religious causes), hatred for and the massacre of the Jews, the destruction of Indian tribes, the enslavement of blacks, and the largely nineteenth-century conquest of other "pagan" nations. It is not a good record, even as compared to civilizations not blessed with a vision of the common bonds of human persons. Each day, it seems, a new savage event confirms the impression that we live in a life-denying world.

Nonetheless, great movements, great reforms, and great persons have graced the landscape of Western civilization. Many of these, as diverse as Francis of Assisi and Martin Luther, Augustine and Aquinas, Sts. Dominic and Ignatius of Loyola, Teresa of Avila and Florence Nightingale, John Wesley and Karl Marx, have established their particular vision of the intrinsic value of persons out of, or in contrast to, the Judeo-Christian heritage.

What is remarkable about our history is the frequency and degree of this fierce vision. Just as the church has always had to reform itself, so too has civilization. Century after century the equality of persons became the rallying cry for uprisings against kings, czars, the church, and even religion itself.

I have called the ideal of intrinsic human value a fierce vision because I find that the constant effort to take it seriously is counteracted by theories of how to compromise it in order to preserve society itself. I will try to answer this dilemma by presenting a theory of choice in the final chapter. Although I suggested, in the brief review of the New Testament, that Jesus did not place any rule or regulation, even his own religious tradition, above the importance of persons, the survival of institutions seems to demand some compromise, some tempering of the fierceness of this vision. Thus Augustine, and later Thomas Aquinas, developed a theory of just war to quell unjust oppression. Enemies are identified as such, and the rule prohibiting killing them is suspended under very specific circumstances (that today no longer seem to apply). On a personal basis, murderers were, at first, kept from membership in the church, so serious was their violation of its creed. Yet, later this view was tempered by mercy, so that such a person could do penance and return to or join the church.

Throughout the history of church and society, the dignity of persons was upheld in some cases, but not in others. In addition to just wars, one could morally defend one's property against an intruder, even by taking the intruder's life. "Turn the other cheek"? Hardly. Hardened murderers, once convicted, could be executed. Persons who did not agree with the ruling power could be executed. Persons who did not agree with that ruling power could also be tortured or murdered, put in camps, isolated like lepers, stoned like prostitutes, ignored like the poor, all in the name of patriotism or some other claim, including the good of the church, the good of society, the good of the state, the good of the revolution. "Love your enemies"? Hardly.

Compared to the vision of Jesus, the compromises are embarrassing. Killing in the name of religion is particularly vicious. It reached its peak in Western civilization during the Hundred Years' War. A loving person had to turn elsewhere than to religion during those tragic times for a vision of human dignity. One readily can understand the emphasis on the dignity of human beings during the Renaissance which later blossomed during the Enlightenment. The emphasis was on the powers of reason, the joy of self-determination, and a wise Father-God who designed the universe but did not meddle in human affairs. These eras bequeathed us the notions of dignity and equality under God. They also exemplified how a new vision of God (one divorced from religious prejudices—a God of reason) led to a new vision of human beings.

Thus the irony. The fierce vision of Jesus is spread through organized religion. In many instances that religion, in its various splinter groups, became the same kind of rules-and-regulations oppressor that Jesus despised. In order to preserve Jesus' vision, organized religion was rejected. Therefore, in the Enlightenment, revealed religion also was rejected, along with a belief in Jesus himself. Nonetheless, the vision of personal equality and the worth of man and woman gradually became increasingly integrated into political life. After losing secular power, many religions themselves joined hands under a common affirmation of the worth of persons.

Today it is not surprising to read of joint religious proclamations against nuclear war, or against abortion, or against racism, or even against the political actions of various nations. The ecumenical era brought with it a measure of reconciliation around the common themes of oppression or major ethical questions, such as the dignity and rights of persons in health care environments.[57] Whether this religious interest in secular rights will be sustained is a matter of conjecture. It does mark a time when organized religion is becoming more important as an alternative to a scientifically discredited rationalism (scientists brought us the bomb, didn't they?) and to politically discredited liberals (they brought us war, depression, and revolutions, didn't they?).

Despite the fact that practice rarely lives up to theory with respect to the equal worth of persons, human worth nevertheless remains a central feature of Catholic-Christian tradition, as well as the Protestant and Jewish traditions. A key concept of the Catholic tradition is that all persons are created equal and are redeemed equally by Christ. Their salvation depends on their graced choices throughout life. This is the basis for religious freedom for every person.[58] For Christians, the call to affirm the dignity of every human life stems from their baptism as coworkers of Jesus and coheirs of his kingdom. For many Catholics and Protestants, it is difficult to understand how other Catholics and Protestants could cogently argue a case for abortion, or infanticide, assuming as it does a theory that some lives are more valuable than others, given their calling to be coworkers with Christ. It is especially difficult if the vision of human value, witnessed to by Jesus, which I have described, is in any way accurate.

In this perspective, Vatican II, in "The Church in the Modern World" *(Gaudium et Spes)*, says:

> For after we have obeyed the Lord, and in His Spirit nurtured on earth the values of human dignity, brotherhood and freedom, and indeed all the good fruits of our nature and enterprise, we will find them again, but freed of stain, burnished and transfigured. This will be so when Christ hands over to the Father a kingdom eternal and universal: 'a

kingdom of truth and life, of holiness and grace, of justice, love, and peace."[59]

That persons have inherent dignity beyond particular political systems and in contrast to all infringements on personal dignity is also recognized:

> Every social group must take account of the needs and legitimate aspirations of other groups, and even of the general welfare of the entire human family.
> At the same time, however, there is a growing awareness of the exalted dignity proper to the human person, since he stands above all things, and his rights and duties are universal and inviolable. . . .
> The ferment of the gospel, too, has aroused and continues to arouse in man's heart the irresistible requirements of his dignity.[60]

These quotations are part of an argument in favor of the social gospel, that the dignity of persons requires just living conditions and that excessive economic and social differences "cause scandal, and militate against social justice, equity, and the dignity of the human person."[61] They also serve as the basis of declarations on freedom of religion, on conscience, and on self-fulfillment.[62]

Similar statements about human dignity have been issued by all major church bodies. Hope for the future of the world can be gleaned from the ideals of these statements, for they represent a long and arduous learning process regarding the importance of human beings over and against other cherished values: The Sabbath is made for man, not vice versa. The vision demands persons sufficiently liberated from narcissism and egoism to understand and to promote the value of other persons as well as their own value as persons. By comparison with more limited visions about the nature and value of human life, such as those we discussed in chapter 2, the religious vision seems to take into account a richer field of human experience.

There is no hesitation in a contemporary religious vision about whether or not human beings have intrinsic worth. They do. I count this affirmation an advance over earlier ages in which extrinsic values could override the value of human life, when religion itself could be counted the most destructive force in human history. But the ethical consequences of this vision still divide Christians just as much as they divide other coreligionists and nonbelievers.

Emancipation from selfishness is not an opium, drugging individuals into submitting to unjust structures. It is, rather, a powerful force for change. Through this religious emancipation, persons recognize the dignity of others and themselves, and the inescapable world-changing duties that follow from that recognition. This is the importance of religion in Western civilization.

## Conclusion

Although a different kind of work would be required to explore this view fully, enough material has been presented to suggest that the inherent and equal worth of persons lies at the heart of the Judeo-Christian vision.[63] The value of human life is always tied to a vision of God. As that vision becomes more universal through the personal history of peoples, so too does the compass encircling those persons by whom the vision is shared. Today we have become accustomed to thinking of all human beings as one, if from no other perspective than that of being residents of the same planet. Questions about the "redeemed" status of other beings in the cosmos parallel those which engaged our forefathers when they met the tribes in the Americas with uneasiness.

The development of the concept of personal intrinsic value, particularly in regard to its application outside one's own group, does not proceed in a straight line. In any one epoch, it may be recognized by some and not by others. On your left at church may be a person who is tolerant of others. On your right may be one who hates whites, blacks, Protestants, Catholics, or Jews. Between epochs, a society may progress in its recognition of the extent of the vision, as America did under Lincoln. Or it may, inexplicably, suddenly regress, as Germany did between the wars, the very Germany that produced Schiller, Kant, and Lessing. Many persons have asked why the Jews went so docilely to the gas chambers. One reason might be that even as they witnessed it, it was impossible for them to believe that Germans could ever do such a thing.

Because progress ebbs and flows, religions can be seen as both syncretic and disruptive forces. That is, in some times and places, a religion may contribute its unitary vision to broader society. At others, it may disrupt the progress which a society already has made toward recognizing the vision. Thus the bigotry spawned by a few religious groups is of concern to everyone. Book and record burnings tend to diminish the ideal of human equality, especially if they are coupled with a belief that no one else is "saved" except those who participate in those actions.[64]

Recognition of the intrinsic value of all human beings might very well provide the normative principle for authentic religious experience. It did for Jesus. Thus, if faith does not lead to belief in the value of human persons, it does not come from God. The covenantal bond between God and humankind is a two-way relationship. Persons believe in God. God believes in persons.

The cultural and social weighting of the value of human lives is especially inimical to a Christian vision. To be redeemed by Christ is to have the life of God within one in a renewed fashion. Charity becomes the basis of personal relations because each person is a mirror image of God himself. Further, a religious view of human life emphasizes the implications of communal existence. With this perspective, it cannot be argued validly that care for some places an unfair burden on others. Care for others is not an unfair burden but a necessary obligation.

Admittedly, major religions of the world have not lived up to their own theology of the equality of all human life before God. Not infrequently the substantial rights of the poor or of those not of one's particular faith are neglected and ignored. But religions progress just as civilizations do. The prophetic element in revealed religions has consistently called these religions back to the theological belief in equality. In addition, this element has gradually universalized the religious perception of equality beyond one's nation, beyond one's own beliefs.

From a religious perspective, therefore, the claim that some lives are worth more than others is not only faulty but also vicious. It gives a lie to the goodness of the Creator of those lives because it substitutes expedient standards in place of moral duties and obligations. I quoted Father Schall's statement early in the chapter that all life is worth living. The Western religious tradition buttresses this claim.

The reasonableness of the idea of the inherent worth of persons is tied to the survival of the race itself. Earlier I mentioned that religion is a symbol of social reality. The cohesiveness of persons is enhanced, to say the least, if all are regarded as having the life of God in them. As this cohesiveness is enhanced, so too is society's resilience to threats of breakdown. Therefore the importance of the religious vision is underscored by philosophical and political views of human dignity, which will be examined in chapters 6 and 7. Even though the intrinsic value of persons is a belief, it has considerable validity as a wellspring of religious faith. Does it have similar validity from philosophical and political standpoints?

# 6

# Our Philosophical Heritage

I wish that every human life might be pure transparent freedom.

—Simone de Beauvoir

How can philosophy be helpful in examining the issue of the value of human life? This question presupposes that it *can* be helpful rather than just "interesting" or "enlightening." By "helpful" I mean that philosophy actually contributes to the practice of respecting the inherent value of persons. Can philosophy help, and how? These two questions are the focus of this chapter.

An outsider approaching the ancient discipline of philosophy for some help in resolving today's dilemmas may well be filled with doubt. In its early adolescence, philosophy was called *alētheia*, "unveiling reality to get at its truth." Surely one could call upon philosophy for enlightenment about problems of human conduct! Aristotle argued, with the characteristic bravado of an adolescent discipline, that the search for philosophical wisdom is justified not only on theoretical grounds but also on practical ones. In his own words:

> To think rationally and wisely, and to acquire rational knowledge, in itself is not only desirable for men (because it is impossible to live a life worthy of man without these), but also useful for practical life. For unless something is accomplished after we have formed a rational judgment about it and acted in accordance with this rational judgment, no real good will accrue to us.[1]

Thus, for Aristotle, as for many early Greek philosophers, the search for wisdom leads directly to a pursuit of the good both in theory and in action. Knowledge of the truth obtained through philosophic wisdom can be used to guide human conduct in all practical necessities.

As philosophy has grown old over the past twenty-five hundred years, though, and suffered bitter internal and external struggles, not only have different opinions and positions multiplied but they also have begun appearing to outsiders as pure cacophony. It seems no philosopher can offer a firm opinion about practical matters, such as the conduct of health professionals with respect to fetuses, because no philosopher has a grasp of the truth sufficient to offer advice.[2] We might call this affliction the senility of philosophy. In fact, in a rare moment of honesty for any philosopher, a modern Spanish thinker, José Ortega y Gasset, said of his discipline:

> The history of philosophy, in fact, has—and there is no reason for hiding it—the amusing aspect of a pleasant insane asylum. Philosophy, though it holds the promise of providing maximum logic—"truth," "reason"—momentarily and in its historical entirety, shows characteristics similar to insanity.[3]

What can be salvaged, what can be extracted from the discipline of philosophy that will be helpful? Is there anything in the insane asylum for those concerned about the value of human life?

### Can Philosophy Help?

My thesis is that philosophy can help by contributing *rationality* to conduct. As Aristotle noted in the early work already cited, "As a rule we must perform those actions well in which reason dominates."[4] Although it may appear that philosophy is a swirl of conflicting opinions, like a Russian saber dance, one of the unities of philosophy in its diversity is a commitment to the Socratic dictum: "The unexamined life is not worth living." If one may play, as did Heidegger, on the word "intelligence," one can see that it might stem from the Latin *intelligentia*, a kind of elegance, a science of choosing the best conduct for a reason (though more often it is derived from *intelligere*, "to understand").[5] Of course, there are many subsets of philosophy, but the major aid can come from ethics and metaphysics, including the theory of knowledge. Why be optimistic, though, at this time in history?

We are in an age like that of the Hundred Years' War. Religious movements, rather than communistic ones, provide the theoretical basis for many uprisings and wars. Thus the Ayatollah's rejection of Western (i.e., secular Christian) values provided the source for the Iranian revolution, and with it the continuation of Iranian violence, not only against other Moslem states but also against its own citizens and, through sponsoring terrorism, many other nations. Moslems and Christians have opposed one another in Lebanon for more than a thousand years. Although many more noncombatants had already died in the "Peace for Galilee" war that Israel waged in Lebanon, and although more than fifty persons died in the bombing of the Christian Phalangist headquarters, including the president-elect of Lebanon, it was the massacre of more than three hundred women and children in the Sabra camp that most horrified the rest of the world at the time of that war.

The picture of men wearing gruesome-looking gas masks, carrying the decomposed body of a child, contrasts vividly with the picture of Mother Teresa rescuing a child from the same encampment (with which I opened chapter 5). This bloodshed occurs in the name of religion. And it continues. Now it has focused on the West Bank rather than in Lebanon, and we are treated to pictures of soldiers using rubber bullets fired in response to stones hurled. It is not just racial violence, as in South Africa. It is religious-sponsored violence

I predict that all of us will tire of religious fanaticism, as did our forefathers in Europe after the Hundred Years' War, and turn again to the powers of human reason to resolve our conflicts. Despite skepticism about philosophy, then, there has been and will continue to be a renaissance of philosophical dialogue about public policy issues. Out of this dialogue must come a basis for agreement. What can provide that basis? Is it to be a common cultural heritage? Probably not, because no two philosophies, even in the most syncretic age, are alike. Is it to be a common political system? Probably not, because variations always exist.

I suggest that the only reasonable basis for agreement in a technological, nuclear, violent age is a commitment to the belief in the value of each human life. In effect, this is a secularized version of the "unity of persons under the sponsorship of God" idea intrinsic to religious faith. As secularized, it does not *impose* a religious belief on others, a major worry that people have and one that causes them to be bystanders, witnesses of horrible events, rather than interlopers or interventionists. As a society, our concern that we not impose our values on others, especially our religious values, is obsessive.

If a secularized version of faith in the value of human life were a universal belief, then intervening to protect another's life would not be imposing a value on others. Instead, it would be an action reminding others of that commitment. Many people feel that America lost some cherished values after World War II, but they have described these in either quaint or old-fashioned terms, terms unattractive to younger generations. One has a picture that what was lost was a quieter life, a farm life, a backward-looking life, a life of corn on the cob and nickel soft drinks. I suggest that what older people actually cherish about the past is the sense of commitment—a commitment to the value of human life, both personal and social.

An objection to the usefulness of philosophy in redeveloping that commitment might take two forms. First, persons who already have a religious belief in the value of human life would often find the philosophical debate tedious and, sometimes, offensive. It would appear tedious because no reasons would seem to be needed. After all, a belief is a belief, isn't it? Why are reasons necessary?

The answer lies in the need to defend one's beliefs, to argue them in the public forum, to contribute their valid, universal aspects to the commonweal. As soon as a religious belief is to be shared with persons who do not hold it, it must be clothed in philosophical arguments. In fact, sharing beliefs has gone beyond the "show and tell" format of the ecumenical movement. We are acquainted now with other beliefs. We might even respect them. But we have not done the more difficult work of agreeing on a central insight that could be the basis of public policy and a future society for our children. This work can be aided by philosophy but must be implemented by politics, as chapter 7 will show. The benefit of philosophy is that it can help transcend religious pluralism.[6]

I said that some people would find the philosophical debate offensive as well as tedious. The Age of Reason, issuing from the twin sources of rejection of religious fanaticism and the rise of science, bequeathed us a sort of cultural positivism about religious persons. This positivism is enhanced when we see demonstrators on television holding up signs that say: *First abortion, then euthanasia!* or *My body, my rights, my abortion!* The first is a pro-life sign; the second is a pro-choice sign. Neither sign gladdens the heart of a reflective person. Both portray a kind of closed-mindedness unacceptable in a pluralistic age. Both signs appear simplistic even though the underlying positions may not be. Abortion does not lead to euthanasia. The two are quite distinct and far more complex than that. Similarly, rights do not lead to abortion necessarily, nor do rights imply so much "me-ness," so much concern for self rather than others.

Reinforced, then, by unthinking religious persons, modern society often views religion as Albert Ellis, the psychiatrist, does:

> The emotionally healthy individual is flexible, open, tolerant, and changing, and the devoutly religious person tends to be inflexible, closed, intolerant, and unchanging. Religiosity, therefore, is in many respects equivalent to irrational thinking and emotional disturbance. . . . Since it is their biological as well as sociological nature to invent absolutes and musts, they had better minimize these tendencies, even if they cannot totally eliminate them. The less religious they are, the more emotionally healthy they will tend to be.[7]

This view is part and parcel of a secular attitude toward religious beliefs. It is, for some, offensive. Unfortunately it is often true as well. Thus a group of atheists can charge that they must be the ones consistently to oppose nuclear war, not religious persons who are irrational. In the words of John B. Massen, director of the San Francisco Chapter of American Atheists,

> Religion is the process by which we are taught to accept the irrational. If you can be taught to accept the Virgin birth, you can be taught to believe that the Soviet Union is our enemy.[8]

Whether or not religious persons can be said to be healthy, it is important in a pluralistic age somehow to combine firm and passionate belief with reasonable and open discussion. I submit that this is the real mark of a healthy person. It is also a characteristic that requires philosophical acumen to examine and critique arguments without destroying one's own beliefs or the dignity of persons who disagree.

A second objection to philosophy's helping to construct a commitment to the belief in the value of human life comes, not from persons with religious beliefs, but from philosophers themselves.

First, the notion that philosophy might support a belief, albeit a belief in human dignity, strikes one as odd, as medieval in fact. Although Thomas Aquinas argued that philosophy was a handmaid of theology,[9] few modern philosophers view their discipline in that light. Second, because of philosophical pluralism, there is little left in philosophy except for what Alasdair MacIntyre calls the increasingly shrill matchup of "assertion with counterassertion."[10] This dynamic, surely part of Ortega's observation about the insanity of philosophy, does not bode well for a genuine contribution, even if one could agree that human life has intrinsic value. Third, moralists are especially wary of efforts to translate theory into practice. They are much more comfortable with discussing and refining theories, matching arguments to historical figures, debating the fine points of a theory, or even contributing arguments to positions, say for and against abortion, for and against capital punishment, for and against infanticide, and the like. Few would, however, in Professor Kai Nielsen's words, want to "be caught dead making a claim to moral expertise."[11] So much for Aristotle's view that philosophy can contribute to practical affairs as well as theory. Social concepts such as the value of human life seem essentially contestable.[12]

Finally, some philosophers might agree with sociobiologists (those who claim that our social behavior is biologically determined by genetic inheritance), like George Edwin Pugh, who wish to reduce all fundamental human values to the genetic inheritance of the race. In his words;

> What is the ultimate source of our basic human values? For generations wise men and philosophers, as well as many religious and moral leaders, have believed that certain fundamental and enduring human values are intrinsic to human nature. . . . A literal interpretation of the philoso-

phers' view would imply that these intrinsic human values are genetically inherited, as an "innate" component of human nature.[13]

It would be hard to imagine a genetic code in which the value of
human life is established. The objection would therefore be that this
value is poorly articulated. If there is any such thing, it would be
found in genetic self-survival codes rather than as a social belief.

These objections against beliefs, against answers, against expertise, and against social concepts are important because they provide
an opportunity to clarify the scope of the arguments to follow. To
answer them in great detail will only divert the chapter from its
purpose. Because they are serious objections, however, some answer must be given to them, no matter how inadequate, before we
move on to the arguments in the next section.

First, the answer to the objection about applying philosophy to
beliefs rests on a clarification of the nature of a belief in the value of
human life. This is not a case of subjugating philosophy to theology
but of using philosophical methods to examine the reasonableness of
a secularized belief. Moreover, philosophy is well suited to just such
a task, since it does not start from faith but from questions. Furthermore, many philosophers have expanded on Plato's theory of beliefs
in order to show that beliefs support statements, assertions, declarations, questions, even philosophical theory itself. The theory of
knowledge includes the analyses of beliefs about the truth of pro-
positions. It is in this sense of belief that the chapter proceeds.

Second, the answer to an objection that philosophy can provide
no answers is that progress has been made through the centuries, as
shown in chapter 5, about the rights of individuals and the respect
that is due them. This progress provides some answers about human
desires, capacities, and social organization that might work, if implemented. It may be true that philosophers have become too engaged
with the trees to look at the forest.

Progress toward respect for individuals is evidenced by many lists
of concerns, about which most people can agree. Massen, the atheist, lists them thus: in addition to curbing nuclear arms, "the preservation and enhancement of the human environment, the abolition of
poverty and reduction of gross inequalities of wealth, the promotion
of legal and social justice, the unleashing of human creativity."[14]
This list could go on and on. You can hear the concerns in any high-
minded lecture, sermon, or talk. Even the simplest examination
reveals that these and like concerns have, as their foundation, a belief in the value of human persons. Otherwise, why would anyone,
from atheists to fideists, want to abolish poverty? provide social justice? care for the human environment?

Although we are accustomed to thinking that science advances in its discoveries, we are not equally accustomed to thinking that civilization and ethics have made similar advances. We saw that Jesus established the view, carried out by many of the reformations and movements in his name, that religious practices must serve persons, not persons religious practices. Similarly, the American Declaration of Independence established for worldwide consumption the thesis that political communities must serve the governed, not the governed political communities, a particularly Lockean point of view.[15] These events represent real, concrete answers about the value of human life. Anyone who thinks there are no answers has not looked in the right places; these persons have not seen the progress even through the retrogression, the backsliding, the many instances of human degradation, the wars, the violence.

Third, concern about posturing as a moral expert usually represents a refined debate about the role of a moral philosopher and the nature of a moral education in a pluralistic age.[16] The hesitancy arises, often enough, too, from a desire to protect the autonomy and self-determination of another person. Obviously we should not tell other persons how to resolve their dilemmas unless they ask for our advice, as a son might ask his father, the athlete might ask a coach, the office manager might ask a friend. Even then, the advice we give should be predicated more on their values than on our own. Thus, at least when we deal with adults in normal circumstances, the reluctance of a philosopher to pass him or herself off as a moral expert should not be mistaken only for a sellout to relativism or an obtuse stand taken on the nature of ethical theory and its relation to practice. Instead, it may well represent an affirmation of the very value under discussion, the intrinsic value of every human person.

Is there a way out of this third problem? I think there is. In the first place, although usual circumstances dictate circumspection in advising others, there are times when philosophers must directly intervene in the events, make a difference in the outcome, give one side a better chance to overcome the opposition, or speak in protest after the fact. The circumstances under which philosophers must move from an objective bystander position to that of a participant in events are those which involve great moral debates of urgent social problems. The days of puzzling over words and distinctions, while other citizens grapple with difficult issues, are past.[17] These are contestable issues but ones in which many persons, especially articulate persons, must become engaged.[18]

In this regard, public policy studies, medical ethics, engineering ethics, nursing ethics, professional ethics, and similar discipline developments represent just such involvement. They represent issues that engage all persons and as many perspectives as possible.[19] These are truly public issues that just now are becoming the basis of state and national coalitions of citizens.[20] Aware of the historical importance of such coalitions, and cautious about the need for sophisticated analysis, Alexander Capron has remarked:

> The grassroots movement changes the nature of our involvement. Just as we individuals, through effectuation of informed consent, change our involvement in our own health care decisions, so too do we in our involvement in grassroots groups stop being observers or even just voters, and become called upon as citizens with a responsibility to have opinions about, to reach judgments that we can defend and to insist that community engage in the process of discussing biomedical ethics—and not just acquiesce to the doctors of health care.[21]

Philosophers are citizens too. But philosophical involvement in events is necessary even more because, as H. Tristram Engelhardt, Jr., has noted, moral policy issues (such as euthanasia, the treatment of the aged, and the rights of adolescents) can be resolved in ways other than rationally and equitably.[22] They can be resolved by a power play, or by court fiat, or by conversion, or by negotiated settlement, or by a number of less desirable means. One of the latter would be to kill off the opposition—a favorite tactic in all centuries but especially popular in the twentieth century. Resolving issues in accordance with reason is an important ideal. It is important because it also affirms the essential dignity of persons. It recognizes their distinctively human power to reason about causes and consequences. In addition, it embraces each disputant in the broader context of brotherhood and sisterhood, the one celebrated by Schiller's "Ode to Joy" in Beethoven's Ninth Symphony.

A problem with pluralistic society always has been that it tries to resolve moral disputes by decisive arguments that appeal to one's own moral community but not to another, quite different moral community.[23] Nothing makes this point more clearly than the abortion debate and political efforts on whether to continue or to repeal the right to abortion in the United States. In these instances, we may try to resolve fundamental value disputes through negotiation. But the problem with negotiation and tolerance is the intolerance of the opposition. In any case, all of these modes, except an authoritarian cloture, require either rational explanation and discussion or, in the case of a less desirable means, prophetic and moral outcries.

One can ask for advice from philosophy, and it can make a contribution. This advice takes the form of an expert consultation on the one hand (when arguments are needed on one or the other side of a debate) or a philosophical testament to the importance of values now being neglected by some country, group, or individual. In fact, the great philosophers like Plato, Aristotle, Hume, Kant, Hegel, Heidegger, and many others have never been reluctant to join in the great debates of the day and to discuss possible solutions. Many prepared social policies. Think of Plato's ideal state or Dewey's proposals for educating for character or Aristotle's outlines for ethics and rights.[24]

The second way out has peeped through the answer to the first way out of the dilemma. It makes sense to decry any attempt to claim that the study of philosophy qualifies one as more expert in moral action than an unskilled person. Saints can come in all sorts of sizes and shapes, only a few of whom might be scholars. Another kind of moral judgment can exist, however. This kind eschews judgment of persons in favor of judging actions. Is killing eight million Jews wrong? Yes. Is dropping any sort of bomb on people wrong? Yes. Is killing infants wrong? Yes. Is demeaning women wrong? Yes. The reason the answer can be given so forthrightly is that a commitment to the value of persons is most likely the single most moral and reasonable path for all citizens of the world to take. In this sense, then, philosophical reflection on events is grounded in a norm established by social covenant. But I anticipate the argument here.

The final form of objection to philosophical arguments in favor of the intrinsic value of human beings was that such value, if it exists at all, is actually an expression of genetic information found in the cells of all human beings. The reason I mentioned this objection is to underline the social nature of the belief in the value of human life. It appears obvious that, if we all inherited such beliefs in our genes, those who degraded others, killed them, mauled them, demeaned them, abused them, would be violating necessary determinants of our nature. Because such abuses occur daily, and because no evidence has ever been found for such "genetic value," it seems best to dismiss the whole sociobiology movement as intellectual faddism. Determinism will be always with us. It is just the newest form, introduced before we have even completed the task of gene mapping.

What is objectionable about sociobiology is its tendency to reduce complex social values to biochemical ones. History has taught us, at least, that such oversimplifications are often found to be in error by subsequent generations. It is important to realize that social values do have a personal, individual character, however. This point will be amplified in the second argument in the next section.

We have now seen that, despite its variegated history, philosophy can help in specific ways to examine and defend a belief in the value of human persons.

### How Can Philosophy Help?

Having established that philosophy can help the discussion and practice of a commitment to the value of human life, I now turn to two major ways it may develop that assistance. In doing this, I do not intend to trace the history of Western thought on the topic of human life, its value, and the respect that is owed to persons. Instead, I will present the ways in which philosophical arguments themselves can help, drawing on the thinking of many persons throughout the history of thought. The two ways are by demonstrating (1) that a belief in the value of human life is reasonable and (2) that an affirmation of life must be a social act.

### Belief in the Value of Human Life Is Reasonable

The first effort draws on John Rawls's "veil of ignorance" method.[25] Picture yourself as a disembodied entity, meeting with fellow disembodied entities. The purpose of your meeting is to develop human society. You are going to be a member of that society, but you do not know what race, creed, class, or country you will be in. You know nothing about your future status at all except that you will have to live in that society. Obviously it will be important to you that certain characteristics of that society be set down in advance, since you cannot judge the particular circumstances of your life to be.

As a disembodied entity, pretend that you are gifted with a particularly refined "sense" of fair play, of compassion, of altruism. In your discussion with other entities involved in the planning, you are concerned that the new society contain absolute provisions for the equal treatment of each person, regardless of status. You argue this position from your sense of fair play. For this position taking, you are nicknamed EFFAP, or Entity For Fair Play. The reasons you cite for treating each person equally stem from altruism; in order that the best occurs in society, each person must be encouraged to act in the best possible way. The best possible way is to treat the concerns, problems, and lives of others at least as equal to oneself. In such a society, where thoughtfulness and compassion reigned, life would be worth living.

Since the beginning, however, SKEPSIS has objected to your line of reasoning. If SKEPSIS had a body, it would include squinting eyes, a sharp nose, and a quick brain. To fellow disembodied entities, SKEPSIS has been quick to point out that, because the society has yet to be designed, there exists no evidence that "the best in society" could be provided by altruistic principles. One could imagine that the eventual individuals in that society would *not* think it best to pursue the achievements of others, the happiness of others. Instead, they might determine that what is "best" is a single-minded effort to achieve power, status, wealth, and honor by either victimizing others or, at least, by enlisting their aid in political schemes. Furthermore, the idea of fair play, leading to a principle that all be treated equally, will clearly falter. For example, SKEPSIS asks whether criminals in the society will all be treated with equality by other members. "What about enemies?" "What about the infirm?" On the other hand, SKEPSIS notes that victims of crime or of oppression or of prejudice and the like might deserve special attention. Thus special attention would tilt "equal treatment" toward "compensatory justice." At any rate, the notion of equal treatment fails.

Another disembodied entity, LIBER, has nodded assent throughout SKEPSIS' objection to your rationale. However, LIBER has been your ally in speaking up for the importance of fairness. Rather than proposing fairness for altruistic reasons, LIBER argues that each eventual person is equal, that society is formed to protect this equality, and that therefore each should be assigned an extrinsic value to protect it. Whether this value is monetary or otherwise, it is always equal to everyone else's. Once points from the extrinsic value have been used up, let us say for education or health care, the members of the society cannot expect extra consideration from those who have not used up their own credits.

The schema of LIBER fails to satisfy you because of its externalism. You object that persons should not have just extrinsic value but intrinsic value as well. In fact, LIBER is more than slightly convinced that its own position assumes the equal intrinsic value of all persons, metaphysically prior to the assignment of equal extrinsic weight to all.

Neither argument, however, has won SKEPSIS over. Instead, SKEPSIS continues to claim that fairness may not necessarily lead to a requirement of equality: "All this claptrap about fairness!" it exclaims. Further, fairness may not be the basic harbinger for a decent society.

At this point, PRAGMA breaks in with a new reason for accepting equality. It is the opposite of yours. Instead of altruistic reasons for treating each person equally, PRAGMA and a friend, EGO, propose that all persons are to be considered equal even if they are not in fact, because the disembodied entities do not know the future. None of you knows what status or class you will assume in this society, so it behooves you to choose the kind of society in which everyone has an equal chance. All of you "nod" in agreement.

The only one who has a hesitation about this argument is UTILITY. In addition, it tenaciously disagrees with LIBER and with you about the reasons for equality. Essentially, UTILITY believes that everyone ought to be considered equal until the common good of the society begins to falter, at which point the principle of the greatest good for the greatest number should begin to apply. The individual may have to be sacrificed for the good of all. At least, UTILITY argues, SKEPSIS' point about the equal regard of all ought to be accepted. Clearly, in any society, not everyone can be treated equally. Some must be punished. Some must have compensation for past injustices. "Even if we accept fairness as principle," UTILITY says, "we can see that fairness does not always mean equal treatment."

The last member of the cartel, VIRTUS, chimes in at this point. It argues that justice is a virtue linked with many others, that justice cannot always be applied in society, because some extenuating circumstances will occur from time to time, and that it concerns equality *and* distribution. Distribution of goods and services ought to depend on an individual's specific needs. After all, VIRTUS' argument goes, both SKEPSIS and UTILITY have constructed valid situations, even in an ideal society, in which everyone may not receive the same resources. In one group, health care might predominate over education (e.g., the aged). In another, educational needs may predominate (e.g., the young). "In fact," VIRTUS continues, "it is impossible to imagine ourselves, as PRAGMA and EGO have reminded us, in a society in which we have not provided for at least some uneven distribution of goods and services to ensure survival."

After endless wrangling about fine points, all the disembodied entities finally agree they will never totally agree. In a spirit of ireny, however, since they are soon to be embodied in the society that they have designed, they do decide on certain fundamental truths. They agree not to tamper with these, finding them rather reasonable. Instead, they will argue later about distribution questions. Here is the testament they constructed:

> We are forming a society of ideal dimensions. Therefore, we hold these truths to be reasonable and beyond current dispute:
>
> 1. That all persons are to be regarded as having equal intrinsic value.
> 2. That this value is both a right that a person possesses and a good for society.
> 3. That the right imposes obligations on everyone else to respect that person's life, liberty, and means of survival.
> 4. That good for society means that, should one suffer injustice, all do.
> 5. That each shall receive distributed goods and services according to need.
> 6. In cases of scarcity, new schemas will be imposed.
>
> Some may abridge the rights of individuals in favor of the survival of the community. Others may propose a lottery, or equal treatment of all. In any case, the new schemas must have the consent of those affected.

This fanciful dialectic has many antecedents in philosophical history. Anyone who is familiar with ancient and modern thought will also recognize some of the positions and names of the disembodied entities. Imaginative thinking was used by Thomas Aquinas in his tract on the angels in the *Summa Theologiae*.[26] There, Aquinas asked himself at great length what powers of mind or intelligence might conceivably be left without the body. Thus his extensive work on the angels actually helped develop his thinking about epistemology (theory of knowledge) and human psychology.

In the modern era, and more to the point, imaginative thinking formed the basis of John Locke's political philosophy. In it he asked us to construct an "original state of nature." In this original state, all persons are equal. They form a political society to protect their rights, their lives, their property. In so doing, they in effect agree to abridge some of their freedoms in order to develop common measures of security and protection.[27] This is the rationale for stop signs, for example. If one would hold that a person had freedom of the road, for that person's safety and to protect the lives and property of others rules of the road would be instituted. Certainly, they abridge one's rights. Equally assuredly, however, they provide for the commonweal. This is Locke's "social contract."

Most noteworthy for our purposes is the fact that John Locke held that all persons were equal prior to their entrance into society, which necessarily abridged some rights with their consent. We will discuss this point in more detail in chapter 7. Important for my claim here, though, is the way the English notion of the consent of the governed, to which appeal is made back in the Magna Carta, is combined in Locke with a deistic view of a Creator God making all persons equal. This powerful combination lies at the root of revolutions and civil rights movements, especially in the West. At its heart is the reasonableness of the claim that human life has intrinsic value. If we were to suggest this wording to Locke, his position might be that the intrinsic value is God-given and that only by a person's consent can some of that value be sacrificed for the common good.

Of course, not all the positions taken by modern-day altruists, skeptics, deontologists (*deon*=duty, the position of Kant), utilitarians, Aristotelians, pragmatists, egoists, and followers of John Rawls are properly expressed in my fanciful thought experiment about disembodied entities. Nevertheless, the experiment does tell us some of the main problems one faces regarding the value of human lives and the affirmations made in the testament. These problems stem from pluralism. A bevy of religious, philosophical, cultural, and social beliefs and practices all strengthen the argument of the skeptic that nothing is sure, nothing is established, no norms are possible, and no appeals can be made to fundamental beliefs or principles. Exceptions from the pool of pluralism can always be drawn like a pail of water from a well.

Once one recognizes that not all persons think alike or share common beliefs and practices, even when they happen to be religious or worship at the same church, a search for common ground on another level is usually launched. Have you ever found yourself disagreeing with someone but hoping to find a particular premise both of you can agree on so you can part as friends? The same spirit often prevails among philosophers.

In a search for the foundations of ethics, in a pluralistic age, Richard Brandt devised an imaginative scenario of disinterested persons designing moral principles.[28] This is an excellent way to try to achieve some unanimity about the moral life. By extracting ourselves from our current interests and plans we are able to consider a wider field of the good of all. A similar method was used by John Rawls in his A Theory of Justice. In it he argues that, despite all the contradictions of deontological, utilitarian, and natural law theories of justice, a method of "wide reflective equilibrium" can be developed. This method includes a thought experiment he calls "the original position," after which the one I offered is modeled. In the original position, without knowledge of future status, he argues, all persons would rationally choose fairness as the basic principle of society. This is so because all disinterested parties in the original position do have one interest left, no matter which moral theory one might prefer. It is this: They want to be sure they will have an equal opportunity to compete for goods and services in that society.[29]

As Kai Nielsen, a skeptic about applied ethics, has claimed, however, it is not really clear that everyone would, in fact, appeal to fairness as a basic principle of society.[30] That is why I added the problem of equity and fairness to the list of SKEPSIS' objections. Rawls tried to avoid this problem by proposing, quite reasonably, that equity does not mean equal treatment. The Aristotelian view of different kinds of justice (the position of VIRTUS) is also applicable here.[31] It is not considered unjust, or a violation of respect for persons, to give some persons in society roads and bridges, while others get higher education.[32] What Rawls does argue is that fairness requires equal access to goods and services, equal opportunity to advance in society. I add that this view presupposes the belief in the intrinsic value of every person.

The libertarian position can be traced back to traditional liberal political theory. Locke's social contract theory, as we saw, requires a view of equal, autonomous persons in a state of nature prior to social organization. Similarly, Immanuel Kant was the first to develop the notion that all of ethics depends upon the principle of respect for persons.[33] Each person is viewed as autonomous. Each person, that is, is to be viewed as the source of the moral law. One acts on principle, on duty, as a self-determining individual. From this moral center, others must respect each person as an autonomous entity, just as they must respect themselves.[34]

Clearly the libertarian position (LIBER) is based on a firm need to believe, to take as a given, the dignity of human life. In fact, this belief has advanced today toward a highly individualistic, antisocialistic point of view.[35] Some libertarians hold that inequalities of access to health care, of privilege, of class, of wealth, are merely "unfortunate," not unjust. These problems deserve our attention, but citizens are not obligated, without their consent, to address them.[36]

It is my opinion that libertarians err on two counts. First, they fail to see that life need not be like a chess game. One can protect the rights of citizens equally while still treating some persons differently from others.[37] Admittedly, this requires a complex, sophisticated system of dialogue and compromise, which I will discuss in the final chapter. Second, libertarians often forget that persons are social entities, a point to which I will turn shortly.[38] Nevertheless, I think that Rawlsians, libertarians, Aristotelians, and deontologists all might agree that a belief in the value of human life undergirds their respective positions, even though they would offer contrasting theories of distribution.

Begun as a new theory of law and social good, the utilitarian principle of the greatest good for the greatest number was proposed by Jeremy Bentham[39] and amplified by John Stuart Mill.[40] Individualism was still desirable, as Mill's *On Liberty* demonstrates, but it is tempered in his writings by contrasting individual liberty with social concerns.[41] Historically, utilitarianism has been contrasted directly with deontologism. The reasons are many and complicated. In a nutshell, utilitarianism emphasizes concern about social outcomes as a means of judging the moral rightness or wrongness of an act, while deontologists proceed from a formal analysis of principles, without regard for the outcome.[42] Be that as it may, utilitarianism still must be seen as a social corrective to excessively individualistic thinking. The purpose of it all, however, requires a substantial commitment to the belief in the fundamental dignity of persons. That is why Mill maintained a strong libertarian stand on personal freedom and supported the equal rights of women. In fact, Mill saw his program as the formulation of a just society in the midst of the injustice of the industrial revolution.

Given demanding or unusual circumstances, however, utilitarians are characterized as willing to put the good of many over the few. A case in point might be a pilot who chooses to accept hazardous duty pay to fly over enemy territory in a rescue mission, knowing that to fail is to die. He cannot return without the freed prisoners. More problematic are situations, let us say a hotel fire, in which triage (deciding who shall be treated first) is performed on the survivors without their consent. In this situation, a "respect for persons" approach might demand equal treatment (egalitarianism). Realistically, however, those who might survive are chosen over those who probably will not. Thus the principle of utility seems to violate a respect for the intrinsic value of each human being. Under normal circumstances, however, utilitarianism would accept the belief in the value of human life.

I have tried to show that the major ethical theories in Western philosophy have, as their foundation, a secular belief in the intrinsic value of human life. Although each does represent a different view of the nature of that life, and a different view of the means to preserve its dignity, the testament of the disembodied entities would receive a majority vote. It would receive mine.

## Affirmation of Life as a Social Act

Let us suppose, now that we have agreed to the testament, that still something about it rings hollow. While it is stirring, it makes our obligations toward others just that—obligations. Surely something is missing from the account of the disembodied entities. Life is not so cut and dried. The testament, in the final analysis, represents only a minimalist set of principles for human interaction. There is more to life than that.

Our unease with the whole scenario can be pinpointed even more sharply. The whole exercise, like that of Locke's original social contract, assumes that persons are individuals before they enter society. Society, with its structure, is seen as the second story over the first story of individualism. Furthermore, even though it was instructive to think about the disembodied entity experiment, it seems a bit too Platonic. There are no such things, at least that we know of, that shape human society. Persons are social. They belong to one another. They come from one another. They all have navels.

Finally, the gnawing question of what to do when individual rights clash with other individual or social rights cannot be resolved by an appeal to justice or equity alone. Is there some other characteristic of human life that imbues it with concern for its dignity, while providing for means to work out problems? Is this characteristic distinct from a divine command theory which might mandate love or charity?[43]

There is. It has been neglected a great deal by ethical theories in the recent past. Yet it is one of the most remarkable features of human social life. It is friendship. As Lawrence Blum has argued, ethical theories that stress principles and reasoning about weights to give norms have spent very little effort on examining the importance of everyday friendship in the moral life.[44]

It was not always that way. Aristotle discussed friendship at length in his *Ethics* because it was based on a psychological construction of human happiness.[45] Thomas Aquinas argued that "in human society it is most necessary that there be friendship among many." In fact, Aquinas appropriated Aristotle's theory of friendship as the framework for his tract on the theological virtue of charity.[46]

If a police officer tears up a speeding citation for a young, harried mother with two screaming babies in the car, he does so out of kindness, out of friendship, out of solidarity with her plight. If your friend agrees to meet you for lunch to discuss a problem you have, she does so out of friendship, not expecting a reward, or even equal treatment. If you sit around after work and talk over your life plans with coworkers, this is done out of friendship. Friendship prompts people to volunteer for crisis hotlines. Friendship is the source of your family physician's care for you as another human being.[47] Friendship is often the basis of love. In this view, if justice is seen as a minimum guarantee of human worth, friendship is its firm and constant affirmation.

Thomas Aquinas' point about the need for widespread friendship in society is an important insight. It is worth pursuing for a moment before the end of the chapter.

Many modern thinkers have deplored the decline in the affability or courteousness of technological societies. This lack of friendliness, they think, is a symptom of deeper trouble—a lack of friendship itself. Impersonality rather than friendship reigns. Anticipating this, the Russian author Tolstoy bitterly rejected the impersonal ethics of the vast state apparatus. In fact, he refused to move to a large city for fear of having to deal with this ethics, which makes ciphers out of persons. In his view, large societies would be based on a morality of general systems, rules, and laws.[48]

Instead, Tolstoy held fast to an opposite ethic. He called it an ethics of intimacy, an ethics that predominates among family members, among friends. One contemporary ethicist, Stephen Toulmin, has based an argument for what he calls an "ethics of discretion" on Tolstoy's refusal to accept an impersonal ethics of utility. In many of the difficult problems that face us today, problems such as abortion, euthanasia, nuclear arms, fairness toward the aged and the incapacitated, Toulmin claims, it is clear that an impersonal ethic is far less effective in resolving our dilemmas than an ethics of discretion. In the latter, friendship and intimacy would prevail. Concern for the value of life and for the values of the person would take precedence over impersonal principles. Toulmin summarizes his position this way:

> So in the ethics of strangers, respect for rules is all, and the opportunities for discretion are few. In the ethics of intimacy, discretion is all, and the relevance of strict rules is minimal.[49]

This view of an ethics of discretion will influence my suggestions for resolving some of the pressing problems of our age. Toulmin and Albert Jonsen have written a book on casuistic methodology in medical ethics[50] that closely parallels thinking about ethics I call "contextualism," and about which I have written alone and with Glenn C. Graber.[51]

Needless to say, the differing opinions formed by philosophers regarding the value of human life will not vanish by a wave of the hand. Nonetheless, many different theories have a substrate assumption about this value. After all, concern for ethics and for a just society is an expression of a deeper concern for persons. The brief discussion of friendship revealed that social exchange is enhanced by friendship. Further, social exchange is thereby based on an affirmation of the special value of individuals. There is no sadder thought than that of a person without a friend. Our natural instinct is to exhale a long-drawn-out "awwwwwww" when we see a cute cocker spaniel puppy sadly begging to be brought home. Surely the instinct would be stronger toward a person without a friend. That is why Aristotle in his *Nicomachean Ethics* defines an individual as a person with a family, with friends, and with associates, because human beings are essentially political animals.[52]

Friendship toward a small number of intimates is not all that is necessary, however. Friendship toward society as a whole is necessary if we are not to succumb to either a sophisticated but superficial urbanity on the one hand (the Christmas basket approach to solving social problems) or an impersonal disregard for human values on the other. On a national and international scale, we therefore face two problems. One is to bring about, at the very least, a recognition of the equal status of all human beings, which can be done through political processes that recognize and enhance the fundamental natural rights of all persons.[53] The other is to bring about friendship. They are not new problems. But philosophy can, at least, make some contribution to their resolution. Even though philosophy's contrasting opinions may sound like the ruminations of inmates at an insane asylum, almost all the inmates can be counted on to support a belief in the intrinsic value of human life.

## Conclusion

I have shown that a belief in the intrinsic value of human life is reasonable. It is assumed by many different philosophical theories, although not all to the same degree. At any rate, one cannot "impose" this belief on someone else if the other person already believes it. In other words, if a society has adopted the belief either through its religious faith or through a social contract, covenant, or bill of rights, then appeal can be made to the belief as a standard of conduct among the members of society. It is not imposed but assumed.

In addition to the reasonableness of the belief, I have added a social theory of human life by briefly examining friendship, the antidote to excessively individualistic thinking. Friendship also buttresses the belief that persons have intrinsic value.

Belief in the intrinsic value of all human beings is sometimes overridden in an emergency to take normally inappropriate social action. Some efforts to establish rules for this reversal arise in the political arena. Thus ethics, as Aristotle saw so clearly, is actually a branch of political theory and practice. To that consideration, and to specific issues of respect for persons, I now turn.

# 7

# Our Political Heritage

The care of human life and happiness, and not their destruction, is the first and only object of good government.

—Thomas Jefferson

As an ethical and moral ideal, the equal intrinsic value of human beings is firmly entrenched in Western culture. Recall that it undergirded religious and philosophical thinking, as we saw in the previous chapters, until late in our own century. Is this also true of our political heritage? After all, even if one's faith and one's reason firmly pointed to the intrinsic dignity of human life, if this were not affirmed politically, such beliefs would not have been put into practice. To affirm the intrinsic value of human life in the political realm is to recognize the equality of all human beings in practice.

## The Problem of Equality

In their comprehensive study, *A History of Medieval Political Theory in the West,* R. W. and A. J. Carlyle divide ancient and modern political theory in Western culture around the precise recognition of the inherent equality of human beings.[1] Ancient theory was based on the ideas of Plato and Aristotle. Perhaps because of the configuration of Athenic society at the time, both political theories assumed a natural inequality among persons. Slavery was justified on that account. As the Carlyle brothers state, "There is no conception which is more fundamental to the Aristotelian theory of society than the notion of the natural inequality of human nature." Thus Aristotle could argue that slavery not only rightly existed but also was a natural necessity. Since recorded history to that date could offer no examples of a society free of slavery, Aristotle took this to mean that slavery, the inequality of human beings, was an absolute necessity of social organization. It was a constant conjunction of human life.

A dramatic shift occurred when the essential and inherent equality of persons was affirmed in political theory. Two sources of the dramatic shift are prominent. The first was the wide-ranging, humanistic thinking of the Stoics. The second was the adoption of Christianity as a state religion in the Roman Empire. We have already examined the religious heritage regarding the belief in the inherent dignity of persons. In this chapter, I will first briefly sketch the importance of that belief in our political heritage; second, examine a number of thorny ethical issues that involve political, that is, public policy dimensions; and, third, proffer three possible positions that one could take on the issues, each of which includes some measure of respect for persons. These positions are the first step toward my suggestion for resolving some of our most pressing public debates that are fully proposed in the final chapter.

## Human Life and Society

A fundamental norm of our political society is the equality of persons under the law. Of course we recognize that persons have different status and different secondary qualities. But to argue that some persons are "worth" more than others by a measure of their income or status violates the very assumption of equality upon which our society is based. As Richard Sherlock has argued, the claim that some lives are not worth living with respect to issues in health care is equivalent to the claim that slaves were not fully equivalent human persons compared to freedmen.[2] Abraham Lincoln's arguments against slavery are the same as those which must be addressed here. At root, equality is a presupposition of any liberal political community.

It was not always this way. Plato's dislike of democracy is legendary. His concern was that unsuitable elements, "evil cupbearers presiding over the feast" when democracy was thirsting for freedom, would rapidly turn the dream into a nightmare. His view rested on an assumption that there was a natural, inherent inequality among persons. With horror, Plato says, "The last extreme of popular liberty is when the slave bought with money, whether male or female, is just as free as his or her purchaser; nor must I forget to tell of the liberty and equality of the two sexes in relation to each other."[3] The very idea was abhorrent.

Aristotle shared this view. He held that every community aims at a good. The state or political community, because it embraces all other communities, "aims at good in a greater degree than any other, and at the highest good." This exalted view of politics is the one I share. It is perhaps not the politics of campaigns and rhetoric but a politics of publicly seeking resolutions for the good of all citizens.

Despite this attractive view of the state, one that contrasts markedly with our contemporary distrust, Aristotle's view of democracy also shipwrecks on the shoals of slavery. It must be said that slavery was ubiquitous in every society at that time. Unable to learn of any society without slavery, Aristotle confidently remarks, "Is not all slavery a violation of nature? There is no difficulty in answering this question, on grounds both of reason and of fact. For that some should rule and others be ruled is a thing not only necessary, but expedient; from the hour of their birth, some are marked out for subjection, others for rule."[4]

A picture of human nature leads to resonances in a picture of political society. The Stoics are a good example. Originally a Greek school of philosophy, Stoicism was adopted by Roman thinkers as well, among whom would be counted Cicero. The Stoics held that nature was orderly, ruled by logos, or reason. One could discern the order of nature by reflection on our human nature. From the laws written into our behavior, what is called the natural law, the Stoics could extrapolate to lists of moral virtues to be followed and opposite vices to be avoided. Scholars believe that some of the lists of virtues and vices cited by Paul in his letters were commonly known Stoic categories.

More important for political design, however, is the universality of the natural law. The Roman Empire was not distinguished for its unanimity of theory. Rather, it is now recognized for its genius in developing a system of laws and administration that held together vastly different people and vastly different ethnic and religious traditions. The empire was able to accomplish this feat because it subscribed to a Stoic view of the nobility of human beings and the general applicability of the natural law to all citizens (though slaves and certain others were excluded). Thus a picture of human nature in which persons are guided by features held in common with all other free human beings led, in Roman times, to a practical political community able to tolerate diversity based on these common features of human nature.

As a young man, I watched a film that extolled the thinking of Marcus Aurelius, a Stoic Roman emperor. The film was made by the University of Chicago as part of its civilization education series. In the film, Marcus Aurelius would utter very noble, farsighted, and uplifting phrases as he penned his *Meditations*.[5] One, I recall, went something like this: "Each morning I remind myself that I rise to the work of a human being!" After all the tragedy that has happened since, that thought would hardly get most people out of bed.

The point that struck me about the ideas in the film, the reason for recounting it here, is that while Aurelius the philosopher had radical thoughts about the greatness of all human beings, Aurelius the emperor was waging war against stubborn Germanic and Anglo-Saxon tribes (my own ancestors) who did not want to be part of the empire. While his thinking was on the mark, it would take centuries to develop, and come to respect, the notion that all persons are created equal.

Thomas Hobbes, the English political theorist, saw only chaos without a state and a ruler, while John Locke and Jean Jacques Rousseau envisioned a simple and alert independence. Once again, a view of human nature lies under the theory. Hobbes thought that human life was "nasty, brutish, and short." Revolution was not possible because of the chaos or anarchy of our primeval state: "They that are subject to a monarch cannot without his leave cast off monarchy, and return to the confusion of a disunited multitude."[6]

Locke shares with Rousseau a comparatively sunnier view of the inherent quality of human beings. We have already touched on Locke's thinking. But the following quote and its comparison with Rousseau illustrate the point that extending the inherent dignity of all persons *to* all persons is an important, unfulfilled task. The state must also recognize some baseline of dignity that can neither be given away nor tampered with by others. Locke, for example, wonders why people would part with their freedom: "If man in the state of nature be so free, . . . if he be absolute lord of his own person and possessions, equal to the greatest and subject to nobody." Locke then answers, with a certain degree of realism, that because everyone is free, and all are subject to no one, "the enjoyment [of these rights] is very uncertain." Locke is willing to admit that, even though "every man be equal," a large number are "no strict observers of equity and justice." Thus one cannot long live in "the state of nature." One must form a community to rule, judge, and execute social activities.[7] It is not far from the mark, then, to say that the purpose of the state is derived from a propensity of equal persons not to respect that equality.

Rousseau's thinking on the social contract was as influential as Locke's. It too assumes a state of independence, which society abridges only by contract or covenant with the governed. Rousseau held that "persons are born free" and that the "social order is a sacred right which serves as the basis of all others. Yet this right comes not from nature; it is therefore founded on conventions." Arguing that families are the only natural societies, Rousseau notes that both father and child "return to independence" after the one's duties to protect and the other's to obey are fulfilled. Thus, he concludes, "this common liberty is a consequence of the nature of man."[8]

The view of equality of persons *prior to* social organization depends upon a belief, as I have called it, a reasonable belief, in the
inherent value of human persons with respect to nature, to society,
and to other entities. The belief is powerful because it relativizes
social structures. Thus this belief formed the basis of Thomas Jefferson's drafts of the Declaration of Independence, even though, as
Garry Wills argues, Jefferson was influenced more by the Scottish
"Moral Sense" philosophers, thinkers such as Lord Kames, Adam
Smith, Thomas Reid, and David Hume, than by Locke.[9]

Specifically, the notion that it was self-evident that "all men are
created equal" cannot mean self-evident the way Locke meant it: an
identity between subject and predicate. Instead, as Wills demonstrates,
Jefferson must have had in mind the meaning of "self-evident" es-
poused by Thomas Reid, that the mind immediately perceives or
grasps the truth of the matter. Thus a simple person without the distor-
tions of theory can grasp the truth of the statement. In this, that person's perceptions are the equal of the philosopher's.[10]

### Affirmation of Equality

I have suggested that the claim that all persons are created equal
is a reasonable belief. This belief commands adherence not only out
of religious and philosophical tradition but also negatively, through
our repulsion at the many instances of murder, mayhem, carnage,
rape, incest, and assault done by one person to another or done by
nation to nation (perhaps this is what Locke meant about how we are
propelled by our own ineptitude regarding our natural freedoms to
seek communal protections). Our repulsion is emotional and instantaneous. It need not be mirrored against traditions alone. It comes
from the heart, if we have not been hardened by evil. That is what I
take Jefferson to mean. All persons are equal not just because our
traditions show it is reasonable to assume this but because this belief
rings true in our hearts. And it never rings truer than when we or
those we admire, respect, or love are faced with oppression.

The characteristics of this belief are firmly established in our culture. The idea, however, needs constant reaffirmation in practice.
New generations must come to believe in it as intensely as the old.
Writing about America as a distinct culture, Edward Stewart says:
"Running throughout the American's social relationships with others is the theme of equality. Each person is ascribed an irreducible
value because of his humaneness. 'We're all human, after all.' Interpersonal relations are typically horizontal, conducted between presumed equals."[11]

Because of this emphasis, Americans tend to view the individual as
supreme and government as an encroachment. Also, because Ameri-

can political thought shares with the Middle Ages a reliance on the natural law, a theory of reason and rule against which minority and majority decisions alike are to be tested, it is difficult to overlay the concept of individual independence on other political systems, particularly those stressing communal or social identity.[12]

It is important to realize, however, that Karl Marx and Friedrich Engels were very much concerned with the inherent dignity of persons, too. The capitalism of the nineteenth century violently subjugated human persons through impoverishment wages and alienation from the products of labor. Concern for the worker did not arise solely out of a class hatred of the wealthy. Instead, it largely rested on a theory of the inherent dignity of persons.[13] Thus, once the worldwide overthrow of capitalism was to have occurred, Marx and Engels thought that a new era of classless society would appear, an era in which industry and technology would function for the benefit and liberation of human beings everywhere.[14]

Self-fulfillment is an essential theme in communism, though it certainly does not appear to us in the West that way.[15] Once the artificial barriers of class and status were broken down, as they are supposed to be in a religious vision of human life as well, then alienation from work, from fulfillment, and from the future will cease. As a totality of "united individuals," human beings could control their own destiny. As Marx wrote in *The Communist Manifesto*, "In place of the old bourgeois society, with its classes and class antagonisms, we shall have an association in which the free development of each is the condition for the free development of all."[16]

History will judge that the American Revolution was more successful in achieving a recognition of the irreducible value of each person than the Russian or Chinese have been to date.[17] This viewpoint is not a call to ignore the many ways within our borders in which the recognition has not yet achieved full stature. We are both a lovely and an ugly country.[18] The reason for quoting Marx and Engels, however, is to suggest that the yearning for the inherent dignity of persons is not confined to traditional liberal thinkers such as Locke, Jefferson, and Mill but includes communist theorists too.[19] In other words, although the specific brand of American individualistic freedom may not be exportable to other political systems, its basis can be the subject of world order assent: the irreducible value of each human person. It comes as no surprise, then, that the charter of the United Nations includes this belief.

## Respect for Persons Baseline

Decisions about ethical and public policy issues such as the ones that will be discussed in the next section arise from a number of factors: different perceptions of the weight to be given one value over another, different perceptions of the relation between law and morals, contrasting views on the benefits or risks of social policy and rules in a complex society, and highly conflicting views of the role of scientific progress and human good. But, as Mary Segers observed in her article on abortion legislation, a fundamental disagreement resides in "the determination of value."[20] Antiabortion groups, she notes,

> generally seem to operate within an older teleological framework, in which the value of a thing is objectively given by external nature rather than subjectively ascribed by human beings.

In this view, the fetus has a nature; it is genetically a member of the human race. She continues:

> By contrast, abortion rights advocates seem to employ arguments that have a more modern philosophical cast and that hold the premise that value is subjectively ascribed by human beings. . . . As applied to the abortion issue, the value of the fetus is not determined by nature but is decided by human beings according to their uses and purposes.[21]

The same observations can be made about all the issues just discussed and their many analogues.

The argument presented in this book is slightly different. Rather than try to resolve conflicting philosophical views about the human person, I have tendered an argument that our heritage is based on a belief in the inherent value of human beings. According to that belief, we are not totally free to ascribe only external value to others for our own use. Although we may value our lawyer for skill in getting us tax breaks, or our car dealer for a willingness to bargain, or our garbage collector for preventing disease, we must also accord them a certain minimum or baseline respect as persons in their own right. Failure to define this baseline or standard, even within the spirit of dialogue about issues I have suggested, is dangerous. As Phillip Heymann and Sarah Hotz caution:

> Society should be and is prepared to pay a great price to define personhood with considerable clarity. Neither doctor, nor parents, nor courts, nor even legislators should be entrusted with discretionary decisions as to whose life can be taken with impunity. Recent history is too full of examples of abuse of that discretion.[22]

Our social instincts in this regard are worthy of some degree of trust. Picture, for example, going out for dinner. While you talk about your values and ideas, you hear in the background, above the tinkle of ice cubes and the subdued clangs of dinnerware and silverware, the soft gurgle of a large lobster tank. In that tank, oblivious to their fate, large and small lobsters dive and surface endlessly. Attached to each lobster, you observe, is a tag. On that tag is a weight, according to which you will be charged a certain price for your lobster dinner. Smaller lobsters weigh less and will cost you less; larger ones weigh more and will cost you more.

In effect, any effort to place only an extrinsic value of human beings is a kind of lobster tank theory of human life.[23] Indeed, we do value animals for extrinsic reasons—they are valued for food, clothing, research, companionship, and security. But should we, without any further distinction, value human life in only an extrinsic fashion? It is clear that we should not. It would be ironic to make only an extrinsic evaluation just at a time when, as a culture, we are beginning to affirm the intrinsic rights of animals to our respect.[24] Not only would it be ironic, it would be anthropomorphically silly to accord more inherent value to an animal than to a human being,[25] although in some non-Western countries this is still done today. For example, cows are still honored as sacred in India. In the West, however, our tradition has always placed human life above animals and nature, often to the detriment of lower forms of life. Nonetheless, we do have a certain baseline respect for human persons that we may not have for lobsters. These form the basis of our social beliefs in the value of human persons.

On this basis, Lincoln saw that one's liberty rested on social recognition as a human being. Without that recognition, one would have no platform from which to argue for one's civil liberties and rights. As Lincoln said about proslavery advocates, they are

> blowing out the moral lights around us, teaching that the Negro is no longer a man, but a brute, that the Declaration [of Independence] has nothing to do with him, that he ranks with the crocodile and the reptile, that man with body and soul is a matter of dollars and cents.[26]

I submit that, in the name of the people, an objection similar to Lincoln's should be made on behalf of all forms of human life that some would wish to reduce to extrinsic value alone. These forms include zygotes, fetuses, the aged, the oppressed, and the infirm.

I say "in the name of the people" because I hold that all persons, under the generalization criterion first introduced by Richard Brandt, if unaware of their own status, would want at least a minimum principle of fairness applied to them. As stated in chapter 6, on our philosophical heritage, one does not "impose" a decision to respect the damaged life of a defective newborn on anyone. It is a belief to be held as self-evident in our society. One does not "impose" rational conduct on nations; one expects it. One does not "impose" burdens in life; they come from life itself.

But does a baseline commitment to an irreducible value inherent in human beings confine us to one particular moral, political, or religious position? The answer is no. Considerable latitude would still exist. Consequently, considerable discussion and debate would still be necessary before our society reached a consensus about macro and micro human life issues. Even if we reject the lobster tank theory of the value of human life, in which persons are only extrinsically valued, even if we adopt a respect for human life posture, at least three positions would remain open to us.

I hesitate to give names to these positions because the names are not neutral enough for us to contemplate which might apply to our own beliefs. Let us call them position A, position B, and position C. If any names could be given them, position A would be a purist view, B an accommodationist view, and C a contextualist view, all representing a belief in the intrinsic value of human life, no matter what its current form or external status. Each will be described and its strengths and weaknesses pointed out.

## Position A

According to this position, all forms of human life have equal intrinsic value. Each form of life and each person is equally free, equally precious. Because of the baseline of infinite value, no government, no court, no other person, no community, no international movement, can abridge or curtail this value without that person's consent. Because, too, of infinite value, human individuals would have inalienable rights toward which the rest of us would have duties. A listing of rights may vary but usually would include the baseline right to life and self-determination. When two infinitely valuable persons clash, or disagree, no other method but dignified, nonviolent negotiation is available to solve their dispute, since any other method may infringe upon the irreducible value of each person. Additionally, not-yet-personal and once-personal forms of human life (e.g., a fetus; a brain-dead human being) are entitled to equal protection of their inherent dignity under the law, even if their survival represents a burden on others or on the state. The reason is that forms of human life are more valuable than burdens they might place on others. In this respect, whether or not the forms of human life are personal does not matter. This is sometimes called the "vitalist" position about human life, but vitalism may not be coextensive with position A.

The strengths of this position are many. No kind of warfare is permitted. No killing is justified. No neglect can be tolerated. Abortion is prohibited, as would be any disposal of fertilized embryos. Dying persons would be kept alive with the use of high technology, unless they explicitly requested not to be kept alive, whether or not family members agreed. The full use of all technologies would be put to saving lives, even of defective newborns or retarded infants. A clear message of compassion and concern for all human beings would be sent out. Racism would be supplanted by brotherhood, intermarriage, and respect. The wolf would lie down with the lamb.

Many moralists take this view of the value of human life. It is at once radical and conservative, radical because it requires the greatest courage to stand against the prevailing zephyrs of popular morality—everyone can do as one pleases, as long as it does not hurt others—and conservative because it represents the best appreciation of what is most exalted in the teaching of the great religions, the most admired philosophers, the finest political traditions. Oddly, pro-lifers join antiwar pacifists at this level of commitment, conservative Christians their liberal cousins, and the right with the left. In response to efforts to establish criteria for not treating certain newborns, this position would echo the words of Eugene Diamond, M.D., professor of pediatrics at Loyola University of Chicago's Stritch School of Medicine:

> American physicians have been the instrumentality responsible for the deaths of millions of aborted unborn children. Now, putting aside the curettes and salt syringes and disposing of the damp pulp of the most recently sacrificed fetus, our profession lifts its eyes above the windows of the abortorium and gazes into the nursery.[27]

The echo would occur because position A regards the right to life to be an absolute, not a relative right. Persons, and all forms of human life, are intrinsically valuable, not extrinsically subject to the whims of others.

But position A requires, along with a vigorous pro-life position, equally vigorous social justice, racial and sexual equality, and antiwar positions, not normally associated with the public position taken by those who oppose abortion. Recall the objection that pro-life positions seem rather monochromatic and focused only on one or two phases of the human value continuum. If all human beings are absolutely intrinsically valuable, then no one, not the state or the church, can tread on this value.

The weaknesses of position A are derived from its strengths. It provides no potential for distinguishing different forms of human life and various obligations that might arise toward those forms. Thus it treats cellular matter as reverently as a fully developed human being. It requires the same protection for this matter under the law as it does for adult persons. Although followers of Christ or of Gandhi might applaud position A for its nonviolent clarity, not many persons living in modern society are willing to forgo their right to self-defense in favor of turning the other cheek. In its wholesale reverence for life, it seems to represent an ideal toward which one might strive rather than any realistic and practical mode of life. Furthermore, by failing to distinguish between the quality of life and life itself, it may cruelly inflict needless suffering on those ready to die, whether they are diseased persons not able to speak for themselves or infants.[28]

## Position B

Position B appears to be more realistic than A. In it, the baseline value of human life is not considered an absolute. Instead, it is considered in relation to other human values, especially the quality of life, friendship, the meaning of life for a person, and so on. No human life is said to have infinite value, even though it has a foundation of liberty and self-determination that must be respected, as in position A. Because it distinguishes between life as surviving and life as having quality and meaning, position B does not regard embryos and brain-dead persons with the same degree of reverence as fully functioning human beings. Nonetheless, because the baseline of respect is equality of opportunity, all forms of life still require others to provide mechanisms for expressing that opportunity.

Thus the fact that a fetus, unimpeded, will become a human person requires certain obligations from the human community in order for the latter to demonstrate its respect for human life, but these might differ from the obligations required toward fully functioning human beings. Within position B, some might argue that, as forms of human life become more vulnerable, greater duties are owed it by others in justice. Other persons might argue that the less conscious, the less "perfect," the less functioning forms of human life may be, the less obligated others may be toward it.[29] Keep in mind, though, that a common basis of respect through *equality of opportunity* is afforded all types of human life, because all types share analogously in the inherent value of human life.

The strengths of this position lie in its ability to maintain respect for persons and for human life while providing a gradation of duties toward persons over and above a basic respect owed to all forms of human life. Embryos, zygotes, fetuses, the retarded, supposed enemies—these would all receive proper but not infinite acknowledgment of inherent worth. The greatest duties, nevertheless, are owed to the fully conscious person functioning in society. In this view, those who violate respect for persons may have some freedoms curtailed in punishment, though fundamental freedoms would still remain. Thus one might lose the freedom of movement, but not one's own life, by being put in prison. All forms of war would still be abandoned because one could not destroy human life. Defective newborns would need to be kept alive, but their quality of life would affect the degree of intervention required. Passive euthanasia would be permitted on the same grounds, even for persons unable to speak for themselves, if their quality of life was irretrievably lost.[30]

The weaknesses of position B are a little less glaring than those of position A. The main weakness is that position B seems to water down a commitment to equality, to equality of value at least, by focusing on equality of opportunity instead. Is that to mean that all persons are not to be considered equal once the opportunity to compete for the world's and society's resources has been offered? By introducing the distinction between life and quality of life, one also introduces the danger of discretionary judgment about whose life is to be considered "not worthy of living." Some philosophers and theologians doubt whether we can ever validly make such a judgment about someone else.[31]

Thus Gilbert Meilaender argues against a theory of substituted judgment and reasonable standard in cases of treating defective newborns on the grounds that

> it makes little sense to attempt to use either of these standards in deciding for incompetent patients such as newborns. The reasonable person standard does not really arrive at a patient-centered decision, and the substituted judgment standard (applied to the case of newborns) is incoherent.[32]

Similarly, we cannot really express what a reasonable person might choose if comatose, since we are not in this condition. How, then, can we rely on a substituted judgment about what this person might decide? The only way is to seek advance directives from the patient or a value history from the family or other significant persons in the life of the patient.[33] Concern about the vulnerability of persons who might have expressed general views before being in a specific condition that might have changed those views have led to stricter interpretations of the living will and other instruments to gaining access to an incompetent patient's previous preferences (see chapter 9). This simply does not apply to newborns, of course.

We do not really know what a comatose patient is experiencing, if anything. A policeman whose brain was damaged by a gunshot wound recovered against all odds after four years of deep coma. He said he thought he had died and gone to hell.[34] But others who have recovered do not remember experiencing anything. A woman severely malformed as the result of cerebral palsy recalled hearing the doctors discuss her case with her parents when she was suffering from burns over a third of her body. The burns were caused by an accident when she dropped a cigarette into her lap and could not put out the fire that resulted. The doctors told her parents that her quality of life prognosis was impossible and that she should be allowed to die. It was like a ghastly nightmare to her. She said that she loved life so much that she gained immense enjoyment out of the simple feeling of clean sheets against her skin.[35]

Examples like these reinforce concern about making quality of life judgments about others. But this objection is not insurmountable in some instances. Criteria regarding the death of the whole brain allows us to judge with great certitude that the person has died as well—that there will be no recovery of any quality of life. Similar criteria regarding the extent of retardation or organic malformation and the resultant quality of life have been proposed for defective newborns as indicators of the level of medical intervention needed to move this quality up a minor notch or two.

Position A, then, establishes an across-the-board basis for the inherent worth of persons as equal and "infinite." No one life can be judged greater than another. Position B also establishes an across-the-board baseline for inherent worth of persons. At the very least this baseline includes a right to life, the liberty to develop, and equal opportunity to compete for a share of resources. But the distinction between life and quality of life permits a range of responses under the rubric of respect for persons.

## Position C

Like A and B, position C holds that there is a baseline of respect for human life that checks our excesses of violence toward that life. Unlike A and B, however, position C holds that this baseline changes with the level or degree of life present and the social context.

Using position C, one could conceivably justify certain wars of defense against unjust aggression. The reasoning would be like that used to develop the just war theory. The lives of persons against whom injustice has been done are, in that context, more "valuable" than the lives of those who have perpetrated the injustice. Capital punishment could be justified, as it is now, by claiming that it is repayment of debt. A convicted murderer "loses" in that context the right to his or her own life, although other kindnesses (visits with relatives, the right to appeal, a good last meal) still demonstrate our respect for the humanity remaining. The life is no longer "innocent." Abortion would be possible. It would be considered a tragic clash between two valued existences. In this situation, however, the mother's obligations and rational choices must be calculated as greater value than an unborn child's. Mechanically motivated, unthinking and uncaring abortions would not be permitted under position C because the clash of two valued entities, the unborn and the mother, would not be tilted in her favor for such extrinsic reasons.

The strengths of position C revolve around an ability to adjust the symbols of respect for persons and human life to the particular context in which the moral issue arises. In contrast to position A, underdeveloped nations would not have an obligation to provide the latest in lifesaving therapy to a dying adult, when their limited economic resources might be better used to help raise the nutritional status of the population as a whole. The individual's life, *in that context*, is less valuable than that of the rest of the citizens. Nonetheless, some form of respect would be required toward the life of the dying adult. Contrary to position B, the value of persons need not necessarily be identified with their life, their liberty, and their opportunities, although in most contexts it may be. It would be conceivable, however, that one could smother one's infant whose cries might alert an enemy to the hiding place of twenty friends. In that circumstance, the infant's life is judged less valuable than the lives of the friends in hiding. Similarly, in the interest of helping persons conceive, spare human embryos could be reverently disposed of, as nature itself does when they do not attach to the uterus. In this context, the embryos carry less value than an embryo that has already been implanted, based upon the goal of the technological process of helping conception itself. If a woman who had been implanted with all her fertilized ova herself decided to eliminate two of the four in her womb to give the others a chance to develop and live, this judgment would be honored.

The weaknesses of position C lie in its arbitrariness. Although it is the nature of human life to debate ethical issues and make difficult choices, our concern about modern society lies precisely in the limited and often violent vision of the persons participating in the debate. Our vicious history, especially in this century, and our reduction of life itself to mechanical processes make it a mark of prudence to exercise caution about arbitrary judgments concerning the inherent value of human forms. Does the community decide what weights to give human life in individual contexts? If so, on what basis does it make these judgments? What about the persons who dissent from the judgment made? Are they to be forced to go along with a disputed and essentially contested plan of conduct toward human beings?

Each of the positions has strengths and weaknesses. My purpose in setting them down has not been to develop them at length at this point. Indeed, they deserve a much more complete treatment than I have given them here. An expansion will occur in the final chapter. Instead, I wanted to show the range of options open to persons who commit themselves to a belief in the inherent worth of human life. The range is not monochromatic. In this regard, all three positions share the belief that human life has an intrinsic value. It cannot be only extrinsically valued. Each position holds that there is a baseline of respect. If this is ignored, one ceases to fulfill obligations toward the value of human life. Additionally, each position requires a certain internal consistency. Thus a position A person must reject as evil all warfare as well as abortion. A position C person, able to accept some situations in which abortion is possible, must also permit some kinds of warfare.

Pro-lifers, who often argue from position A about abortion, tend to adopt position C about the possibility of war. Oddly enough, many pro-choicers adopt position C about abortion but position A about war. I will say more about these positions, and traditional resolutions of the problems that arise, in the final chapter.

It should be noted that to skip from one position to another with changes in the moral issue under consideration is to adopt position C. If one does not consistently apply A or B, one automatically moves into C, a position that permits variations in the baseline "respect for persons" depending on the context. This means that a pro-life person, adopting position A about innocent human fetuses but favoring capital punishment (position C) because that person's life is now no longer innocent, has adopted a general position C view of the value of human life. If, then, the context alone determines the degree of "value" that will be honored, one has moved into the ballpark of "the other guy" and is playing that person's game. "The other guy" in this case is the position C advocate, who, like pro-choicers, points to the context to resolve conflicts among intrinsically valuable individuals or beings.

One cannot have it both ways. Either one adopts a "consistent ethic of life" or one adopts a more moderate, contextual approach. This is the reason, consistency, that some people are put off by extremist arguments on both sides of the human life debate. Nevertheless, no matter which position is adopted, one can still be committed to the multiple heritage of Western culture regarding the inherent value of human life.

## Conclusion

In this chapter we saw that beliefs about the value of human persons underlie our political heritage. Political beliefs are either essential to or disruptive of resolution of some of the difficult ethical issues of our time. The reason that we cannot, as a society, reach a consensus about some of these ethical issues is that we no longer seem to hold as self-evident certain truths about the intrinsic value of human life. One of the dividing lines between attitudes about abortion, test-tube babies, nuclear war, and the like, is a different way of valuing human life. I have argued that a solely extrinsic valuation of human life neglects our religious, philosophical, and political heritage.

Even if one were to accept this heritage as it occurred in the past, however, an additional objection can be raised to its use today. The objection would run as follows: Although thinkers and political communities in the past were preoccupied with the moral status of human persons, modern technological society poses an entirely different kind of ethical issue. In fact, the concern for the status of human persons is now somewhat old-fashioned and misplaced. What is germane to the modern era is a concern for the responsible use of technology rather than the older metaphysical questions about the nature of human life. Note that technology poses the nub of the ethical dilemma in the issues examined in this book: precision computer aiming of missiles, nuclear technology itself, in vitro fertilization techniques, hormonal manipulation of the body to accept embryo transplants, resuscitation techniques and machines that can save the lives of defective and retarded newborns. The list goes on.

In the next two chapters, therefore, we must consider the question of the responsible use of technology. In chapter 8, I will examine some issues that demonstrate the wisdom of a lengthy public discussion for the formation of moral policy. Chapter 9 will suggest some policies about problems that are only now surfacing. I will show that any resolution of this question of directing our technology, despite the above objection, does include taking a stand about the inherent value of human persons, and the proper ends of good human life.

# PART FOUR

# A Life-Affirming Society

# 8

# The Complexity
# of Human Life Issues

The dominant cultural fact, present in both modern warfare and
modern medicine, which induces a sharper awareness of the fragility
of human life, is our technology.
——Joseph Cardinal Bernardin, *Consistent Ethic of Life*

Challenges to any commitment to the value of human life occur
across the generational scale as well as developmentally within a
generation. These are seen in massive public and moral policy debates in our time. This chapter will examine several of these debates
in some detail, showing how the outcome favoring compromise and
explicit policy seems to work best to protect as many interests in the
policy as possible.

Granted, now, that belief in the inherent value of human persons
is reasonable from the standpoint of religion, philosophy, and political theory in the West, the time has come to discuss difficult issues
that test this belief. As we do this, some problems of resolving a
clash of rights will emerge. I will argue in this chapter that when
equal weight can be given to both sides on a difficult issue of moral
principle, one should "err" on, or give greater support to, that side
which tends to sustain our belief in the value of life. The fundamental reason for taking this position is that it is as reasonable as any
other and that it reaffirms our religious, cultural, and political traditions.

The ethical problems to be discussed all call into question our
commitment to the value of human life. I will discuss nuclear war,
defective newborns, teenage abortion, and death and dying. Our
current problems are hardly exhausted by this list. But because
these problems involve our belief in the value of human life, they
may function as examples, prototypes as it were, of all ethical
problems that require public policy resolution.

## Nuclear Armament

The industrial revolution created the greatest ethical challenges of the nineteenth century: slums, rural migration to cities, alcoholism, breakdown of family structure, unionization, child labor, and the like. Many of the problems have not yet been resolved. The great moral issues of our age have been caused by the technological revolution discussed in the previous section. The greatest of the moral problems bequeathed by technology to the twentieth century is noncombatant warfare. And the greatest form of warfare in which noncombatants are killed just like combatants is possible nuclear genocide.

The ethical problems arising from a consideration of nuclear warfare are so immense as almost to break down conventional rational discussion. Because of the number of people involved, the possibility of nuclear warfare can serve as a prototype case of other ethical issues that have the same structure, such as the redistribution of income to third world nations, overpopulation, mass starvation, liberation movements, and the rights of workers and communities versus international corporations. In each of these ethical issues, politics is an essential component. Further, politics is a necessary consideration because large numbers of persons are at risk. Finally, it is a consideration because the resolution of the problem will require worldwide consensus.

In the buildup of nuclear arms, the whole world is at risk. A 20-megaton bomb is over 6,000 times more powerful than that dropped on Hiroshima. The Hiroshima bomb killed about 100,000 people instantly, 40,000 within the next month, and 100,000 from long-term effects of radiation. The human suffering was incalculable.[1] Just one moderate-sized bomb dropped on San Francisco, it is now calculated, would kill 2.5 million people, displace most others, and create lethal radiation for 400 square miles downwind.[2] The United States and Russia have 16,000 nuclear weapons and warheads, enough to destroy the world four times over.[3] Four bombs exist for every population center of 50,000 or more. Yet both nations continue to spend $250 to $300 billion on "defense" each year, at a severe cost to social services such as health care and education. A direct, cause-effect relation exists between military spending and loss of productivity. The more a nation spends on its military burden, the less its annual growth in productivity.[4] Both major nations are finding this out and are seeking ways to cut military spending and to reduce the arms effort.

The human impact is more severe than facts and figures. Life as we know it would end. There would be no more cities, no more lights, refrigerators, parks, zoos, concerts, music. There would be no more friendship. Uncontaminated grain and water would be the objects of fierce fighting. Persons who did survive the immediate blasts would break all rules of human decency—ignoring others who plead for help, their skin peeling off, their eyes liquefied by the blast and firestorms, searching the rubble for their own loved ones. The Reverend Tanimoto, a Methodist minister, survivor of Hiroshima, and one of its Peace Center founders, remembers passing by the living dead with the apology, "Excuse me for not having a burden like yours."[5] Every minute outside an underground shelter would mean increased risk of radiation sickness and death or, later, rampant plagues and infection. No death in a nuclear holocaust is peaceful. Neither is life after this level of destruction.

There is a range of responses to the possibility of nuclear war. Some responses are more appropriate than others from the standpoint of the intrinsic value of human life. Of course, the first is to continue on the course of massive buildups. This is part of the policy of "mutual assured destruction" (MAD) pursued by the superpowers. In it, the argument goes, no nation will attack, because it knows it will be destroyed. Aside from the absurd spiraling of overkill that this policy represents, it is to be rejected on grounds of human worth. In particular, any plan, even for "limited" nuclear war, is a plan to destroy people. In that plan, one claims that the lives in one's own nation are more valuable than the lives in another. As we have seen, however, this claim runs counter to our religious, cultural, philosophical, and political beliefs.[6]

Recognizing that continued arms buildup never makes the other country secure enough to stop its idiotic buildup, both the United States and Russia began new limitation talks labeled START; superseding the aborted SALT II agreements, START would reduce current weapons. Although the talks have been going on for almost a decade, they originally had and continue to have the backing of many Americans.[7] About 50 to 60 percent of Americans support bilateral reduction.[8] Even local communities have recently voted to freeze or reduce nuclear arms. The effects of nuclear war, and the impact of the large defense budget on the economy, may have much to do with this national sentiment. No more encouraging sign could be given than the Russians' own unilateral reductions and agreements mutually to reduce arms that occurred during 1988. A regard for the value of human life and improved social conditions is behind these hopeful activities of the major powers. There is a sense, as we end this century, of the futility of war and its incredible power for self-destruction. Building on this sense to "make peace" will be the challenge for the future. As a Russian writer noted about the promise of the times:

Indeed, there is a deep meaning in what is happening. It is quite clear that everything occurring today stretches with its branches into the

future, into the third millennium. . . . You and I are preparing the
ground for this future.[9]

Freud and Einstein exchanged letters on war and peace in 1932,
at the encouragement of the League of Nations and one official,
Leon Steinig. They were as confused as we are about the causes of
war, citing industrial greed, power, and reluctance to limit the rights
of sovereignty. Einstein's theory was that persons have in them a
need to hate and destroy. Freud felt that the "death instinct" was
the cause of that need and that war was a natural consequence of the
death instinct. Against that nature, civilization tended to control
passions and produce pacifists. Both men seemed to agree that there
was no known ideology that could bring all people into a single
group, thus transcending the divisions that lead to war.[10] My suggestion is that the ever-widening recognition of the inherent value of
human life on a global scale can function as the missing ideology.

The heart of nuclear arms policy is defense. And the heart of defense is the claim that a nation will retain the right to fire first. This
was the political policy of the Reagan Administration. The National
Conference of Catholic Bishops issued a pastoral letter in June 1983
that expressed deep skepticism about the morality of nuclear deterrence as a defense posture: "The Challenge of Peace: God's Promise
and Our Response." The bishops say, "We have profound doubts
about whether the use or threatened use of nuclear weapons can be
truly reconciled with traditional principles of self-defense and just
war." Considerable controversy surrounded this position. In particular, the bishops dialogued with representatives of the then current
Administration about the morality of nuclear war, the Administration attempting to maintain its right to "fire first."[11] The bishops'
position, later echoed and even enhanced by other religious groups,
such as the Methodists, based on principles of self-defense, contrasts
markedly with scriptural pacifism, based on religious nonviolence.
Thus Archbishop Raymond G. Hunthausen of Seattle, having joined
an earlier pacifist stand taken by retired Bishop Carroll T. Dozier of
Memphis, and other churchmen and churchwomen, claimed that we
are controlled by "principalities and powers," by the demonic realities of nuclear weapons. "The possibility of unilateral disarmament
seems incomprehensible in this country," Hunthausen says, "only
because we worship the nuclear god."[12] Later suppressed by Rome
for a time, until the American bishops conference worked out a compromise, Hunthausen's cause created concerns that the stand he
took was too strong for the universal church.

Writing on the respect for persons, resources of nonviolence, and
their applicability to the nuclear arms race, Professor Gerard
Vanderhaar notes: "Nonviolence takes two forms: a firm no to the

forces that propel us on the road to nuclear destruction, and a strong yes to ways of affirming human life and dignity."[13]

In a nonviolent view, one may still accept the principle that nations have autonomy and that they have a right to defend themselves, even others, against unjust aggression. That form of defense, however, does not rest on destroying the life of another human being. Instead, it rises from respect for the values of that life. Its challenge is that it is more difficult to talk than to hit, to negotiate than to strike out, to dignify than to destroy. Later, I will propose at least one position that would require pacifism as a commitment to the value of human life.

## Abortion

The same forces of hatred, greed, destruction, laziness, and selfishness occur in the less global sphere of care for defective newborns and some of the other human life issues I will now discuss. To develop some points further, I single out abortion and the right to die. So much has been written on these topics that one despairs of shedding any new light. They must all be seen within the extremely complex context of sexuality, family life, and personal worth in our society.

Society encourages teenagers to be active sexually, and then it encourages abortions or ostracizes girls if they get pregnant. One out of three marriages ends in divorce. In the last two decades, out-of-wedlock births have tripled, from 5.3 percent to 17 percent. Over 1.5 million babies are therapeutically aborted every year. One out of 4 pregnancies ends in abortion. Teenagers end 42 percent of their pregnancies, while women over forty end 51 percent. Most women who have abortions are not married. Nearly 70 percent of women having abortions are white.[14] There are thousands of children in homes with only a single parent, 90 percent of these being mothers. Herpes, a lifetime infection transmitted sexually, is rampant among 30 million Americans. As a society, Joan Beck observes, "we still haven't reached a comfortable new consensus about sexual morality."[15]

In this context of sexual and family turmoil, an enormous number of ethical problems arise. There is no easy middle position on most of these issues. Resolving them by appeal to the Supreme Court or by efforts to develop a constitutional amendment may allow one side to win over the other but does not truly examine the conceptual issues and commitments to the value of human life.[16] Politicians and pressure groups abound.[17]

Without an ethic of sex and family in which the value of individuals is recognized, the state is often asked to resolve questions through its courts and legislation. Once the state enters, it jeopardizes the chance of grappling with questions of morality according to the communal beliefs of the persons affected. Of course, the state can and does act against popular opinions, as it did by mandating speed limits and the use of seat belts, but this intervention does shrink moral discussion and decision making. Once made legal, abortions also seem, for many, to have become moral. This happens because the state must resolve the issue on the basis of the common denominator found in the national community. When there is no consensus in that community, as there was not regarding the beginning of human life, the Supreme Court and legislators must appeal to another value (such as privacy) about which we do have a consensus. In effect, the state selects a secondary value in the absence of a missing primary one (belief in the dignity of life itself).

While I do not intend to belittle the judicial or the legislative branch of government, I wonder whether either is the proper place to resolve human life issues. It seems that justice for the unborn, in the abortion decision, was certainly overlooked. One of the last speeches of President Reagan, before he left office, was on the abortion issue. The theme of the talk was that if people are so interested in choice, what about the unborn fetus which cannot choose to live or die? This is a powerful concern in our country, one that will not go away in the public arena.

In this respect, the issues now under discussion are different from the global issues exemplified by nuclear war. In those, the political process is essential. In the personal human life issues, the political process occurs but is not essential to resolution unless a community consensus cannot be reached. Let us see how important this consensus is.

To start, let us take abortion. Our lack of consensus quickly will become evident. As it does, it can only make a reflective person sad, sad that the vulnerable have had to suffer while we tread water. Furthermore, the connivance of the Missouri legislature to introduce a law governing abortion that was planned to be appealed all the way to the Supreme Court, now less liberal than in the past, is a good argument for keeping moral decisions and moral policy out of the political arena.[18]

The Supreme Court of the United States judged in 1973 in *Roe v. Wade* that a zygote and a fetus could not be called a person. As a consequence, the normal protections of the Constitution did not apply to these entities. That is, the inherent value of persons, a belief underlying the Constitution and the Bill of Rights, could not, without great dispute, be applied to fetuses, even though they possess the potential to become human persons. Although the court is now to review the Missouri law that defines the moment when an embryo becomes a person ("the life of each human being begins at conception") and restricts abortion ("unborn children have protectable interests in life, health, and well-being"), it is not expected to reverse *Roe v. Wade* completely, which affirmed a woman's constitutional right over her own body.[19] Nonetheless, constant pressure by conservatives on this issue has now reached a watershed. It appears that the Missouri law was deliberately designed to test our national consensus, as it most clearly exploits the ambivalence we have in thought and in law regarding the status of unborn human life.[20] Additionally, the court has now become much more conservative,[21], a point that makes pro-life groups very hopeful.[22]

Attempts to legislate against abortion by constitutional amendment have failed, precisely because we still do not possess a consensus about the start of human life. Further, abortion now has become our most-used surgical procedure. Further still, feminists have taken the stand that support for abortion is support for women's rights and that resistance to abortion diminishes the personal worth of women, because they must have control over their own bodies.

The debate has been vitriolic and will continue to be so. Candidates are elected on their stand for or against abortion.[23] Some figures, like John Lipsis, argue that *"all* life is precious, and equally deserving of protection under the law [author's emphasis]."[24] Of particular concern is our attitude toward burdensome life. Others, like Valerie Vance Dillon, argue that in modern society we have new control over the destiny of human life requiring a new kind of responsibility, especially toward the unborn.[25] Still others are aghast at the curious euphemisms used by supporters of abortion, the worst being a reference to living fetuses as "products of conception."[26] Who could disagree with the important values of the preciousness of life and our responsibility toward it, especially if one follows the heritage regarding the value of human life I have spelled out so far? Admittedly, the fetus is not clearly a person, not, that is, to everyone involved in the debate. But do we want to become the kind of society that does not respect the inherent worth of human life, even in its incipient or in its final stages?

On the other hand, pro-choice arguments also rest on some extremely important values. Who would wish to have others control his or her body? Who would want his or her privacy invaded? Who would want to reenslave more than half the population? And who would want to claim that an incipient human life is more valuable than one now existing? How is it possible to decide such a thing? The Jewish tradition permitted abortion for the sake of the mother's life, while Catholic moralists used to argue that the unborn must be given a chance to live, such that the mother must be sacrificed for its sake if both could not be saved. The fetus cannot be sacrificed to save the mother. Thus, in this conflict situation, unlike ones in which there might be an unjust aggressor, the fetus cannot be considered such an aggressor, although the Jewish tradition sometimes did make this judgment.[27]

Who would want to bear the offspring of a rape? It is difficult for a man to imagine the feelings of repulsion and hate that surround a rape. How saintly can we expect a victim to be, asking that she bear the child regardless? And should men be involved at all in moral policy about how women should behave? Recall how angry men were after World War I when, in their absence, the women in the country organized and imposed on them prohibition to solve an enormous problem of alcoholism, abandonment of wives and children, and violence. It took years to repeal that amendment to the Constitution, and we learned in those years that people will drink anyway. We established a powerful underworld that controlled liquor and all the bad things that went with it. Crime flourished. Regressing on abortion rights, the argument goes, would simply reintroduce criminal activity; respect for law would decline; women and abortionists would develop an underworld, an unholy alliance.

What will most often happen happened in Kalamazoo. An eleven-year-old girl, raped by a man living with her mother, was denied an abortion by the courts because it was past the second trimester. The girl herself was a victim of neglect. It comes as little surprise, then, at twelve years of age she was later found unable to care for her baby properly. Thus she faced a charge of neglect of her infant. Both child-mother and her child were put in different foster homes.[28]

Efforts by pro-life groups to have these issues resolved with legislation are attacked on the following grounds. First, many women consider abortion a matter of conscientious moral choice. We have seen how moral choice is a very important value, one that is closely identified with the very value of human life that pro-lifers are supposedly supporting.

There is a pro-choice "seamless garment," or "consistent ethic of life," argument that accompanies this one. According to the Catholic bishops in the United States who adopt this approach, a respect for life reaches from womb to tomb; one must be concerned about the value of human life across the board. For this reason, church leaders of all denominations point to needs of the poor, the uneducated, the homeless, the need for peace and justice throughout the world. A pro-choice version of this argument is an accusation against pro-lifers, that they neglect the battered child, the beaten wife, the homeless. In a "Letter to the Editor," Nancy Degnan says:

> I have not heard of any pro-lifers starting agencies or shelters to care for these physically and emotionally bruised kids. . . . I call the major-

ity of women who seek abortions responsible, because they recognize
their own limitations and the limitations of society. They do not want to
hate their offspring.[29]

Of course, not all women choose abortion for such noble reasons.
And that is the problem of the "responsibility" argument. Most
women getting abortions are white and unmarried. Should they not
exercise some responsibility for birth prevention before they take
the life of another potential being? But the accusation against the
pro-life movement is to some extent accurate. It seems to be a one-
issue concern, just now branching out into death and dying issues as
well. While the arguments they advance about the dignity of unborn
life ring true (especially against the backdrop of the Nazi experience, of the ways in which people can disvalue and destroy other
human lives), an awareness of the context and social problems that
lead women to abortion seems lacking. This detracts from the persuasiveness of a pro-life position.

The pro-choice lobby is traditionally more concerned with
broader issues. A meeting of the Religious Coalition for Abortion
Rights of Illinois in the winter of 1989, for example, had workshops
on fertility control, family planning, child abuse, infertility treatment, ethical perspectives on fetal rights and fetal medicine, teen
sexuality, the family unit, and so on.[30] Typical of the concerns was
that expressed by the keynote speaker, Daniel Maguire, a theologian:

> We are living, right now, at the end of what I see as the most mean
> spirited presidential administration of this century. . . . What would
> you make of an administration which would cut aid to the homeless by
> 78% in seven years and, at the same time, . . . that same administration
> would pour hundreds of millions of dollars into the destruction of some
> 50,000 peasants [in Nicaragua]?[31]

The speech continues with a host of social ills underaddressed by
the Reagan Administration, the point being that a commitment for
life must be borne out throughout the lifetimes of a people, not just
in the narrow confines of the womb.

In addition to the moral choice argument, there is another. It is
that amendments and legislation about morality are efforts of the
new right to revive civil religion. Robert E. Webber, an evangelical,
criticized the Moral Majority in these words: "They want to restore
morality to government by supporting legislation that will produce a
moral country. . . . at least externally. But true Christianity is not
moralistic. Moralism is do-goodism."[32]

A third argument against legislating morality rests on prudence. If
Congress could overturn rights interpreted by the Supreme Court in
*Roe v. Wade* based on public clamor, as Mary Segers argues, then it

conceivably could do the same for hard-won civil rights.[33] Consider the possibility of a reinterpretation of *Roe v. Wade*. Suppose the Supreme Court decides that the constitutional right of privacy actually cannot be extended to such an extent that individual women have a right of choice over their own bodies. If this precedent does occur, then it would seem that the state or some other power will be able to control reproductive and other functions of the body. Is it hard to imagine that in the future, when the state decides it wishes to control reproductive rights (as is now done most extensively in China), it would have the constitutional right to do so? Or is it hard to believe that in a time of depression or economic crisis the state will usurp for itself the right to "put people out of their misery or old age" by active euthanasia? This is precisely what happened in Nazi Germany. Look at this argument about lives considered to be meaningless, called by two physicians "ballast existence":

> The question of whether the expense of maintaining these categories of ballast existence is in every aspect justifiable was not an urgent one in former times of prosperity. Today conditions are different and we have to consider it.[34]

Thus the rightness or wrongness of the ethical issue, if brought to the public forum, would be settled on political grounds rather than on moral ones. The three arguments—for moral choice, against legislating one group's morality for others, and for limiting the power of Congress and the states regarding human rights—are all too powerful to ignore.

### Defective Newborns

Another related moral issue is that of treatment for defective newborn children. For at least ten years, retarded persons have been steadily gaining rights: rights to be consulted about sterilization, rights to marry and have children, rights to receive special education, rights to be protected against discrimination.[35] One "right" stems from laws against child abuse—the "right" to survive against many odds. This right has not yet been won. The Supreme Court did define three rights: safety, freedom of movement, and training. What is not defined is the retarded person's right to life in any and all circumstances. And even though training is a right of a retarded person, after the school years parents of these young adults find it increasingly difficult to gain access to structured programs.

It might be best that a right to life for all retarded or special persons has not yet been defined, not because the retarded do not have a constitutional claim to protection of their life, but because as a society we do not yet fully support the retarded and their families.

For every heartwarming story of family love and the courage of a special or retarded child, there is one (or more) of bitterness. The heartwarming stories tell how a child adapts to the challenges he or she faces with the love and support of the family.[36] The bitter stories tell of the agonies of social rejection and of caring for children until their death.[37]

Following dramatically publicized cases at Johns Hopkins University Hospital, special protection for defective newborns was included under various laws. When the case of *Baby Doe* arose in Indiana, the national uproar about not treating a defective newborn was immense. A baby, whose real name is protected by confidentiality, was born with Down's syndrome and a closed esophagus. It is very difficult to predict the level of retardation in Down's syndrome children immediately after birth. Some children do rather well and others do not. Apparently judging that Baby Doe's affliction represented a burdensome life to themselves and to the baby, the parents, with the doctor's accession, decided against surgical intervention to correct the malformed esophagus. The parents were both intelligent. Both had once taught the retarded. As a result of refraining from surgery, the baby died on April 15, 1982.

In cases of babies like this, dying occurs rather simply. Only water is given (but when the esophagus is malformed, it can be given only intravenously). The baby's cries are distressing to the staff, especially since Down's syndrome children appear more normal to the staff of an intensive care nursery than other children they are working hard to save. The baby cries because it is starving to death. To stifle the cries, the baby is oversedated, until it finally dies.

Before Infant Doe died, many public activities occurred. Under Indiana law, the baby was initially considered to be the victim of child abuse. The Monroe County assistant prosecutor filed suit under this law to remove the child from the custody of the parents, to make it a ward of the state, and to try to save its life by mandating the operation. Two hearings occurred before the case went to the Indiana Supreme Court. While the court considered the case, at least six families offered to adopt the baby. The court decided the case in favor of the parents and doctors, a decision parallel to the recommendation of the American Medical Association Judicial Council and the recommendation of some ethicists. If we did not have the technology, the baby would have died naturally. We therefore should act to use that technology responsibly. Further, parents normally have autonomy in a decision to treat or not to treat their child, when unusual treatment is involved.

After the state court judgment and the death of Baby Doe, the federal government put hospitals on notice that to allow defective newborns to die is to violate federal regulations and legislation, the

Rehabilitation Act of 1973, regarding the rights of the retarded.[38] Federal legislation was introduced by Rep. John Erlenborn (R, Illinois) to mandate the treatment of *all* defective newborns, in spite of the large body of philosophical and medical literature that attempts to establish sophisticated criteria for treatment and nontreatment.[39] The sadness that a child needlessly died affected many people, precisely because the issue about who should decide in such a case is so complex. Erlenborn's view is that the case was "a shocking example of a newborn baby being allowed to die slowly of starvation," while third parties battled in vain to adopt the baby or to summon help.[40] Beverly Draper wrote sadly in a letter to the editor of the *Chicago Sun-Times*: "Yes, my heart goes out to the parents of 'Infant Doe' from Bloomington, Indiana, but it breaks for the little boy who will never be."[41] And Susan Benes wrote the same day to the *Chicago Tribune*, "As I sat holding my beautiful, happy, 10-month-old Down syndrome infant, I felt as though I'd lost someone close to me."[42]

As in the other issues examined so far, though, it is at least clear that we lack a necessary consensus about the inherent value status of retarded (and defective) newborns. As a consequence, courts sometimes decide in favor of parent and doctor decisions, sometimes against. Nonetheless, the Department of Health and Human Services and the Reagan Administration issued a notice to health care providers on May 18, 1982, that the department will withdraw all federal funds if withholding decisions are based on "the fact that the infant is handicapped" and "the handicap does not render the treatment or nutritional sustenance medically contraindicated."

On May 20, 1982, Illinois moved to gain custody of and find adoptive parents for a child born with spina bifida.[43] Eventually a family willing to adopt the child and have it treated was found.[44] Consensus about legislating treatment automatically, however, is far from secure. Representative Erlenborn's district was quite evenly divided on support for his Handicapped Infants Protection Act aimed at amending the Child Abuse Prevention and Treatment Act (42 U.S.C. 5101 et seq.) to give powers to the Secretary of Health and Human Services to intervene to save lives like that of Infant Doe.[45] After reviewing legislative recommendations, Norman Fost said, "Like so many other attempts at legislating morality, it is difficult to know whether this one will result in more harm than good."[46] Reviewing his work with children who suffer from spina bifida, Chicago surgeon David McLone put his finger on our social attitudes regarding "special" persons when he said,

> But if we don't find a way to bring them into society, then we've created a situation where we may end up with a thousand children with normal intelligence sitting and looking out the windows of nursing homes. And that's my nightmare.[47]

Eventually an amendment to the child abuse legislation was passed by Congress, giving the Department of Health and Human Services the power to protect defective newborns against decisions made by their parents and doctors. Notices went up announcing a hot line. After only a few cases, this power was reviewed by an appellate court, which suspended it, and then by the Supreme Court. Finally, guidelines from the department made it mandatory to treat all defective newborns, unless, in the opinion of the managing physician, the newborn was dying. If that was the case, appropriate medications, pain control, and fluids and nutrition could not be withdrawn. This position too was protested and amended by the department itself to include the judgment of a physician about whether such treatment might prolong the dying process. Consultation with an ethics committee, called an infant care review committee, is suggested.[48] The latter had the support of the American Medical Association and the American Academy of Pediatrics during the several years of debate about this issue.

Treatment of defective newborns is hardly a closed issue today. As I noted in chapter 2, the vulnerability of these infants and their families, and of the health professionals who care for them, is high. But the debate and the mix of legislative efforts and court cases, as well as the vigorous discussion of ethical issues, led to a compromise that may not satisfy all parties but is certainly reasonable. The effort by Surgeon General C. Everett Koop to argue in a case similar to the Indiana one, called *Baby Jane Doe* (from New York), that such infants have a constitutionally protected "right to life" seems to have failed, since that effort was interpreted to mean that in such cases treatment should be mandatory for all infants without regard to outcome.[49]

On the other hand, society has judged that such infants are vulnerable enough to the decisions of others that it will not tolerate variability from case to case, depending on the judgment of the family and the doctor. This is seen as inappropriately making quality of life judgments for other persons.[50] For some people this is tantamount to infanticide.[51] The major issue in this, as well as in abortion, is what the child would decide in case it ever could.[52] This is not the only reason for trying to protect vulnerable forms of human life, but it is the main reason we are cautious about making quality of life judgments for others. Freedom of choice, for pro-life and pro-choice proponents, is a central value, even though it is interpreted differently and issues in diametrically opposed public policies.

### The Right to Die

Conflicting court decisions, differing opinions about the value of legislation, concern about "imposing values" on others, and lack of public consensus are not confined to the incipient and vulnerable forms of human life. The same confusion exists with respect to the dying and euthanasia. Just as in cases involving defective newborns, most of the decisions are made by the family or the dying patient with the doctors. No direct killing is permitted, but many forms of withholding treatment take place. Now increased efforts are being made to regulate the discretionary decisions being made by individuals. Here the principle of choice should predominate, especially if persons express their wishes through advance directives and living wills.[53]

Should doctors agree to a request by a possibly senile eighty-five-year-old woman to withhold the medication that was preventing another stroke? Should they agree to withdraw a respirator from a dying patient? In New Jersey, doctors refused to do so for Karen Ann Quinlan, even after the New Jersey Supreme Court ordered that no further "extraordinary" treatment would be required.[54] They agreed only to wean her from the respirator. Karen lived, unexpectedly, and in a nursing home was fed by tube, dying finally about ten years later. By contrast, a court in Massachusetts decided against giving potentially lifesaving leukemia therapy to a sixty-seven-year-old retarded ward of the state because of the uncertain outcome. The man had a mental age of only three, and there was concern that he would not understand the therapy.[55]

Should doctors have to agree with the family about treatment decisions? In New York, the state's highest court of appeals ruled that blood transfusions should not have been stopped for a terminally ill, severely retarded adult cancer patient at the request of his mother, an apparent contrast to the Massachusetts decision. The same court approved a request by an eighty-three-year-old terminal patient to disconnect the respirator because the patient consistently expressed views against life-prolonging treatment when no recovery was possible.[56] Yet in California, the Los Angeles district attorney charged two physicians with murder in the case of Clarence LeRoy Herbert. The family gave the doctors permission to discontinue the respirator three days after the fifty-five-year-old patient suffered severe brain damage following intestinal surgery. After the patient breathed on his own, the charge was that the surgeon and the internist then gave orders to discontinue intravenous fluids and nasogastric feeding tubes. The patient apparently died, as did Baby Doe, of starvation and dehydration but without gaining consciousness. If a nurse had not complained to the county health department, the incident, which occurred in September of 1981, probably would not have come to light.[57] What, if anything, makes the case of Clarence Herbert different from that of Infant Doe? Why "murder" in one case and "approval" in another? The district attorney in the Herbert case found it difficult to substantiate the charge of murder, and initially no indictment of the physicians was issued. An appeal by the district attorney led to their eventual indictment for murder. This was dismissed after a hearing involving debates about the nature of intravenous feeding and nutrition. These debates continue to this time.

Although the principle of the right of patients to determine their own treatment has been firmly established in subsequent cases, such as *In re Conroy, Elizabeth Bouvia,* and *In re Jobes,* more recent court cases in New York *(O'Connor)* and Missouri *(Curzan)* call into question the quality of advance directives, that is, their specificity, and even the right of privacy as governing one's own treatment while dying. I mentioned these in chapter 2 to show how vulnerable people are to whims of others during the dying process, especially if their own wishes are not clear. As a consequence, these general principles are not always operative in the dramatic cases that reach the court system in some states.

The problem of what to do about vulnerability has not yet been decided in this ongoing concern about incompetent persons, those whom society so often regards as post-persons. This debate will continue for many years. In chapter 9, I will address some of these issues by focusing on a policy for the right not to suffer.

## Conclusion

We are clearly in a state of chaos about the status of human life in our society. Can any sense be made out of it at this time? I think some norms have begun to emerge, but still lacking is the underlying ideology about human life that Einstein and Freud wrote about. We ought therefore to discuss thoroughly and then rededicate ourselves, internationally if possible, to the proposition that all persons have an irreducible, intrinsic value. Does this mean that they all must be treated alike, or that quality of life considerations cannot be taken into account? I think not. Instead of rushing pell-mell into legislation and even judicial decisions about ethical issues at "the edges of life"—that is, about incipient forms of human life (embryos, fetuses, and the like), burdensome forms of human life (severe retardation, severe handicap, or debilitation due to age), or vulnerable forms of human life (inability of persons to speak for themselves)—I would counsel a long period of public discussion and practice which would take place under the umbrella of a commitment to a basic concept of the intrinsic dignity of persons. I will argue this position in more detail in the final chapter, when I present a theory of choice.

Of course this position is open to the criticism that we ought not to stand on the sidelines and do nothing while others take radically repulsive actions that destroy our sense of the value of human life.[58] I agree with that objection. Instead of "doing nothing," we must try to persuade others as much as possible about the evil of their ways, without destroying their own freedom of choice. Otherwise we treat them as if *they* were objects to be manipulated by our own visions. A good example of the more difficult work of persuasion comes from John Woolman, an early Quaker who became convinced that slavery was wrong. He then traveled through Virginia and Maryland, going from home to home, trying to convince his coreligionists about his view and bring them to it. Eventually he was successful.

Many of the references in this section came from newspaper accounts, calling our attention to the issues. They are quite thoroughly discussed by experts in professional journals, yet we are only just beginning serious, well-informed community discussion. Instead, we tend to let the issues be decided by televised documentaries or, worse, soap operas and talk shows. In practice, people with their doctors do resolve difficult issues. Only when other parties get involved are the issues put into a legal, rather than moral, framework. This is not to denigrate the law. It quite properly acts to resolve conflicting claims. But it cannot create a consensus that does not yet exist.

No consensus about the status of human life—that is *my* nightmare. Without it, we will continue to have confusing and conflicting decisions about human life. People will needlessly die. People will needlessly live. Rightful life will be snuffed out, while dying will be prolonged. Experts will draft theories that, as Richard Westley quite honestly notes about his own views, have little or no community support.[59] People seem instinctively to know that letting Baby Doe die was tragic but letting a Clarence Herbert die was probably merciful. In other words, they know that life is not always worth living, even though it has intrinsic value. A baseline about respecting life is needed. I will next discuss that baseline.

# 9

# Taking Responsibility
# for Our Technology

"You tell him he's unnecessary and that is a . . . sin. . . . It's abortion at the other end."
— Nat, in *I'm Not Rappaport* by Herb Gardner

Precisely because life is sacred, the taking of even one human life is a momentous event. Indeed, the sense that every human life has transcendent value has led a whole stream of the Christian tradition to argue that life may never be taken.
— Joseph Cardinal Bernardin, *Consistent Ethic of Life*

The Presbyterians have joined other religious bodies in the United States in taking on the morality of nuclear war. In 1988 the 200th General Assembly of the Presbyterian Church (U.S.A.) examined a draft of a statement that the three million member church had hotly debated for about three years. The statement argues that Christians should "normally" support their governments but that pursuit of nuclear deterrence is immoral "as an end in itself."[1]

In Stockholm, on the same day, international health officials met to discuss the AIDS crisis. The first item, and most important, was a plea for an international antidiscrimination effort on behalf of AIDS victims. Anyone infected with the HIV+ virus should be considered in need of care. Dr. Jonathan Mann, director of the World Health Organization AIDS program, told seven thousand delegates to the Fourth International Conference on AIDS on June 12, 1988, that fighting discrimination against AIDS victims is not just a necessary public health measure (that all persons be identified and helped) but also a humanitarian stance for all victims. "The protection of the uninfected majority depends precisely upon, and is inextricably bound with, protection of the rights and dignity of infected persons."[2] Given the general reluctance of the population to "identify" with persons with AIDS,[3] this statement is an important insight into the ways in which we must work out our social policy. The new chairman of the Presidential Commission on the Human Immunodeficiency Virus Epidemic, James D. Watkins, said, "The epidemic provides us with an opportunity to reaffirm our basic American values and improve our ethical treatment of others."[4]

Concern for the rights and dignity of all persons, including those who fall "outside the norm" of our pluralistic society, is a refinement of the twentieth century that will stand us in good stead in the next "Century of Progress." Thus we find churches also grappling with their ancient teachings (some say biblically based) on human sexuality. The Episcopalians published a booklet that is recommended (but not as official teaching) as a teaching guide for pastors and laity regarding sexuality. The title of the booklet is *Sexuality: A Divine Gift*. But because both heterosexual and homosexual love are depicted, critics call it a sacrilegious "sellout to contemporary culture." The central feature of the guidebook is the notion of sexuality as a sacrament: "When sexual intercourse is recognized as a Christian sacrament, our bodies become the means by which God teaches us what it means to give ourselves without holding back, to love another person with generosity and enthusiasm."[5]

These are but a few of the current efforts to take responsibility for our human values in a technological age.[6] Each such effort, some of which will be discussed in this chapter, shows a high regard for the value of human life while kneading the dough of a new moral policy. As Joseph Cardinal Bernardin puts it, "Every human life, at every state of development from conception to natural death, and in all circumstances, is sacred and beloved of God."[7] Praising the American Catholic bishops for taking stands on social issues, Robert Johnston says of a general thrust by religion in human life issues, "The religious conscience in this country does have a positive effect on national policies and has brought a new awareness to problems like poverty, lack of decent housing, unemployment, the homeless, racism, sexism and the scandalous neglect and poisoning of our environment."[8]

Just because each human life is to be taken as sacred and loved by God does not mean that we have the same obligations to all forms of human life. Recall at least three positions about the inherent value of human life sketched in chapter 7. But if we take the value of human life seriously, we must develop equitable policies in the future that apply our burgeoning medical technology fairly. This chapter looks at some examples of what we might do about aging and the end of life.

Little can be gained by assuming simplistic postures about any one of the incredibly complex issues that do arise when technology meets human life. But there does seem to be a difference between issues at the beginning of life and those at the end of life, of obstetrical and pediatric issues as compared to geriatric ones. In the former instances we are dealing with transient and potential beings. Although such beings have rights, they may be more restricted than fully functioning human beings. Thus a frozen embryo might, in the future, acquire the right to be implanted (as it apparently now has in Australia) but not, of course, the rights of free speech, assembly, suffrage, and the like, that we honor in persons (those who are able to make moral choices).

In the latter case, at the end of life, we are dealing with persons who have constructed a value history.[9] Even if both the pediatric and the geriatric patient are now considered incompetent, there is a world of difference between them.

The heart of the difference lies in the fulfillment of the capacity to make decisions either upon values that we already have or upon values that emerge after reflection on the decision. Although all beings should be valued by us, and their integrity preserved as far as possible, when a tragic choice is forced on us it is far easier to decide about applying a medical technology or withholding it altogether based on values constructed by a patient over a lifetime than on a "value-less" field presented by the embryo or the newborn. That is why the abortion debate has divided us politically, and much more so than debates about the living will and other forms of controlling the dying process (though the latter too have been vigorously argued).[10] Honoring the values of individuals as part of decisions to be made about them, once they are incompetent, is the primary way we can respect their inherent dignity. If they are dying, we should never strip them of the lifetime of choices their values represent.

Again it is instructive to note our ambivalence about human life values in our public behavior. Although abortion is legal, what do we do with the problem of protecting the fetus from a mother who is destructive? Should the protection of the unborn extend to jailing mothers, such as was done in Washington? There, in order to protect the fetus, a pregnant cocaine user was given a longer sentence than usual for forging checks.[11] Up to 10 percent of all babies born are born with addiction, in pain, and often disabled (being born without eyes is just one of the gifts a cocaine abuser bequeaths to a child). The prosecuting attorney of Butte County, California, has a policy of zero tolerance toward such women. He claims that this policy forces women dependent on drugs to seek help and that it has reduced the number of drug-dependent births to zero.[12] In the end, however, jailing does not seem like a decent policy. Sometimes, the drug-related injuries have already occurred by the time the mother is discovered and jailed. Also, people can get drugs in jail. This public policy issue demonstrates the problem of protecting the unborn from the capriciousness of their mothers. How can it be distinguished from abortion itself? Is abortion also a kind of capriciousness?

By contrast, a position of solid commitment to the value of human life, even that which may not be a human person as we normally understand personhood, produces the safest insurance against bigotry, repression, neo-Nazism, and murder. There is much to be said of this position. As we saw, it is in the natural law tradition of the founders of our country.

If curtailing our technological possibilities for human life is not the answer, what is? As I have suggested, the best approach for the future is not to suppress the inquiry and action that flow from scientific judgment. Instead, our science and technology must be directed to good human ends.

This suggestion becomes a truism if there is no attempt to define the kinds of efforts that will be required in directing technology. Some important examples are worth discussing: controlling life-prolonging technologies, regaining personal control of dying, limitations of access to health care resources, ways of forming conscience, the social problem of a dependent population, and the amelioration of suffering. I can only sketch the outlines of a possible moral policy in each of those categories; the purpose is to indicate how our society can direct rather than suppress modern medical technology.

### Controlling Life-Prolonging Technologies

Controlling life-prolonging technologies is but one aspect of the larger problem of directing technology to human aims. Nowhere is that more apparent than in the application of medical technology and its various interventions to the dying patient. Not surprisingly, studies have confirmed that it is not the technology but the care that persons receive that determines their well-being, and in the case of the dying patient, the protection of their human spirit to the end.[13]

Dying is at once a personal and a social ritual. In ancient and medieval times, and even today, persons were able to sense that they were dying. At that time, they would assemble their families and friends for some last words. During this assembly, they distributed their goods (later they were able to make out a will ahead of time for this purpose). After talking and praying, the dying person assumed a ritual posture to await death. Sometimes this was a seated posture (as among Native Americans); sometimes it was a posture of folding one's arms across one's chest (as seen on sarcophagi of knights, kings, and queens).

The social ritual of dying paralleled the personal ritual. The family and friends assembled. They kept vigil around the dying person to assure him or her that the community support the person had enjoyed through life was maintained. That same community recorded the last thoughts, the wisdom of the dying person. Psalms and prayers were said. The burial ritual simply extended this vigil until the body was in the grave.

Dramatic changes in health care have also changed this personal and social ritual. There has been an enormous increase in the technology of care. Where once a cold compress might have been applied and the patient's hands held, now all sorts of interventions are possible, ranging from intravenous fluids and nutrition, nasogastric feeding tubes, tubes implanted directly in a vein or in the stomach for feeding, bypassing cancerous obstructions, blood products and agents to prevent clotting or bleeding, and cardiopulmonary resuscitation all the way to experimental treatments such as advanced chemotherapeutic agents, radiologic implants, artificial hearts, and transplants of other organs.

With the increase in technology came a corresponding increase in the institutionalization of care. Whereas formerly patients died at home in the midst of family, relatives, and friends, now they die in hospitals. Almost 80 percent of persons who die each year die in institutions. Many of the personal freedoms enjoyed by dying persons were lost as a result. Hospitals are excellent places to go when one wants to be cured of a disease, but they are terrible places in which to die.

With the increase in technology and institutionalization came a corresponding increase in the specialization of care. No one person attends to the dying patient. Often different services are stacked up like planes at O'Hare field, waiting to attend the dying person. At risk, then, is the former freedom to control one's own dying process.

In our hospitals it is actually difficult to die. There is little possibility of maintaining the personal and social ritual of dying.

In a technology-intensive hospital, it is difficult to sense that one is dying. The patient and the family have no clues about what will be the final outcome. The dying process is disrupted in favor of doing all one can to preserve life. Hence it is hard to assemble family and friends for a last conversation. How many persons have gone to and from the deathbeds of their relatives, wondering whether each trip would be the last? Even if one knew that death was approaching, there is a diminished chance that last words could be spoken. This is true because the prolongation of the dying process, if it were successful and provided a few more good days, weeks, or months, usually terminates in a process of pain during which the patient is severely drugged.

People's bodies die in pieces. First the kidneys might go, then the liver, then the heart, and finally the lungs. During this process, they have invited into their bodies fluids, nutrition, antibiotics, surgeries of various sorts, respirators, nasogastric feeding tubes, and all sorts of other interventions. There is no one to preside over the moment of death, since the dying is spread out over so many moments.

Even though persons have always died in pieces, that is, the body has deteriorated or parts of the body have shut down, in the past because of the social ritual and community support the person did not disintegrate from a metaphysical point of view. Each person was assured of support, convinced that loved ones were near and that a smooth transition to an afterlife would be provided by religious ritual at the deathbed.

### Regaining Personal Control of Dying

Personal control of the dying process can be regained by appealing to a number of principles of medical ethics. Some of these have now been recognized in the law as well. An obvious one is that of Informed Consent. This standard originally applied to medical research, but in *Canterbury v. Spence* in 1972 it was applied by the D.C. Circuit Court to regular medical treatment.[14] The principle is that individuals have a right to decide about their own medical treatment and must have sufficient information and freedom to make that choice. As Russell McIntyre notes about a New Jersey Supreme Court adoption of the "objective prudent patient standard" in regard to informed consent, the obligation of providing information and being sure the patient is free to make the decision falls on the physician, and that the requirement to pursue this obligation is linked to New Jersey's other supreme court judgments regarding the right to die.[15] These judgments involve protection of the rights of patients to avoid abuse.

First, all patients should have a right to refuse treatment, even if this refusal might lead to their death. Court cases, such as *In re Bartling* in California and *In re Conroy* and *In re Jobes* in New Jersey, have confirmed this right, even for incompetent patients. An incompetent patient does not lose the right to refuse treatment; the guardian or family member must speak for the person's wishes. Thus the family does not have a right to say what *it* would want so much as what the patient would prefer. This right of the patient perdures whether or not there is a living will law in the person's state. Of course, a living will strengthens the advance directive a patient gives about his or her care. Perhaps the strongest statement comes from California in the case of *Elizabeth Bouvia*. There the California Second District Court of Appeals stated explicitly that a patient has the right to refuse any medical treatment and that the exercise of this right requires no one's approval.[16]

However, in what was characterized as a setback for the right to die movement, the Supreme Court of the State of Missouri forbade the withdrawal of artificial nutrition and hydration through a gastrostomy in the case of Nancy Cruzan, who lay in a permanent vegetative state for five years as a result of an automobile accident. She was then thirty years old. If the feeding continued, she might be expected to live another thirty years in this condition. Her family had argued that she did not wish to live in this condition. Their argument was based on a "somewhat serious conversation" in which Nancy had indicated that if sick or injured, she would not want to have her life continued unless she could live "halfway normally." A trial court found this to be sufficient evidence that she would not want to live maintained only on artificial food and hydration, and it ordered the state employees who were caring for her in the Mount Vernon State Hospital to carry out the request of her legal guardians to withdraw the fluids and nutrition.

But on appeal, the Supreme Court brushed aside the nearly one hundred court cases in twenty states, and the living will statutes in thirty-eight states, including Missouri itself. The overwhelming majority of the court cases were decided in favor of the right to die.[17] These cases also affirmed the role of families or other decision makers, who are able to say in the absence of written preferences from patients that the patient would not have wanted the treatments in question.[18] The statutes are based on the right of individuals to determine their own treatment, especially when they are dying.

The court considered that euphemisms made their way to the fore in the cases they considered, particularly the concept that by withdrawing fluids and nutrition the patient died of the underlying disease. The majority opinion (4–3) held that the constitutional right to privacy is not expansive enough to apply to livesaving treatment. Other court decisions, different from the Missouri one, were simply based on a desire to interpret the law in favor of one's right to die. Clearly, only the United States Supreme Court will be able to make the final interpretation of the constitutional right to privacy.

The decision demonstrates that one can interpret the law in many ways.[19] This is certainly not the way a principle of choice would apply to such decisions. Patients who express their wishes about their death ahead of time must be respected, if their values and their lives are not to be denuded at the end.[20] At risk too, and not very well examined, is the right of the family to advocate and interpret the preferences of their loved ones who become incompetent. Another case, like the Cruzan case, involved a young mother whose brain was severely damaged in a car accident. Only in this case, Nancy Klein, the mother of a three-year-old daughter, was pregnant. The doctors in the case told her husband, Martin, that she had a better, though still slim, chance to live if her pregnancy, in its early stages, would be terminated. Presumably they could try to keep her alive until the baby was about twenty-four weeks old, when it would have about a 20 percent chance to live if they took it through a Caesarean, but that Nancy might not live to that point. Martin Klein sought a court order to authorize him as a legal guardian in order to issue such an order. But antiabortion forces entered the case to protect the unborn child. It went all the way to the U.S. Supreme Court, where Justice Thurgood Marshall gave the authorization (by rejecting a lower court stay) to Mr. Klein. Nancy underwent an abortion in the eighteenth week of her pregnancy.

Martin Klein said of the experience: "No other family should have to go through what we have gone through." His view about the right of the family to make such decisions, though, was upheld: "This was not an antiabortion case. This was a matter of who can make the decision for a wife who could not make one for herself. The decision was made by a husband and family in unity, who know her and love her."[21] Although attempts were made by the antiabortion forces to contact a more conservative Supreme Court judge, Justice Antonin Scalia, he, in effect agreeing with the stay, put the appeal on the agenda for a regular court conference for a time after the decision went into effect.

This decision may have an impact on the review of the restrictions on abortion in the State of Missouri. Of equal importance, however, is that the Missouri Cruzan case is being reviewed by the Supreme Court as well, since in that one, remember, the family is not only trying to act in the best interests of their loved one but is doing so based on fairly strongly expressed wishes about not having her life prolonged.[22] In California, as well, a measure by the legislature to broaden the situations under which a living will may apply (usually it covers only the final days of a person's dying process) was vetoed by the governor, apparently in concern that it might relax too much the definition of death, making it easier for doctors to remove life-sustaining technology.[23] But that is the whole point! Controlling technology by shaping its use to an individual's values is the struggle of this century and the next. Fortunately, for over a decade, as the Society for the Right to Die points out, "legislatures and the courts have elucidated patients' rights to reject life-sustaining treatment through Living Will statutes in 38 states and over 100 court cases in more than 20 states."[24] This constant and perduring effort will continue into the next century.

One problem in the Missouri case was with the specificity of wishes. In this regard, the court built upon an earlier and less restrictive judgment handed down in New York regarding Mary O'Connor. The decision in New York is considered less restrictive because it did not deny the right of patients to express advance directives, or that the family might have a legitimate role in witnessing those directives, but rather denied that O'Connor made any specific reference to fluids and nutrition in her wishes. She was seventy-seven, a widow, with two daughters who were practical nurses. During her later years, she frequently had to confront issues of life prolongation with relatives and her husband. The daughters and friends were able to testify to her constant and explicit desire never to "be a burden to anyone," "not to lose my dignity"; that it was "monstrous" to keep someone alive using machinery when the person was "not going to get any better." She held that people who were suffering very badly should be allowed to die. Several times she told Helen, one of her daughters, that if she became ill and could not take care of herself, she would not want her life to be sustained artificially.[25] A trial court approved removal of fluids and nutrition after her progressive deterioration following a series of strokes. She was in a geriatric institute at the time. The appellate court affirmed that ruling, but when the institute went to the New York Court of Appeals, the court issued a surprise ruling. After affirming the ideal situation of having advance directives from the patient herself, or a living will (which is not yet legal in New York), and acknowledging that repeated oral expressions are important, the rulings of the lower courts were overturned because the patient's statements, as expressed by family and friends, were "not clear" about application for withdrawing fluids and nutrition.[26]

The Society for the Right to Die commented on this case, with respect to the role of the family:

> The underlying assumption is that to permit ending treatment without clear and convincing evidence would lead to abuse of the vulnerable elderly. Other courts and authorities . . . have strongly held that decision-making when the patient is incompetent is best discharged by family members who know and care for the patient, rather than health care provider or courts, to whom she may be a stranger.[27]

The court's position is that there is nothing more than conjecture about whether O'Connor would have wanted the fluids and nutrition withdrawn. One suspects, however, that a more conservative concern about many vulnerable individuals has now surfaced. This concern has as a deep background the Nazi experience already noted in chapter 8. Yet the question remains, How specific can or must individuals be about the future contingent possibilities of their health? It seems sufficient to take the "family principle" seriously, that, lacking any other data, families are the best interpreters of their loved ones' wishes, unless, of course, the family itself is judged incompetent to speak for its loved one for one reason or another.[28]

highest of the developed world.[38] A poll of Americans published in 1989 indicated that 90 percent wanted key health care changes. The Canadians and the British were also polled and only about 1 percent would exchange their national health plans for the American systems. Since Americans have a worse birth rate and lower longevity rate than the Canadians and the British, this does not come as a surprise.[39] When Margaret Thatcher offered a plan for the first overhaul of the British system by introducing more competition, she was roundly criticized, even by doctors who vowed to fight the changes (though they once vowed to fight the National Health Service itself, not unlike the American Medical Association which fights any changes in our own). Although overburdened, the Service was called "poor" by only 15 percent of the British polled. As one observer said about Thatcher's plan, it might "prove the first step on the road to the horror of the American health system."[40]

When uninsured persons of such astounding numbers cannot get access to health care, many observers think that "some form of universal health care" is "inevitable." These same persons can point to surveys that show "consistent support for a tax-supported egalitarian national program."[41] Mainstream groups, like Consumers Union, criticize the current system and argue that consumers cannot look to the private sector to finance and support long-term care. We must look to government.[42] Yet sufficient concern about such a plan, which would also "inevitably" ration by means of "first come, first served," that backs up surgery, for example, for almost six months,[43] brings us to the point of this chapter: control over technology. The real efforts will lie in strengthening cooperation in the patchwork system that now exists.[44] Among more creative plans are those which emphasize more local and personal control over allocation decisions.[45] An example might be a systematic process developed between patients and physicians, using the hospital ethics committee itself.[46] As Carola Eisenberg, M.D., emphasizes, "We must mobilize our natural allies—our patients and the public at large. It is they who have the greatest stake in the battle to preserve excellence in medical care."[47] It is within this context that discussions about access to health care for the aged should be discussed.

A right to health care for all citizens must be defined and implemented. It would be good to do so within a rationing context. I will not examine the rationing methods for the general population but will give examples of how that might be accomplished for the aged. The components of an argument for a basic right to health care might be the following. They are presented by way of summarizing this section of the chapter.

The right to health care will become the next major human rights issue in the United States. Most other advanced and even many nonadvanced countries (Nicaragua springs immediately to mind) have established a constitutional or legislative right to basic health care for all citizens. Already in the United States there is an entitlement to health care for veterans, to kidney dialysis for all citizens under Social Security, and to the poor and the elderly under Medicaid and Medicare. Recognizing the crisis in health care, a broad coalition sponsored by the American Medical Association recommended increasing Medicaid coverage so that the poor and the uninsured would get better coverage and doctors and health care institutions would receive better compensation for this care. It is estimated to cost $13 billion more. This is proposed without attention to the fact that the United States spends almost twice as much on health care without any better results than other advanced countries.[48]

## Ways of Forming Conscience

In any reasoning about rights, claims that rights do in fact exist are worthwhile for argumentation's sake but in reality cannot be implemented without the political process. Conscience requires speaking out about this issue. Conscience can be informed by the following components.

1. **Experience.** The experience of a well-designed social system in which all persons have access to health care can easily be gained by consulting Canadian, British, and European models. Americans can be embarrassed by our nation's lack of resolution of the problem of access, especially when confronted by European colleagues. Uwe Reinhardt, a medical economist at Princeton University, who is familiar with different models from different countries, has very clearly laid out the strengths and weaknesses of the American system of access to health care as compared to the European. Its strength is freedom; its weaknesses are all expressed in its lack of compassion and justice.

2. **Data and Demographics.** We are unable (read "unwilling") to provide access to health care for almost 38 million underinsured and uninsured Americans. These people are not all poor: some work for companies that do not have policies, or some have temporarily lost their jobs. The poor have access squeezed by virtue of hospital closings in inner-city or rural areas such that their access to care, while still available (e.g., at a county hospital), becomes less and less convenient. Since we cannot now address the needs of our citizens, unless there is a drastic change in the near future, a social revolutionary kind of change, major unmet needs will rupture our society.

For this reason, support for some sort of national health insurance such as that discussed by the Physicians for a National Health Plan is required. What might emerge would be a multitiered social program, like one I call Eldercare, rather than a program by which the Federal Government is the sole insurer.[49] In any case, the disparity created by uneven access is a violation of general principles of justice and a violation of the principle of treating each person as if he or she were a class instance of the human race.[50]

**3. Philosophical Reasoning.** A social decision is required to determine fundamental rights to health care.[51] At the very least, all persons should have a right to primary care or a right to a certain minimum basic health care. Americans might be appalled by the reasoning of libertarians such as Robert Nozick, H. Tristram Engelhardt, Jr., and recently Michael Rie. The latter two authors published an article that proposed skimming and dumping (getting the paying patients and dumping onto the public system those who can't pay) as "virtues," since private enterprise hospitals then teach society to make its own commitments to the poor.[52] The libertarian view of society is essentially flawed, because it is based on a social contract theory that emphasizes autonomy as a condition of possibility for ethics.[53] In this view, the fact that some persons cannot get access to health care is unfortunate but not unjust. No one has a claim on the resources of others unless by social and explicit contract. This is not the kind of society we ought to be. The reasons were explored in chapter 7. The issues of the right to health care are to be played out in conflicting views of the nature of human society.[54] Respect for autonomy is important, but beneficence-in-trust is the primary ethical principle, not respect for autonomy (which is included in the principle). This principle governs especially the relationships of need and meeting needs that occur in health care.[55]

There is a social obligation of health care professionals, but the primary obligation is not to the economic goals of society, as Robert Veatch seems to hold,[56] but rather to correct the imbalance of need. The obligation stems from the needs of individuals who cannot provide for these needs themselves. David Ozar has developed a theory of social justice based on this insight about health care,[57] from which can be drawn the common conclusion that health care is not a commodity but a human need. More about this in the next point.

A critique of different models of access to health care and theories of justice can be done from the point of view of the principle of medical need.[58] Each person should receive help according to his or her need. But if this principle is adopted, as it has been in the past by the health care system, some access principle must also be proposed. I will suggest one based on functional status care categories in examining the problem from the point of view of the crisis of aging in our society.

**4. Theological Reasoning.** If the problem lies in the kind of community we wish or ought to be, then the real support for the idea of a right to health care must lie in a theological vision. If Christians believe they are a form of eucharistic community, this vision can sustain an obligation to offer assistance to others; for example, there might even be an obligation to donate our organs to others when we can no longer use them ourselves.[59] Theology can certainly enhance our understanding of social interdependence. Biosocial interdependence is a physical phenomenon of human society, but it has moral and religious implications. It can form the moral basis for the right to health care. As noted earlier, Erich Loewy has argued that the morally significant thing about beings is their capacity to suffer.[60] One of the religious foundations of medical practice is this capacity, but another is the very capacity of human beings to heal one another, a point I will make in the section on the duty to ameliorate suffering, below.[61]

Finally, Laurence O'Connell, a theologian and president of the Park Ridge Center, has argued that while the preferential option for the poor is a principle rooted in a Christian vision of health care, it can be sustained in secular society as well.[62] At any rate, the most vulnerable persons ought to have first call on our resources in any Christian community. These considerations can lead to a conclusion that every human being has a right to health care. Further, the church should be a leader in establishing and fostering this right from its own self-reflection on the nature of the ideal human community.

If we ration by age, serious difficulties arise for justice and for the nature of our society, as I pointed out in chapter 2. Among those difficulties are inequities of access, a lack of respect for the aged in return for all they have done for the younger generations, the creation of institutional dumping grounds for elderly, incompetent persons, and the cutting off of care for many elderly persons who could profit from it and return to a normal life. Stephen Miles, M.D., of the University of Chicago, described a "feeding ward" of a chronic care hospital, two wards, each with eighteen beds, where aged persons were quietly fed through tubes, with one nurse in attendance. Families and physicians were no longer really involved in the care of these patients, all of whom had suffered irreversible and progressive brain damage. The patients themselves were not involved in the decisions to continue to feed them through medical interventions. Many were contracted into a ball, into a fetal position. Miles reflects: "Medical technology is a way we care. But it is the caregiving, not the technology, that we honor. The automated silence of the feeding ward where families' and patients' voices may not be spoken is not a human caregiving."[63]

Is there some way to avoid the ageist social policies discussed in chapter 2 that will pay attention to the human aspects of care, the dialogue between doctor and patient, and the role of families in care decisions? Can there be a sophisticated and complex policy that would empower individuals in a grassroots medical ethics and social policy movement?[64] The basic problem is to provide for the autonomy of the elderly patient as well as the sometimes competing interests of the family and society.[65]

## The Social Problem of a Dependent Population

There is a major social problem shaping up with an increasingly dependent population. As noted already, the number of dependent persons is increasing more rapidly than the number of workers.[66] Currently over 50 percent of the cost of long-term care is borne by public funds, and we face a crisis in catastrophic insurance. Imagine what will occur in the future when we are faced with these demographics:

| Age | Current | Year 2040 |
| --- | --- | --- |
| Over 100 | 200,000 persons | 1,000,000 persons |
| Over 95 | 300,000 persons | 3,000,000 persons |
| Over 85 | 2.2 million persons | 15,000,000 persons |
| Over 65 | 11% of population | 33% of population |

As these staggering statistics become a reality and our children become a problem for our grandchildren, extremely sophisticated norms for withholding and withdrawing expensive forms of care will have to be in place.[67] These will most probably be based on current guidelines that cover terminal illness, but the major ethical and legal issues today surround disputes about certain conditions, such as advanced Alzheimer's disease or a permanent coma, that may or may not be seen as terminal states.[68] A Congressional Study by the Office of Technology Assessment is helpful in this regard, as it enumerates the areas in which the application of technology to the elderly causes both ethical and economic problems.[69]

Bear in mind that the most expensive form of care right now is not life-prolonging technology in an acute care setting but long-term care in a nursing home. According to congressional studies, the average family can go bankrupt financing just four months of care in a nursing home for a loved one. As Dr. A. R. Somers in the New En-

*gland Journal of Medicine* put it: "Of all the difficult health-care issues facing the nation today, none is more complex or more urgent than the formulation of a viable policy of long-term care for the elderly and the chronically ill and disabled."[70]

Ideally, all decisions to withhold or withdraw care, whether clinical or in public policy, ought to be based on the value of enhancing individual autonomy. This would mean that a national policy that respects the value of elders' lives would establish the means of allocating care on the basis of self-determination largely through advance directives. When these are not present, families should be permitted to influence decisions by constructing a patient's value history or even by insisting on a minimal quality of life.

Even when diminished capacity occurs, individuals can still preserve their dignity through a preservation of freedoms. Not all freedom is centered on the freedom of choice. Other modes of freedom are:

> Freedom to act on life plans unless there is harm to others
> Freedom from obstacles and interventions
> Freedom from hidden obstacles, propaganda, choices by others that limit one's choices
> Freedom to know one's options, e.g., informed consent
> Freedom to choose goals and relate means to goals
> Freedom to act such that (a) actions are one's own and (b) one can commit oneself to new values (even if a patient loses freedoms 1 and 2 because of illness, freedoms 3 and 4 can still be protected)
> Freedom to create new options. The "will to live" might be one form of this freedom; so, too, might be the will to die.[71]

### Balancing Autonomy with Quality of Life

Perhaps the most difficult clinical problem in working out an equitable system of access to health care is that of balancing the patient's autonomy with his or her quality of life, particularly if the person becomes increasingly incapacitated by the effects of age and disease. Some moral rules could be established that would assist in making the necessary decisions. These would grow out of the experience of caring for the aged. Examples might be as follows:

**The rule of illness.** "All illness represents a risk to autonomy."[72] Therefore one might wish to conclude that paternalism toward the elderly is justified. Yet not every illness diminishes all forms of freedom noted above.[73] There is still a chance to enhance the individual's autonomy.

**The rule of mutual dependency.** "All care is between mutually dependent persons."[74] There is a common identity among those who care for the elderly and the elderly themselves. This recognition diminishes the danger of a loss of advocacy for the aged among the caregivers. It also underscores the need for a national health policy that includes, rather than excludes, the caregivers, whether they are professionals or family.

**The rule of dependency.** "The greater the patient's dependency on others, the greater the care must be to act to enhance his or her well-being."[75] Special care must be taken to ensure that individuals do not suffer the ultimate humiliation of having their lives and values subject to the override of the agendas of other persons. Well-being and freedom are always circumscribed by social duties and physical limitations, however. Thus the context in which the patient is cared for and the physical condition of the patient are valid components of decisions about the care of that person.

**The rule of objective treatment.** "When wishes of patients are not known, and the patients are now incompetent, they should be treated as others in their condition have chosen to be treated."[76] Thus it becomes possible to avoid providing unlimited care for each individual now incompetent in cases where valid directives are not present. Social justice is also objectively ensured using this moral rule; that is, treatments are not decided upon on the basis of subjective quality of life judgments. Instead, they are based on an objective, medically indicated standard.

The foregoing rules are just four of a set of possible moral rules that could be developed to limit access to health care. Note how they depend much more on individual and caregiver decisions than the proposals in chapter 2 of limiting treatment on the basis of age. Any just policy would also have to balance an honor to individuals and to society.

The first way to honor individuals who are aged is to decouple age from disease. Not all older people are sick. Age in itself is not a disease. Age has a meaning all its own, and this meaning contributes to an individual's self-image.[77] One example of this is when senior citizens discover that volunteering or working in child assistance programs improves their view of their life as well as their view of society.[78]

A second way to honor aging individuals is for society to assist them in preparing for old age. The best way to accomplish this is to emphasize their freedom to be themselves. No one wants to be subject to others after years of independent living. Autonomous decision making is still an obtainable ideal in geriatrics.[79] As we age, of course, we must learn to rely on others. Some dependency does occur. So the effective method of emphasizing the freedom of elders is to free them from unnecessary dependencies.[80]

The third way to honor individuals is to provide outstanding geriatric care by providing the basis for good nutrition, good interventionist medicine when necessary (adjusting goals of that intervention appropriately), control of polypharmacy (avoiding too many and conflicting drugs), and enhancing their relationships with others.[81] Home care is a major provision in this plan. Many nurses are now leaving institutional care for home care, because it is more personally rewarding, although more difficult.[82] A case management approach to each individual is also required. This will entail the creation of a new kind of liaison health professional who directs all aspects of the care of the individual and coordinates the home care and institutional care programs for that person.[83]

### Honoring the Common Good

The common good of all citizens is honored when we do justice to the elderly, since all of us will eventually age and be part of that population. Proposals to include the elderly and the poor in a national health plan are part of this commitment, because justice is a kind of transforming process; it changes the way we deal with one another in society.

Among the behaviors that must change are our paternalism toward the elderly, effectively neglecting their wishes in favor of our own. But another is our interventionist tendency to "fix" things up. This cuts out the possibility of the aged being asked to help to be responsible for the aged.[84] The long-term care insurance package passed by Congress in 1988 is a bad example of this, since it covered almost nothing. Hence, what A. R. Somers said in 1982 remains true to this point: "Of all the difficult health-care issues facing the nation today, none is more complex or more urgent than the formulation of a viable policy of long-term care for the elderly and the chronically ill and disabled."[85]

Why not ask senior citizens to be involved in the creation of social policy governing their care and to monitor social protections against violations of their civil rights in cases of age discrimination and forced retirement? An example of work that needs to be done on a national level, legislatively and clinically, would be the creation of new forms of guardianship that may not depend so heavily on family.

Institutions can enhance the autonomy of individuals by creating mechanisms both to protect and to implement directives that patients initiate, or to enable them to implement those directives themselves when they enter a critical care facility or long-term care home.

Second, patients themselves can be asked to participate in shaping the rules governing their care, including the rules of long-term care settings.

Third, elders can be promised a death with dignity. At the least, this can mean a dying without technical fuss, free from the vitalist assumptions of others,[86] and with an expectation that the community of healers (caregivers, professionals, society itself) will ensure that pain control will be used and the suffering involved in dying will be addressed, a point for the next section of this chapter.

Finally, institutional ethics committees can play a role in helping both in case decisions and in the setting of moral policy for institutions.[87] Ethics committees are immersed in the "clinical realities" of decision making and are the structures best able to formulate appropriate care policy recommendations about withdrawing or withholding care from elderly patients, given the notion that the elders themselves would play a role in this clinical reality.[88] Nursing homes ought to have such committees as well.[89]

### Critique of Ageist Proposals

Armed with the above case-specific and autonomy-enhancing proposals, we are in a better position to see how enormously unjust are the ageist proposals of Richard Lamm, Daniel Callahan, and Norman Daniels discussed in chapter 2. No effort as well thought out as theirs should be dismissed without considerable countereffort. But the problems created by the use of age as a cutoff outweigh the merits of their proposals.

First, even with the best-laid plans individuals are often not responsible for illnesses they contract, especially later in life. Hence prudent plans cannot always be made. Further, while one person requires more than another at age seventy-five, the proposals would not allow us to meet those different needs. While it certainly seems reasonable to curtail spending on high technology medicine, the most spending done by the elderly and their families is for nursing home care and chronic care, something Lamm and Callahan would not deny for the elderly (though Daniels might).

Furthermore, Callahan's concept of a "natural life span" is hard to defend in a society so well developed as ours. What are we to do with the many patients over eighty or eighty-five? A number of persons are operated on when they are over one hundred years of age and do well. Would it be just to deny such persons the opportunity to return to their own, quite comfortable, quality of life? On top of that, Callahan and others who propose cutting off high technology care do not seem open to voluntary active euthanasia,[90] or even, in Callahan's case, withdrawing or withholding food and water at the request of patients.[91] Both euthanasia and assisted suicide are seen by him as being disrespectful of the elderly. Yet these activities would surely cut down on the expenses of dying. Approximately 40 percent of the costs of Medicare and Medicaid are incurred during the last three months of life. Admittedly, other values must be protected in any scheme for allocating health care. It is right for Callahan to protect the intrinsic value of human life. But once external factors, such as the social welfare of all, economics, or a national health policy that limits treatment on the basis of a natural life span, are used to allocate care, the intrinsic value of individuals is at risk. If life can be curtailed for social policy reasons, why could it not be curtailed for other reasons, such as active euthanasia or even involuntary euthanasia of the elderly? Once the principle of medical need is abandoned, external market forces and public policy values are brought to bear on allocating health care and on the very lives of individuals. The intrinsic value of the individual suffers.

Even though we might think in an ideal world that we could have a national consensus about rationing care for the elderly on the basis of age, it should not be pursued on that basis. Instead, health care should be provided to the elderly out of love and devotion to them. The supposed "squeeze" on the resources available to younger generations can be avoided by honoring the elderly's exercise of their right to die.

There are so many unique factors among individuals that ageism can never be just. A different method must be found, one that would rely on a multitude of factors, such as primary intergenerational assistance, economic incentives to care for persons at home, stress on advance directives, openness to a therapeutic plan to bring about death, and assistance by the government for independent living. But the fundamental purpose of any social policy governing care of the elderly ought to be individualized care. Persons have individual needs that cannot be met by rigid social policy and arbitrary ageist cutoffs. As Joseph Fletcher says, "We ought to decide whether there is an obligation to die in terms of particular individuals in particular situations, not in terms of generalized categories of human beings."[92]

One piece of a more flexible social policy would be the notion of health professional stewardship as advanced by Fletcher elsewhere.[93] According to this notion, a steward is "somebody who acts on behalf of a principal. He or she is an agent who carries out the principal's wishes."[94] As Fletcher argues, this role has been exercised less frequently than is realized. Often in the clinical setting, older patients, say those over eighty, request that nothing further be done to prolong their life. They do not want to die any more than any of the rest of us. But they seem to have passed beyond the stage of grasping onto life the way younger people do. Fletcher has noticed this too: "In actual practice, physicians often ignore, compromise, or even deny a patient's right to die, probably more commonly than we like to think. . . . Physicians are less prone than some patients and ethicists to acknowledge that the patient has a moral right to choose to die."[95]

Stewardship of the elderly also entails helping them achieve the more limited aims of life in a body that no longer works as well as it once did. But it need not overburden a society through high technology interventions. Most elderly persons maintain a balance like that sought by Callahan in society as a whole. They often express dismay at what they consider to be inappropriate, disproportionate interventions. Usually the family itself is the main source of this inadequacy at protecting the loved one's values.

Following the notion of stewardship, a national or social policy about allocating health care to the aged at the very least should underscore and protect:

1. The right of each person to refuse medical treatment that might prolong life, no matter in what condition the person finds himself or herself. This right should be supported even if the person is not "terminally ill."

2. The right of the physician to act as the patient's surrogate against the family when inappropriate care is requested,[96] inappropriate both from the standpoint of medical indications and from the standpoint of the patient's own value system.[97]

One of the most important efforts in this regard would be the "decision not to leave home." Gene Stollerman's "Decision to Leave Home"[98] pointed the way toward the next major effort to take control over our modern medical technology. In the old days, people rarely thought of taking their loved ones to a hospital to die. Instead, farmhouses were equipped with a coffin door, a door wider than the others, through which the generations exited.

Today the hospital and, with it, high technology intervention are no farther than a phone call away. When a seriously ill loved one suffers a heart attack, a stroke, greater confusion from kidney failure, or shortness of breath, it takes extraordinarily stalwart and resolute souls to stand by. How much easier it is to grab the phone and call Emergency Medical Services. We always think we must do something, especially when someone we love is dying. Upon their arrival, Emergency Medical Services' direct communication with the hospital means that the ethic of intervention will supersede all other responses.

Instead of a coffin door, there is an emergency room door in our modern homes. Normally invisible, it beckons powerfully when someone we love fails to thrive. It is therefore immensely important that families receive support to help them "do nothing," as they do in home-based hospice programs. The attending physician should thoroughly discuss with the families the need to control technological impulses in favor of personal care, to bring about a humane dying process.[99]

This will take a reversal of traditional physician instincts as well. As Dr. Stollerman notes, the precedents set by DNR orders can lead to DNLH (Do Not Leave Home) orders as well. But there still exists an enormous gap between DNR orders in principle and in actual practice.[100] The same gap between an individual's preferences and their implementation occurs at home as well.

3. A system of functional care categories that would define a range of medically indicated treatments for various categories of function.[101] Outside this range, no discussion would take place of other medical interventions or technology. The lower the functional care category, the less would be the range of indicated treatments to be discussed. Economic considerations nationally could shrink this range, but it would shrink it for all persons falling within objectively described functional status measurements. Justice would be served.

These categories would be developed into a national health care plan from clinical experience of medically indicated treatments for elderly patients. According to the American College of Physicians, "Primary care physicians should incorporate functional assessment techniques into their routine medical management of older adults, and the skills and procedures necessary for assessing functional capacity should be taught to medical students and residents."[102] As experience grows with these techniques, our national categories can continually be improved.

How might these categories work in the clinical setting? Functional status chart orders could be written on behalf of an incompetent patient whenever the potential benefit of therapy might be disproportionate to the cruelty or harm inflicted by the therapy or the potential benefit to the patient. Typically, status one, in which the patient still enjoys significant functional ability, may limit only highly disproportionate care. Such a patient may normally be treated for infection, heart attack, stroke, even cancer such as adult onset leukemia. This is because there is a reasonable hope of returning the patient to a functional status equal to the one enjoyed before the onslaught of the disease. Disproportionate care in this first category may include only organ transplantation and some forms of highly technical cardiac procedures that carry a high degree of risk.

Persons in the fourth functional status care category, by contrast, are currently in a severely compromised state. They may not be able to interact at all with their environment, may not be able to feed themselves, and may be weakened by irreversible disease processes.

People in the "feeding wards" described by Dr. Miles are examples of these patients. The proportion between intervention and outcome in such cases increases to such an extent that these persons may not receive antibiotics, resuscitation, pacemakers, and cancer therapy in the event that additional diseases strike them. The reason is again past medical experience, not quality of life judgments. Recall the point made earlier under the discussion of quality of life that one may judge that interventions are inappropriate while bracketing out any judgment about the merit and worth of a person. The proposed intervention is now seen as out of proportion to any increased benefit to the patient.

Cases of never-competent patients often do not fit a stereotypical pattern for which moral choices have been thought out in advance. Clearly the situation demands ethical decision making, but that decision making has to be innovative. There is no possibility of appeal to the usual standards of moral choice.

Such a chart order, indicating to which of several functional status categories a patient may be assigned, should be written when two conditions are met: (a) Other established criteria for withholding therapy are absent; and (b) the patient's family and/or doctor concur that the patient's best interests do not merit treatment for diseases of specified levels of severity. Regarding the first condition, other criteria already exist pertaining to irreversibly, terminally ill patients. These ethical and legal criteria govern all treatment, including food and water medically delivered.[103] No further criteria are needed. Regarding the second condition, placing persons within treatment ranges (this is effectively accomplished by assigning them to an arm of the functional status categories) should be done only when the best interests of the patient call for it. Prior to that time, all treatment options should remain open.

Thus the functional status order can be seen as an action for patients, without abandoning them, on the basis of medically indicated ranges of treatment. It goes without saying that no prior patient choice can guide our decision, since the patients being discussed are those who have never been competent. Extrapolating back from this restriction, the same conditions would apply for all patients, except that the first condition would now be guidance in treatment options by previously expressed wishes of the competent patient.

4. The flexibility of the dialogue and adjustments within the doctor-patient relationship. Each decision within the medically indicated range of treatments would still be individually tailored. Ageist social policies destroy this individualized tailoring altogether.

There is an enormous range of options to be discussed with a patient who is fully functional versus one like Claire Conroy, who was confined to bed in a fetal position. The former might include angioplasty, chemotherapy, cardiopulmonary resuscitation, and the like, while the latter category may embrace only measures to increase comfort. Precedents exist for such assessments as the basis of care. These include a broad spectrum, from screening for hearing loss[104] to the differential diagnosis and treatment decisions for dementing diseases.[105] In each case, the physician should function within a dialogical framework of the doctor-patient relationship, factoring into the decision the patient's or surrogate's value system, the medical indications, and the functional care category.[106]

Finally, stewardship requires a different kind of education in medical school and residency programs. In addition to cost control as a function of ethical decision making, physicians need education about the value dimensions of patient decisions and how those extramedical values can supervene medical indications. The covenant between the physician and the patient takes place within a context, an institutional and social context, that shapes their joint decision making.

## Euthanasia

It is clear that a broad range of euthanasia is practiced in the United States, some forms of which are more acceptable than others.[107] Independent of the many philosophical, theological, social, and political questions about voluntary active euthanasia is the most pressing one of all: Is euthanasia the best way to support suffering persons?[108] When the physician and other caregivers in society approach a dying patient, is the option for terminating that life an important part of the care to be offered? Patients have complications that require compassionate care that borders on killing, yet physicians especially have a traditional duty to respect the life of patients. If the physician or other caregiver is committed to preserving the life of the patient, is there an alternative to active euthanasia that will not neglect the suffering of that patient?

### *Technofix Society*

The greatest concern of persons opposed to active euthanasia is the creation of a new sort of Nazi society. Commentators point out that Germany between the wars had many enlightened groups, similar to those present in the United States today. Among these groups were physicians and laypersons interested in fostering voluntary active euthanasia. When this idea was taken by the Nazi party and embedded in initiatives to eliminate the retarded and other genetically and (later) racially impure persons, it was, of course, an aberration.[109] But the misuse by political power of a technology available in medicine and the reasoning of active euthanasia is a danger of all modern states.

For the United States the danger exists in the economic sphere. Will it be easier to use a simple method of dispatching those persons whose care costs too much, or who are now considered to be a burden on society, such as the aged and the poor, than to address their suffering, which sometimes is overwhelming even for the most dedicated caregivers? As Joseph Cardinal Bernardin noted in an address on euthanasia at the University of Chicago Hospital, "We cannot accept a policy that would open the door to euthanasia by creating categories of patients whose lives can be considered of no value merely because they are not conscious."[110]

The "technofix" solution is not only easier to conceptualize and implement than the more difficult processes of human engagement but is also "suggested" by technology itself. The training and skills of modern health professionals are overwhelmingly nurtured within a bath of technological fixes. By instinct and proclivity, all persons in a modern civilization are tempted by technical rather than personal solutions to problems. This is the real issue for Cardinal Bernardin, for example, who poses this question: "What would we be suggesting to one another and to our society, if, seemingly with the best of motives, we were to say that those who are sick, infirm, or unconscious may be killed? How could we allege that such actions would not affect us individually and collectively?"[111] Such actions are a form of "privatizing life," denying its social and communal dimensions as both a private and a public good.

Therefore the concerns of disvaluing human life through technical responses to human suffering should not be dismissed as hopelessly conservative and neurotic. The overbearing experience of the twentieth century is one in which persons have been put at the mercy of technology. Caution about this reversal of the creative process is not only justified but important in developing any social policy and legislative process.

The proper kinds of caution can be seen from the reaction of physicians, members of the Hemlock Society, and the lay public to the "It's Over, Debbie" case published in the *Journal of the American Medical Association*. Concerns were expressed about the lack of feeling on the part of the resident who dispatched Debbie with an overdose of morphine. There was no engagement with Debbie, her values, or her suffering (except to eliminate it as easily as possible). Annoyance at the interruption of the schedule of the resident was expressed. The resident did not try to find out what Debbie meant when she said, "Let's get this over with." Nor did he discuss the values of the patient and the family with the person in the room. Nor, most damaging, did he try to contact the managing physician.[112] All these problems portrayed vividly the dangers of the "technofix" mentality drummed into the heart of all of us.

## Obligations to Address Pain and Suffering

The movement toward voluntary active euthanasia rests on the following principles:

1. Autonomy. A person has a right to do what he or she pleases with the body.

2. A person should not have to suffer unduly at the hands of a rampaging modern medical technology. Uwe Reinhardt has suggested that the modern American health industry is the fourth largest "country" in the world. The right to control one's own destiny should be seen, in the light of this remark, as a major civil rights effort in facing the power of modern medicine.

3. When a person decides that continued life is meaningless, that decision ought to be respected. No one else has a better sense of the value and meaning of one's own life than that individual.[113]

These arguments are for the most part valid. They can be met by a social policy that ensures, through double-effect euthanasia, that no one will suffer unduly and that all suffering will be eliminated as far as possible.

An important distinction must be drawn here, however. The distinction should be between pain and suffering. Persons ought not to have to suffer pain; but all dying involves a kind of suffering that cannot entirely be taken away. As Eric Cassell has argued, suffering is distinct from physical distress. The former is undergone by persons and the latter by the body.[114] Since persons experience suffering, personal engagement by health providers and caregivers is essential to relieve it.[115]

Pain control is not only required but possible.[116] In this respect, the focus should turn to the obligations of the community and away from rights of patients. The patients cannot control the pain; they are entirely in our hands.

This social policy would be an obligation on the part of the community to control the pain and address the suffering of dying persons. This is how John Liebeskind and Ronald Melzack put it on behalf of the International Pain Foundation: "We are appalled by the needless pain that plagues the people of the world—in rich and poor nations alike. By any reasonable code, freedom from pain should be a basic human right, limited only by our knowledge to achieve it."[117]

As Cassell has also argued, the primary obligation of physicians and other caregivers to the dying patient is to control the suffering and pain of that person.[118] In all respects, Cassell says, confrontations about the person's right to make treatment decisions within this context are "ugly" if they do not take into account the structure of that person's life and value choices.[119] This obligation includes, as Dame Cicely Saunders indicates from her long association with the hospice movement, an obligation to address the spiritual suffering that patients experience.[120] Although modern medicine offers many means for such control, it is an irony, perhaps stimulated by the overwhelming sense of responsibility for the lives of patients, that physicians are reluctant to use the means at their disposal to control pain.[121]

The commitment of modern medicine to engaging persons and their spirits on the level of biosocial interdependence is strongly impeded in modern society by technological barriers. Technology influences training. It makes people think that the only intervention into the lives of others must be through technological means rather than interpersonal ones. Recall Miles's observations about the "feeding wards."

If the focus turns to the obligation of caregivers to control pain and address suffering, this requires a rethinking of the goals of modern medicine, especially during the dying process. The goal of medicine in this instance must be to assist persons to accomplish (however small) some life plans.[122] One way of rethinking these goals is to introduce a duty not to prolong dying at the point:

1. When the patient suffers from the effects of a terminal illness, however long that illness may take to play out its course.

2. When the patient judges, on the basis of his or her own self-worth and attendant quality of life judgments, or has given advance directives in this regard, that the life he or she now lives is no longer of meaning.

3. Or, alternatively, when the patient has left no advance directives, the condition of the patient is such that the terminal illness is now in its imminent phase and the patient is no longer able to participate in the spiritual and material goods of human life.

Finally, a rethinking of the nature of the human community is required in any social policy stressing the obligation to address suffering. This requires, at the very least, the kind of thinking that informs the hospice movement itself.[123] The community must become a community of healing, even in the presence of death. Saunders refers to this as a "friendship for each individual person in pain."[124]

Another way of putting this is to note that a morally significant aspect of all beings is their capacity to suffer.[125] But even more remarkable is the moral significance of the capacity of *human* beings to heal. Animals feel pain and can sympathize, but they cannot heal beyond the most elemental licking of sores. Only humans can heal.

This capacity grounds a view of human society as capable of being a community of healers. Perhaps this aspect of human life is most jeopardized, in the view of many, by a social policy permitting voluntary active euthanasia. Will human persons neglect the admittedly difficult task of addressing suffering, and their own capacity to heal, by too quickly dispatching others who are clearly suffering pain and the loss of self-worth and the meaning of life?

The social policy that might support a commitment to control pain and address suffering could include:

1. Legislation to hold physicians harmless who, while meeting these needs of dying patients, with the proper documentation, induce their death through double-effect euthanasia.

2. Support for traditional commitments of health providers to the value of human life as an important component of a life-oriented human society.

3. A requirement that all caregivers in the health professions be trained in appropriate methods of pain control and that certification examinations include this educational requirement.[126]

The increased debate about active euthanasia in our society should be welcomed. It will force the medical profession, ethicists, the legal system, and churches to provide more profound responses to human suffering than has been the case so far.

At this time, there is little need for active euthanasia if more attention is paid to controlling pain and suffering, more attention is paid to the patient's value system, much firmer responses are made to patient requests to die, and plans are made with the patient and family about the best way to bring about a kind and merciful death.

Arthur Dyck, in his *On Human Care*, observed that in the early days of the discussion of the principle of beneficence by William Frankena and W. D. Ross, "Do no harm" was considered virtually equivalent to "Do not kill."[127] Today, however, the problem has become one of interpreting beneficence from the point of view of the patient's need not to suffer and the community's obligation to address the suffering in its most profound and intimate ways.

Under the heading of "Quality of Life in the Twenty-first Century" ought to be included all our efforts to aim at a decent human society. Rights and obligations such as the few discussed in this chapter need major development not only in our country but worldwide.

There is so much to do that is noble that we should not have time for evil actions that destroy the quality of life for any person. As we prepare for the challenges of the next century, may the balance tilt in favor of human life!

# 10

# A Life-Affirming Society

Although human life is priceless, we always act as if something had a greater price than life . . . but what is that something?
—Antoine de Saint-Exupéry

The Deuteronomist says, "I set before you life or death. . . . Choose life." In the modern era, it is even more necessary than ever to affirm the value of human life. As we have seen from the preceding chapters, our traditional heritage clearly stamps our culture with this value. Further, despite astonishing scientific changes in our society since World War II, the direction and the character of our technological society require a firm footing in a belief about the value of human life. In this final chapter I wish to spell out the virtues of a society that stands committed to the value of human life. As I set these forth, the necessary changes in our own brand of social activism or political action become readily apparent.

Spelling out the virtues of a society (and therefore of persons) that chooses life will require four steps. First, I will reexamine positions A, B, and C, which were left at the end of chapter 7, to see which is the most viable in society today. Next, I will spell out the changes needed in society to adopt this position. Better put, I will be showing how intellectual assent to a position should transcribe into a new kind of social structure. Third, I will propose a theory of human choice. Fourth, I will discuss a mature form of ethics, an ethics of discretion, needed to continue to develop an environment that affirms life. Finally, I will summarize the contributions this book has made to reflections on a life-affirming society.

## The Commitment to Choose Life

When do the good things start? They start with a commitment to respect human life. Admittedly, our century has excelled in its appalling depth and excessive range of destruction.[1] But for every terrible story, for every story of pillage and injustice, there are a multitude of stories about good deeds. For example, wife and child abuse are terrible tragedies. They represent learned behavior from the perpetrator's own insecure childhood. But programs to protect children and wives are based on a belief in their inherent value. Rehabilitation for offenders, male or female, is a mark of respect for their personhood, however repulsive their actions. Our century also has seen that alcoholism is not a crime or a sin but a disease. Compassion and counseling for the alcoholic most often replaces ostracism. The 1980s may be called the decade of "coming out of the closet" on alcoholism and drug addiction. Famous persons by the hour confess on television and in the newspapers their problems with dependency. *Co-Dependent No More* became a best-seller in 1988.[2] Similarly, the retarded and the mentally ill have been treated with a greater sense of compassion and assistance than in previous eras.

The Rev. Gerald Oosterveen in a speech about the retarded noted that Paul told the Corinthians, "Those members of the body which seem to be weaker are necessary. And those members of the body which we think to be less honorable, on these we bestow greater honor."[3] Once called "God's mistakes," the retarded have been approached by special ministries in churches. One such has been a $1 million ecumenical Christian instruction program for the retarded sponsored by the Christian Reformed Church, a Dutch Calvinist church in the United States. "We need to understand," said Rev. Oosterveen, "that the retarded person does not have a disease and does not represent a threat to society. We must be taught that we need them in our lives just as much as they need us."[4]

An exquisite sensitivity to a wide range of human life and human conduct is the mark of a society that respects human life. Joyful acceptance of the infirm, the retarded, the aged, the unborn, in short, anyone who might possibly be a burden to us, is certainly part of a religious vision of life. I have tried to show that it is part of a philosophical and political vision as well. Even if we were completely selfish disembodied entities, we would want to create a society in which we could command at least the same respect as others. Thus, though we might want to neglect the many inspiring arguments of philosophers about the value of human life, we would still retain an interest in this value if we did not know the outcome of our social existence. From the point of view of politics, we saw that an acceptance of the "self-evidence" of the equal value of persons is required to continue American democracy. No one can infallibly judge that someone else's life is not worth living.

Despite these arguments, why is it that we persist in a defective social policy? Why is it that we sometimes value others and, at other times, get caught up in personal and social violence? The main reason seems to be that we receive mixed messages. On the one hand, we vigorously act to protect the rights of the downtrodden. We like to think of ourselves as a nation devoted to freedom from repression, to "Truth, Justice, and the American Way." On the other hand, however, we pour billions of dollars into destructive weapons, guns, missiles, ships, and planes. We balance our national imports with enormous arms sales around the world. We watch, gleefully perhaps, as Israelis armed with our jets prove the superiority of our weapons over the Russian arms used by the Syrians. We glory in the "nice kill" of Muammar al-Qaddafi's pilots in their planes. We count planes downed and ships sunk rather than lives lost.

In a 1982 address to the United Nations General Assembly, President Gemayel of Lebanon said that foreign armies on his soil had led to the death of 100,000 civilians since 1975. The figure of 100,000 persons rolls off the tongue just as it rolls off our mind, like droplets of water off a newly waxed car. We do not stop to think how horrible that number of deaths really is, not to mention the many thousands more displaced, homeless, foodless, struggling in poverty so that nations can buy more weapons. Nor do we stop and think about how that occupation by Syria and by Israel of Lebanon was only part of a continuum of violence and divisiveness that has dominated that country for years. Ironically, Americans were asked to help rebuild what their own weapons destroyed and did so generously through a $10 billion aid package.[5]

Similarly, we might have glanced right over a story that some hospitals may limit second-trimester abortions because nurses refuse to work on them. "This is not a stand against abortion," an administrator is quoted as saying (perhaps to appear open-minded or fearing what other women would think of her), "they are just saying when it is that late in the pregnancy, they can't handle it. Their psyches just won't do it. It was difficult for them to be involved with a fetus the same size as babies they were trying to save."[6]

The tragic destruction of life will continue, we are assured, but at a lessened pace. In the same issue of the daily paper, we could read of Dr. Denton Cooley's rapid and practiced technique for saving hundreds of persons, from around the world, through open-heart surgery.[7] The contrast is obvious. If a space traveler from another galaxy arrived here and learned our language, as E.T. did, what would he or she think of this dichotomy: using surgery to kill; using surgery to heal?

If one mark of a respect-for-life society is an exquisite openness to burdensome life, then a second mark must be a consistency about affirming life. Briefly put, an inconsistent affirmation is no affirmation. It is rather like hedging a bet. It is not a commitment. It is a wager. "I'll put six chips on death and destruction, and six on life-saving surgery, so nobody will think I'm a bad person."

A third characteristic of life affirmation is straightforward language. Look back at the story about the nurses and second-trimester abortions. Note that the hospital spokesperson seemed reluctant to say that the nurses had a conscience and that their conscience bothered them because they were killing a form of human life very much like babies. Instead, their "psyches" would not let them continue. Moreover, we are told that their refusal to assist is not really an argument against abortion. What is it, then?

Of course, whether or not abortion is a moral evil is not settled on the grounds of a few nurses and their consciences. Perhaps that is what the administrator meant to say. The nurses have taken a stand that goes beyond good and evil, however, a stand that transcends customary moral debate.[8] In it, without attesting to ethical arguments one way or another, they have acted not to use their considerable professional skills to destroy life. The fact that life has recognizable human properties nudges their conscience. Presumably in the first trimester, it would not. At any rate, the nurses who refuse have taken a small step toward life-affirming consistency. Their step has been ill-served by reducing its rationale to a vague sort of psychologism, by substituting "psyches" for consciences, psychological difficulties for moral ones.

Given the dichotomy in modern society between life-destructive and life-affirming policies and behavior, which of the positions mentioned in chapter 7 is the best upon which to build a more decent social structure? Although I did not mention which I thought was best when I introduced positions A, B, and C, the time has now come to do so.

We have seen that a modern society requires a commitment to human life to gain control over the direction of our technology, and we have seen how sophisticated policies, such as those about pain control, can foster the value of human life and our compassion toward it, but which position should we take as a society to gain that control? Which position will offer us the greatest possibility for human responsibility and action? Which position will permit the greatest diversity of religious and political beliefs while retaining a baseline commitment to the values of human life? This respect for diversity follows from a respect for all forms of human life, as I shall soon propose.

To decide between positions A, B, and C is to decide between beliefs. Recall that the positions themselves have grown out of beliefs more than out of rational arguments. I have tried to show that a belief in the inherent value of human life is reasonable. In discussing the right-to-life debate, Richard Westley has pointed out:

Catholics are the ones usually singled out by their opponents as having nonrational (religious) elements hidden behind their arguments. For some strange reason, the Catholics vehemently deny this charge, as if to match the quality of their opponents' arguments which is supposedly purely rational. If that were the case, then we should expect their arguments to be conclusive. But they are not conclusive either, because *all* the arguments in the debate rest on other than rational grounds; it is just that everyone seems afraid to admit it. [Author's emphasis.⁹]

This is what I meant by going beyond good and evil, moving beyond customary ethical arguments. The arguments all lead to a perception. And the perception leads to a belief, confirmed by our life experiences.

Glancing over the shoulder of a secretary as she typed an early version of chapter 6, a typewriter repairman objected to the antiwar sentiments expressed at its outset on the grounds that he was in a war and killing wasn't all that bad. We could argue forever about that statement. But his perceptions have come from his own immunity system. He learned to survive in violence, like a small fish might learn to swim through an oil slick. The oil gets on the fish. It goes in the gills. It poisons the body. So, too, does violence. After a while, you get used to it. It does not seem wrong anymore.

One's beliefs about the world, about human beings, and about society have been fundamentally altered. Even so, sometimes persons come up short and refuse the violence of the context, like the soldiers from both sides thrown together in Erich Maria Remarque's *All Quiet on the Western Front*¹⁰ or the soldier's World War II story told to Studs Terkel of coming upon a group of German soldiers in a valley and not being able to kill them, since they were telling jokes and eating just as American boys did.¹¹

Opponents have often scoffed at the domino argument advanced by many pro-lifers. In this argument, allowing abortions will eventually lead to direct killing of other burdensome life, like the aged and the dying. Opponents disregard this argument, quite rightly, because there is no evidence that one form of conduct toward the unborn will result in the same form of conduct toward other expressions of human life. We are too sophisticated for that.¹² If one peels back the arguments to the beliefs, though, a more basic picture emerges. Pro-life advocates, in the abortion debate, seem to believe that human beings will become immune to violence as they might to war. Further, they believe that human judgment about life and death issues is often not to be trusted because of the somewhat infectious impact of society on our own vision. By contrast, opponents seem to believe that people are trustworthy and relatively immune to the creeping violations of life in modern society. The point of raising this dynamic of conflicting beliefs is to note that these beliefs cannot be settled by arguments. They require a conversion from one perception to another. That is why I stressed persuasion so much in earlier chapters.

Therefore, in an attempt to decide among three different positions, each of which is devoted to the value of human life in its own fashion, several caveats are in order.

First, by arguing for one or the other position, one cannot convert persons. Actions, rather than words, count. Conversions always occur based on some intriguing conduct in persons and society. The conduct is intriguing because one has come to question one's own beliefs. This questioning is brought on by a cognitive dissonance, a difference between what one perceives and what one thinks. Hence, to create a climate of conversion to one position or another, one must demonstrate by action that one is better than another. This position will be elaborated in the next section.

Second, arguing as I did in the first caveat is not the same as arguing that one belief is as good as another. In fact, we do decide between beliefs. These decisions are based on criteria we establish. Arguments are helpful in this regard. Most disputes about the merits of one position over another actually hinge on what will count for evidence, what weight different pieces of evidence will have, what definition the problem will carry, and what criteria will be used in the dispute.[13] It is in this way that a group of detectives solve a murder case. In the same way, we use criteria to develop models of reality. Thus we ultimately decide that someone is suffering from a paranoic delusion system if the system itself, internally and logically coherent though it may be, creates aggression or fear, self-centeredness rather than communal trust, in the one afflicted. Overaggression, paralyzing fear, self-directedness rather than other-directedness, and lack of trust are criteria by which we judge a belief to be abnormal. In this sense, it is much less desirable than other beliefs.

The object of this book has been to develop some of the criteria by which we would judge that, when push comes to shove, even when we cannot prove it, it is always better to come down on the side of the value of human life than to permit its destruction. By presenting these criteria, in showing the reasonableness of the belief, I have not claimed that I have demonstrated the all-time truth of the value of respecting life. Instead, I wish to make a much less exalted point. The point is this: Given the state of our society today, it is much better to choose to support the value of life than to participate in or to direct violence against human life.

To summarize, then, how do we choose among beliefs? First, we examine the impact of a belief on the conduct of a person or society.

Does the belief make the person or society more open? More
happy? More forgiving? More understanding? More human? Improved animal entities? In a word, does the belief make them more
virtuous? Does the belief lend itself to a fresh and vital perception
about human life that we share as a matter of instinct or nature?
Based on these criteria, which in turn are an outgrowth of our considerations thus far, if a belief belligerently regards all other points
of view as false, if it has no provision for internal adjustment based
on new data, if it does not lend a follower any happiness, then it is
less to be desired, from the standpoint of the human community,
than one that would correct these deficiencies.

Does the impact criterion help us judge which of the respect-for-
life positions would be better? After all, even if we agree about the
criteria used to judge one belief to be better than another, may we
still not disagree about their application to a particular belief system? Of course.

Recall that the positions differed from one another on the nature
of the baseline. Position A holds that each person is equal and
"infinite" in value. By "infinite" is not meant mathematically
without bounds. Instead, what is meant is a quality of deserving
respect, deserving the same respect perhaps as God, or at least
deserving of so much respect that no one life could ever be judged
more valuable than another. A great deal of human happiness evidently is reaped by those who hold this belief. The position certainly captures, more than the other two, the ideas of the Judeo-
Christian tradition, as well as many others. Further, it can provide
for an intense devotion to social justice and nonviolent responses
to many current problems, including war. Its consistency is without peer among positions that respect life, but it demands the most
social change. If our goal is to adopt a belief about the value of
human life most apt to produce in those who profess the belief,
humane responses on the level of saintly virtue, then this position
is preferable to the other two.

Again from the point of view of the human community, position A
does have a flaw. The flaw is that position A is the most likely to
produce bigots. Because of its consistency, it is the belief least able
to provide for adjustment to new data, least malleable, least dialogical. Further, this position is most likely to lead to protection of all
human life through unchanging rules. If human life is of irreducible
merit, then universal laws must be designed to protect that life in all
circumstances. A society governed by such rules may appear to
many persons as too "pat," too "settled," too "monolithic." Even
medieval society under the church contained much more flexibility
than this. America's one experiment with a monolithic, religious-
based culture, the Puritan, ultimately proved to be less forgiving

and understanding than most of us would want. We therefore shy away from legislating morality.

It should be noted, however, that the objections to position A are actually worries based on previous belief systems. In these, the value of human life failed to be affirmed to the extent we desire. No one has tried to build an international society on pacifism, nonviolence, and the absolute value of human life since early Christian times.[14] Perhaps in the movements that have shared this vision, like Gandhi's and Martin Luther King's in recent times, failures obstructing worldwide implementation stemmed from an inability to follow the belief rather than from the system itself. Hence the position itself would overcome, somehow, the concerns represented by the objections.

Position B is to be preferred to C but not to A. Using the same criteria, B would be more consistently affirmative about the value of human life than C. In its recognition that some lives are less to be valued than others, however, it can provide for more malleability and responsiveness to different situations than A without falling under the criticism of arbitrariness leveled at C. Remember that B provides an ability to judge that one life is more valuable than another but establishes a universal baseline of equal opportunity and freedom to compete for resources. We saw that a sophisticated policy of access would include this provision. A range of skills and innate abilities exists that will make some persons and some forms of life of greater merit to the community than others. In this sense, position B most clearly provides a common ground for establishing political communities when persons cannot live up to the rigors of position A.

As with Albert Schweitzer, position A would require its adherents to live in uprightness. Its reverence for life is so awesome that it borders on the holy. Schweitzer would not willingly step on an ant. It seems to require supererogatory sanctity of normal human beings. By contrast, position B just asks for equal treatment for all with respect to rights and liberty. There is no need to stand in awe of life, but just to acknowledge it. One need not withdraw to mountains, deserts, or forests to be able to practice position B. It can be accomplished, with difficulty of course. What is more, it can be accomplished in a modern community, city, state, or nation. There are no zealots to make us uncomfortable, just everyday persons trying to live up to their duties.

But just as there are no zealots, there are no prophets to call us on to greater respect. There is a tendency in position B to consider that the task of affirming life has been accomplished. If political societies are formed on the basis of B, it is all too easy to forget that rights must be won daily—otherwise the community will slip into repres-

sion rather easily, as one sees from the great film, *Citizen Kane*.
There is also a danger in adopting position B that we will forget that
constant progress toward more universal recognition of the value of
human life is not only possible but is obtainable. Does the position
set our sights high enough?

Position C seems, at first blush, to be the most realistic. In it, the
baseline of respect for human life is adjusted depending on the context. Although it is the most desirable from the standpoint of flexibility, it is the least desirable from the standpoint of what is needed in
our troubled times.[15] Its flexibility is to be highly prized. This belief
would surely provide for continual adjustment and critique. If we
take the concerns for the value of human life in violent and deper-
sonalized societies around the globe seriously, however, the very
flexibility of position C becomes a detriment. Its allowance for context and case-by-case judgment neglects the fact that complex societies must establish some rules of conduct to govern in the best
interests of divergent groups, a strong point of position A. Its flexibility can easily be twisted into capriciousness by twisted persons.[16]
"These people must be moved out of their homes to make way for
progress." "Globs of tissue are less important than adults." "A criminal has no rights." In short, position C can too easily slip into a lack
of commitment to the value of human life *under our present social
conditions*. If society were to become more life-affirming, position C,
adopted by many civilized persons, would be more desirable.

Given our present conditions, then, I suggest that A, B, and C
ought to be our priorities. Since no one position is a clear-cut winner—all are capable of miscue—we must try to detail the best features of each in a picture of a life-affirming society. I will do this in
the final section of the chapter. First we should look at a second way
in which we judge some beliefs to be better than others: social consequences.

## New Social Structures

The social consequences of position A are enormous. I also mentioned in chapter 7 that consistency must be maintained in positions
A and B or one automatically adopts C, judging each situation on its
own merits. Because of that requirement for consistency, the following social conduct must be present to be able to fulfill a commitment
to the belief embodied in position A:

1. A tolerance for widely divergent forms of human life. If equal
intrinsic value is to be assigned to all forms of human life, then
respect is owed to all of these forms. That respect demands tolerance for special needs of each of these forms. In the "original position" of Richard Brandt, the philosopher who developed the idea of

disinterestedness as a basis of moral principles, a basis of respect grows out of the very lack of knowledge about personal status or ends of our moral policy. I adopted this idea in the thought experiment about the disembodied entity. Regardless of personal philosophy or even beliefs, the community value that all agree must be present is a respect for the needs of whatever form of human life we may eventually become.

2. An instinctive reaction against any demeaning act. One cannot flush human embryos down the drain. One cannot browbeat one's children. One cannot kill anyone for any reason. One cannot farm out the elderly to die far away from loving arms. One cannot commit abortion. One also cannot drop bombs. One cannot harbor prejudice against anyone. One cannot resist interracial marriage, fair housing, equal employment opportunities, and so on. When Jefferson coined the phrase "We hold these truths to be self-evident" (not without editing other starts), he meant just that. A belief need not be justified each time we encounter opposition, if we all believe in the same values. In this case, if position A is adopted, debates about war, abortion, women's rights, and capital punishment would end. There would be an instinct against any violation of the human creed: It is self-evident that all forms of human life are equally to be valued because of their irreducible inherent worth.

3. A concentration of all social and technological effort on resolving clashes between two or more absolutely valuable beings, in favor of the value of human life. Consider one absolutely valuable being who earns a living and employs many other absolutely valuable beings in the disposing of hazardous wastes. Everyone agrees that the common good is served by such disposal. The hazardous waste person cannot, however, place the value of his business or the well-being of his employees over the value of the lives lived near his dump. Suppose he clashes with a mayor, he arguing that his dumping methods are safe and that new guidelines would ruin his ability to employ so many persons, and she, the mayor, arguing that the waste methods used endanger the lives of absolutely valued persons in the nearby town for which she is responsible.

Inevitably clashes will occur. When they do, do we switch from a deontological position of duty to respect every human life to a utilitarian one in which we attempt to solve the problem on the basis of the greatest good for the greatest number? To do so would be to violate the consistency of position A by adopting one more like C in which a quantity of absolutely valued human beings is judged more important than a lesser quantity of absolutely valued human beings. This quantitative fallacy (from the point of view of position A) means that another path must be sought to resolve the dispute.

Precisely at this point we may summon our best technological effort. It may be that all hazardous wastes must be hurled by rockets toward the sun to be vaporized in space or buried on the moon where no life forms would be threatened. Expensive? Yes. But a reduction in weapons budgets would easily permit this solution, one that respects all forms of human life, at least until our cosmic neighbors appear and object to our methods.

In the same vein, the abortion debate would require more humane technologies. Think of the debate about abortion and the right to life as a clash of two equally valuable forms of human life. According to position A, there can be no inherent distinction of merit between one form of human life and another. The mother and the unborn are equally to be valued. What are we to do? Even though we reject a utilitarian solution, it is hard to see how to fulfill duties to both the mother and the unborn. As we said before, the abortion debate admits no convenient middle position. With respect to the mother, we would wish to support freedom of choice, freedom from coercion (if the conceptus is the result of rape), freedom from imitation of others (in a case where a poverty-stricken girl "imitates" Mom in hard times and becomes pregnant), and the like. With respect to the unborn, its basic inherent value requires that it not be subject to dismemberment or scalding in a saline solution. We cannot kill it.

It seems that technology can be used here for a good human purpose. We could develop better techniques for implanting an unborn, unwanted child in the womb of a carrier or a woman who does want a child. Not all implantations would be successful, but neither are nature's own efforts to implant an embryo in the womb. If there should be more unwanted or undesired unborn than carrier wombs, then artificial wombs should be created to keep the unborn alive to term. If some of the unborn are not wanted because their genes are faulty, then every effort should be made to develop the ability to alter those genes. Better still, we should inaugurate a massive reeducation about our responsibilities toward life and reproduction. Rather than the horrified vision of Orwell's 1984, a room full of artificial wombs keeping unwanted infants alive at least would be an instrument of a just, equitable, and compassionate social policy. This would also require a commitment by society to raise such children in homes and families. The Vatican Instruction argued that all conceived human entities deserve to grow and develop in a family unit.[17]

4. A readiness to accept the major consequences of a commitment for life. Most of us stand ready to shed prejudice if everyone else will. But are Americans ready instead to adopt the 1.5 million babies who this year, in the United States alone, will have been aborted? Remember that some of these babies will be of a race,

skin color, and genetic background quite different from ours. If we are not ready to adopt them, shall we just institutionalize them or let them run around the street like children of American soldiers in Vietnam?

Are we ready to employ everyone, regardless of intelligence or training, even if we must accept a drastic reduction in our own salary? After all, if each of us is equally valuable, then each must have equal job access, equal starting positions in the work force. What is more, if all persons are inherently valuable, then our help is required around the world. We can no longer, as only about 30 percent of the world's population, consume over 60 percent of its goods and services. The human creed of position A would decry that imbalance.

These brief descriptions of social consequences show that to believe in the value of human life requires a much greater "social conscience," a much, much more demanding change in life-style than heretofore normally considered. It is not enough to demonstrate in front of a women's clinic against abortion, carrying one's children.[18] Society itself, for no one of us can bear all the burdens, must provide alternatives of care. It must respect the life of the unborn, its right to be cared for, to belong, really to belong to someone, as much as it must respect a woman's agonized decision to let the unborn in her womb go elsewhere.

The rigors of position A may tempt us to move to position B or C. Position B may certainly be used as a temporary respite from or platform for achieving A beliefs. It may not always be possible for every society to achieve A at all times, because of a sudden depression or a natural catastrophe. In an emergency, we must even adopt triage decisions (in which some persons will receive treatment rather than others) more decidedly arbitrary than position C. But our sights should always be set on reestablishing a normal effort to achieve position A.

The basic reason is that in C, and to some extent in B, a consistent stance toward the inherent value of human life is hard to maintain. Thus, in C one might argue that war is unsuited to a respect for the human life position, while holding that abortion or research on spare embryos is all right. Or one could argue that war is all right because, after all, we are defending a good way of life against evildoers, although abortion, infanticide, or euthanasia would be wrong because it harms innocent or advanced human life. In neither case is a belief in the intrinsic value of human life properly maintained.

A society that chooses life begins to let some "good things happen." Position A is held as the basis of its social policy whenever possible. It is the guiding hand on technological design. A commitment to the absolute or "infinite" value of human life helps direct technology and sciences toward the proper ends of a good human life. These ends are widely discussed and implemented. Computers that help one work at home with one's family are judged helpful because they affirm an important value in human life, constant in its history until the industrial revolution drew us from home to factory.

Space-age industrial techniques used for modular housing throughout the world would employ more persons than a much-diminished defense industry. Indeed, the best "defense" against aggression is to share what one has rather than hoard it. If one shares, everyone depends on everyone else for well-being. Attacking some nation upon which one depends for energy, for example, would make little sense. Hoarding goods and services causes jealousy. It would also be impossible to justify in position A.

Position B should be used as the platform to launch efforts to achieve A. Respect for liberty and equal opportunity, the hallmarks of B, are essential to A as well. It is especially helpful to have B as a backup when disputes arise among equals in A. While efforts are under way to resolve those disputes, like the toxic waste dispute discussed, all parties may "fall back on" a baseline commitment embodied in B. It is a temporary retreat, while dialogue occurs. Contrast this behavior with immediate efforts to resolve disputes of contested values by submitting legislation inimical to the interests of at least one party in the dispute. Are hospitals not treating defective newborns? Let's have legislation to protect them. Instead, all parties in a dispute would have an opportunity to agree on the terms of a slightly less rigorous belief while the public discussion of the interests at stake continues. If that discussion is left to run its course, it will take less than five years for some consensus to build. Also, time will have been set aside for technological research and application. Of course, I am not so naïve as to think that all disputes may be settled or that technology can help solve them all. But I do hold that a waiting period, a cooling off period, often produces good results.

Position C is available for emergencies. If there is an earthquake, we must treat those who can help rebuild the town first, before we can turn our attention to the helpless. A frankly utilitarian approach, trying to achieve the good of survival, can be temporarily adopted. No other goods and services, no quality of life, no life itself, is possible without the survival of the community. All ethical positions are ultimately based on the survival of the community, ensuring smooth and positive relations among its members. Even if happiness seems to be the object of the moral life, this happiness is transcribed as political. Hence Thomas Aquinas could hold that the virtue of politics was the highest virtue one could attain in this life. He meant by this the virtue of fostering and maintaining the community so that one had friends, strong bonds in the community, and sufficient means to live a virtuous life. This is how a community survives. Whenever demand exceeds resources, position C can be adopted. It is always an exception rather than the rule.

In fact, we do retreat from position B to C whenever a scarce or expensive resource is in limited supply. When kidney dialysis machines were first invented, there were too few for the number of persons needing them. Criteria for selection to be put on one of these machines were developed. In every case, these criteria included some reference to choosing those who stand a chance to contribute to society. The possibility of implanting artificial hearts required a panel to establish similar criteria. That is how Barney Clark was chosen to receive the first such implant. Triage decisions are even more evidently utilitarian in their approach.

Indeed, Pope Pius XII's famous distinction between ordinary and extraordinary means for keeping people alive was, in part, based on the notion of scarce resources.[19] If a person is dying, and the means for keeping him or her alive are draining the family budget, there is no moral obligation to continue to use those means if by doing so one merely prolongs the person's dying.[20] In this way, economics and availability enter into our moral decisions. Position A, respect for all life, is temporarily suspended.

At least one thinker, Robert Veatch, writing on medical ethics, has held that exceptions to our social duties are suspensions of justice. As such, they ought to be spelled out in contracts or covenants between persons.[21] What I have proposed, a fallback to position B, a platform from B to A, and a temporary suspension of A when demand exceeds supply of resources, goods, and services, should not be viewed as a "suspension" of all respect for life, however. Of course, a particular system of belief, A or B, is temporarily dropped. Remember, however, that C also represents a respect for life. The baseline changes with circumstances. Because a small dosage of care to everyone in an emergency fire would actually help none of them, those persons who have the best chance of survival must be treated first. They are the ones to be sent to a burn center. But that does not mean we turn our backs on the others. We should provide them with care to make their dying comfortable. As Paul Ramsey has argued, we have no ethical responsibility to prolong the dying process.[22] In this sense, then, although some are chosen above others when we do not have enough space for a high technology treatment, everyone should still receive the respect due to him or her as a human being, even though we could not provide even the remotest possibility of cure. Not to treat when it is time to stop can also be a mark of respect for persons. Recall my suggestion for "functional status treatment categories" for the aged as one example of this mark of respect for persons.

From the above considerations, it is clear that a nonviolent, pacifist position (A) of respect for human life is the most consistent. It can function as an ideal toward which we aim our technological society. Vast social changes are necessary to implement this ideal. Particularly when clashes occur, it will be necessary to step back to a basic liberty position (B) while we try to resolve that clash. This is necessary to protect fundamental liberties during dialogue and dispute. Finally, in emergencies, when the survival of the community is at stake, or when demand exceeds resources, we may temporarily retreat to a triage position (C) in which some lives are judged more worth living than others. Note that the triage position cannot be justified for long periods, as Lincoln pointed out regarding the treatment of slaves. It is justified only for the period of scarcity or emergency. Meanwhile, our social action is directed toward removing the scarcity and returning to or achieving normalcy.

## A Theory of Choice

In this section I wish to grapple with the difficult question of conflict among inherently valued individuals. If, as position A would have it, each form of individual human life, whether it is or is not a person, has absolute intrinsic value, then we are in a terrible bind whenever the rights of these inherently valued individuals clash. Conflict resolution, in fact, is the reason why positions B and C are also required to sketch adequately our commitment to the value of human life.

By suggesting that a single position is not adequate, one automatically is forced into position C, for that position provides for contextual changes in the way respect for human life might be expressed. My own convictions have led me to embrace position A. Yet I realize that other committed persons may adopt position B or C. All of us would be affirming the value of human life, each in an entirely consistent way, unless while in position A or B we began to hedge (e.g., argue against abortion because fetal life is innocent, but for the possibility of war because others might be just aggressors). If we did hedge like this, we would automatically be "bounced" into position C. That is perfectly all right, but it does not permit us to use certain favorite arguments that can only be consistently applied in A or B.

For example, if we argued that fetal life is innocent, but are now, almost against our will but by reason of logical consistency, in position C, then we cannot adequately refute those who are also in position C but who place more value on the life of a functioning adult (the mother) than on the unborn child (the fetus). In other words, once having admitted that, even when life is intrinsically valued, it is not absolutely so (by agreeing that war is possible or that abortion is possible or that infanticide is possible), we cannot then refute others who appeal to different standards than we do to decide which lives are to be contextually diminished.

On the other hand, by maintaining a rigorous position in A or B, we may be able to act *consistently* but will find it difficult to *act* in our society at all. For example, if one adopts position A, then all killing is impossible. Yet even while one discusses pacifism and the gospel at the church,[23] one might be contributing (by using the air conditioner) to an unjust distribution of the world's goods and resources and thus contributing simply by being a member of society to a diminishing of the status of other infinitely valued entities, causing some indeed to starve to death. Position A is therefore subject to scrupulosity and fanaticism even in its idealism.

All of this is to say that human life is essentially social. As a consequence, conflicts among rights, duties, claims, and values will occur. This conflict means that we must appeal to complicated methods to resolve problems, to redress wrongs, and to treat losses compassionately and justly. In position A, the method of choice can only be negotiation. Thus, for the fetus to "speak" for itself, it must rely on the law. The negotiation can only be about resolutions that do not do violence to the individual, infinite value of human life. Thus abortion would be ruled out as a negotiable item. Instead, as I have suggested, new technological means must be made available to preserve the life of unwanted fetuses until they might speak for themselves. This position holds true even for defective children.

For persons who are dying, a policy of treatment decision status can be developed, as I have suggested elsewhere, in which all options are discussed with the dying person.[24] Our obligations to the dying are different from preserving life. Instead, they express our duties to provide comfort and peace during the last days by permitting persons to die on their own agenda rather than on someone else's. Thus, when the dying can speak for themselves, their wishes about treatment ought to be respected. While negotiated settlement is required by position A, it also demands a most sophisticated ethics of discretion which I describe in the next section.

Conflict resolution in position B is not quite as difficult. In this position, remember, each individual form of human life is seen as having inherent value, but that value is not infinite. It is therefore possible to permit infanticide if certain criteria for viability are not met, for this reason: If those criteria are not met, then the resources of society would be spent unfairly and unjustly on trying to keep that child alive. A similar argument could be advanced for nontreatment of the disabled and the dying. The reason that these are consistent within position B, although they would violate the vision of position A, is that if no life is infinitely valuable, it may be comparatively valued. If it may be comparatively valued, it may be judged not as valuable as another life. In order to avoid position C, the reasons for the comparison cannot flow from external circumstances but must flow from the inner development of the form of human life affected. This is an important point. One may withhold or withdraw treatment from a dying person if that person's condition, that person's life, would not change with the planned intervention. The basis of this decision is really a medical indication, not a quality of life judgment. Does the intervention make a difference in the outcome?[25]

Even though position B resolutions are not as difficult as position A negotiations, they are nevertheless dependent upon sophisticated technical and scientific data about the prognosis for a certain standard quality of life. In many cases, we simply cannot judge outcomes. Thus it is very hard to predict at birth how a Down's syndrome child will do. It is hard to judge at what point an irreversible illness switches from only threatening death to being actually on the verge of death. It is hard to judge when and if a convicted murderer will ever be able to be rehabilitated.

In each of these instances, therefore, the inner development of the form of human life affected by our decisions regarding conflicts cannot be adequately predicted. That is why many physicians reacted negatively to the proposal by Duff and Campbell that criteria for the treatment of defective newborns be established based on their projected quality of life. Quality of life is almost impossible to judge. Similarly, Gilbert Meilaender argues that the reasonableness criterion, whose champion has been Richard McCormick, is inadequate. According to this criterion, we should only offer to incompetent patients (those who are not able to decide for themselves: the senile, the retarded, the newborns) treatment that a reasonable person might want to choose for himself or herself. But how might we make a rational decision about acting in the best interests of another when we do not know the life plans of the entity?[26]

Paul Ramsey's medical indications policy is an attempt, in position B, to skirt these problems. In proposing it, he holds that, when a person is incompetent to judge for himself or herself, then we simply should ask whether or not the treatment is *medically* indicated (will help the development of that person). If it will, we should employ it, regardless of its costs and burdens either to the life threatened or to society.[27] This policy, however much it is centered on the inherent but not infinite value of individuals, does seem to require from us sometimes needless and heroic efforts.

Conflicts are resolved in position C by traditional theories of philosophy, such as the natural law theory adopted by many Roman Catholics,[28] the theory of the greatest good for the greatest number (utilitarianism), or by the libertarianism we considered in chapter 7. Thus, when inherently but not infinitely valuable entities clash, one is asked by position C to consider external circumstances, by which one decides which of the two entities should receive attention. Hence, in this position, abortion might be judged wrong because it represents killing an innocent life (not the life of an unjust aggressor), while war is conceivably "just" (the just war theory); capital punishment is possible, or killing an intruder is possible, when certain conditions indicate that a serious wrong to another has been done.

These are conditions that spell out the the external circumstances under which one life, inherently valuable, may be considered more or less valuable than other lives, other duties, or other values. Freedom of speech, in some theories, is judged of sufficient value to throw millions of persons into the breach of war to defend it, asking them to value this freedom higher then the human lives they must destroy. Similarly, dropping bombs on the innocent children of our enemies, as we did in the Vietnam War and in earlier wars, is judged less serious than aborting an innocent child, simply because of the fortunes of war or because we have properly declared war on another nation or because we have created from persons enemies.

Frankly, I find all attempts to resolve conflicts in position C flawed, not because this position fails to respect the inherent value of human life but because the position leads so easily to externally valuing human life through its appeal to circumstances. That is why I hold that the position may be used only in emergencies, leaving to the public forum the debate about the proper definition of an emergency. Certainly, from this perspective, the temporary suspension of our normal behavior regarding the value of human life may have been warranted during World War II in order to stop dictatorship from covering half the globe and the loss of so many innocent lives. Even so, persons who in conscience objected to this violence from a position A or B standpoint would be free to appeal to conscientious objector status, in order to pursue nonviolent alternatives. This argument would easily be developed from the natural law and utilitarian stances, and it has been. But as a policy for our nonemergency, everyday world, position C arguments water down too much for comfort the vision of a belief in the value of human life required by our culture.

But what should we do if we are faced with a conflict among persons who choose one or another of these positions? Or what should be used as a criterion for resolving conflicts between those who hold that human life is intrinsically valuable and those who do not make this commitment? Until there is a greater consensus in our society, one toward which this book is aimed, I hold that it is better to err on the side of human choice than artificially to "resolve" the issue through legislation. One component of this view, however, is that there be a distinctively different kind of ethics, an ethics of discretion, as a condition of possibility for respecting human choices.

Fostering both autonomy and the needs of the community requires a delicate balancing act.[29] Yet too much is at stake to sit on the fence. What to do? Each age has had its crises about the value of human life. The best lesson learned from the struggles about those values is a virtue of tolerance even while remaining committed to one's position. If one's vision is accurate and true, convincing arguments can be made for it. If not, the vision will fail.[30] But this does not mean that one becomes hopeless about moving the cause along. It may not happen in one's lifetime, but each of us as a citizen must avoid lawlessness while urging our fellow citizens to consider the impact of what we are doing in all sorts of human life issues, from birth to death. Sidney Callahan says on this point that

> societies do change; moral progress often accelerates after long periods of acquiescence to evil. We have seen the civil rights movement, the women's movement, and the peace movement make progress, and we should never underestimate the flexibility of human social systems to respond to new visions of reality.[31]

Earlier I mentioned the story of Adam and Eve. The point of the story was that God was willing to admit wholesale evil into human history (the results of the choice) in favor of human freedom. From the perspective of theology, it is difficult to consider reasons why human beings should not be as lenient as God was in this regard.

But there are other reasons besides a theological one for promoting human choices as a social policy during times of conflict. First, as a matter of social engineering it is a good to society to reinforce altruistic actions. Nonetheless, when these actions require of some individuals greater sacrifice than of others, the greater sacrifice ought to be freely chosen.[32] Second, it is a good for society to reinforce that aspect of human life which most sets us apart from animals—rational choices. We ought therefore to be encouraged to make these choices whenever possible, even if they conflict with the cherished values of others. Thus, even though I have argued that respecting the inherent value of all forms of human life is not a value "imposed" on those in our culture but one that is its foundation, until a consensus of belief is reached on this point, and for reasons of both theology and social engineering, human choices must be respected.

There are at least two additional reasons why liberty must be respected as far as possible in matters of public concern. The first of these is pragmatic. When there is no consensus within a plurality of views and commitments, it is a good for society to permit choices in order to detect the true beliefs of its citizens, as long as actions in this regard do not violate the rights of others. Of course, this is precisely the point at issue in moral dilemmas like abortion and infanticide. Natalists especially argue that the unborn and the defective newborns have rights that are viciously disregarded. Unfortunately this point is hotly contested. In fact, one and a half million abortions a year demonstrate what persons actually believe. The number of abortions speaks louder than concepts in debate.

While the pragmatic viewpoint has merit, of course it is open to attack on grounds that it is too socially permissive. Because millions of people think abortion or infanticide or killing or racism is just fine does not make it so. Further, the state ought to intervene to teach its citizens about correct conduct rather than passively permit moral chaos. These arguments are well taken. That is why almost everyone could agree that Charles Manson should rightly have been jailed upon being judged guilty of horrible murders. Murder takes lives, takes rights from those who we agree have them. The state must act to protect these rights. But in the abortion debate, whether or not the fetus has those rights is essentially contested and apparently, given our pluralistic climate today, is unresolvable. With respect to severely damaged life forms, the same question is being asked. Thus the pragmatic reason for permitting human choice about moral issues applies, and is strongest, only in cases when the rights of the entity are contested. I say this with extreme reluctance, because the thesis of this volume has been that all forms of human life have intrinsic value and are thereby worthy of having ascribed rights.

The most persuasive argument for respecting human choices, however, stems from that thesis itself. A philosophical restraint on resolving moral issues through legislation rather than free discussion is that to respect the infinite, or finite but inherent, value of human life means that we must respect the decisions others make, even if we believe them to be wrongheaded or, worse, an offense against God. Because so much evil has been introduced into our history by intolerance, this argument for tolerance rests not on a vague, soft-shell, romantic kind of American pluralism. Rather, the requirement of tolerance for choices stems both from a respect for human life and from an abhorrence of the brutal consequences to that respect when one point of view dominates all others.

John Stuart Mill grappled much better than I can with the problem of human choice and social constraint in his *On Liberty*.[33] One example of the tolerance thesis he uses is this. For many religions the eating of pork is abhorrent, more abhorrent than murder or war, because it is a direct offense against the Deity. Should this practice then be abolished because a minority in a nation is offended by it?

To this we could add, from a theory of choice, that the practice should not be abolished even if there were a majority in favor precisely because the morality of the practice is contested. Only if there is widespread consensus about its offensiveness might a society instruct its citizens in right conduct.

With respect to the philosophical reason for a theory of choice, contestants in the antiabortion and women's rights movements sometimes fail dismally to honor one another. They do not listen to the fears and despair our society has caused in them both. I hope readers will scrutinize their own thinking based on the three positions enunciated, perhaps deriving some new ideas and social plans from the consequences of the position they do adopt.

In a word, I hope the reader will have developed some tolerance for the convictions of others. Similarly, the arguments presented should help convince those readers who have wondered about the disvaluing of human life, or who have contributed to it directly or indirectly by not becoming involved in plans to rectify injustice, and lead them to some renewed belief in the value of human life.

### An Ethics of Discretion

When we were children, we needed a lot of rules to help us establish our own internal virtues. The rules were necessary to keep us from harm and to protect others from our inexperience. But as we became adults, the rules were no longer as necessary. They could be dropped in favor of our own discretionary judgment. The same should be true of society. As its citizens mature, discuss, accept, and apply the values about human life they inherit from their elders, an ethic of rules or an ethic of strangers, as Tolstoy called it, ought to be supplanted by an ethic of intimates and colleagues. The former relies on sweeping policy. The latter relies on discretion among friends.[34] The former seems to be based on a presumption that persons will not obey the rules (so penalties are attached). The latter is based on a presumption of virtue or character.[35]

The more mature and civilized we think we have become, the more some rules seem to be unnecessary. Hence the strongest objection to position A was that it presented us with no room to negotiate about issues of human value. Equally, when we are at the bedside of the dying, or are counseling a pregnant twelve-year-old, or when national leaders are in the council of war chambers, commitments would be unflaggingly in favor of the absolute value of human life. There would be no American Civil Liberties Union lawyer protesting our decisions because they violate a "solemn right to abortion." Similarly, there would be no free enterprisers calling for cutbacks in social programs for the poor. There would be no War

College, training bright men to lead us in battle. In short, there would seem to be less room for the diversity of opinion and calling we now protect in our myths about America. After all, a particularly strong American contribution to the world is a recognition of pluralism and the skills to negotiate differences of viewpoint to get things done.[36]

The answer to this concern about position A is, of course, that establishing a baseline commitment to respect the inherent value of human life does not cut off political and ethical debate. It merely reaffirms the "self-evident truths" we need to hold after more than two hundred years of existence and for which we need to stand in the world community. By holding them as "self-evident," we say in effect that they are beyond debate. Richard Westley calls them a gift.[37] They are a belief we inherited. We examined them again and they seem reasonable. What is more, they can function as a foundation of a better society in a technological age. They can function as the source of international accord.

Establishing a baseline does not negate debate. It shifts the debate from a right to life to other rights, ones desperately in need of resolution now: education, health care, a standard of quality of life, a decent workplace, a decent job, and so on. Thus the Palestinians would still be claiming a right to a homeland but would have to recognize the right of Israelis to exist. Only in 1988 did this commitment come finally to voice. Vice versa, retaliation by Israelis would not destroy the lives of human beings because they are Palestinians. The dispute would still fester, but both peoples would have to grow up. They could not resolve the dispute by whacking each other to death. We would stop them if they were kids on the playground. "You don't have to like each other, just respect the other's right to exist." But on the world playground, we sell them the bludgeons to continue to destroy each other and, thereby, encourage the conflict to continue.

So, growing up is an important part of international and national conduct, as it is for individuals. If position A is to be adopted in some international day of dedication to the universal rights of persons, it must be adopted within the context of certain virtues of life-affirming societies. I call this set of virtues "an ethic of discretion," and conclude the book by discussing them briefly here. They are the virtues necessary for living on behalf of the graciousness of life.

1. **Acceptance of life.** This virtue is grounded in a recognition that human life is a gift. I mentioned that Richard Westley found this point significant. He said, concluding his book on the right to life:

I have been at some pains to suggest that the kind of "knowing" involved here [about life] has little to do with arguments and reasonings
and that it is more like insight, vision, or revelation; it is given as a gift,
not acquired by study.[38]

Thus the virtue of acceptance of life is one that urges us to profit
from our own experience of it, and from the experiences of others.
Attempts to reconcile difficult questions about the value of life using
narrow arguments cannot be sufficient in this view. Narrow arguments from one or two disciplines can never capture the fullness of
human experience about life. They are thus a dangerous basis for
policy. That is why my position has borrowed from many disciplines
(even though it may appear to some to be too eclectic). Policy cannot be formulated by taking into account only one position.

**2. Tolerance.** Tolerance is a natural consequence of accepting life.
The incredible richness of the forms of human life, individual and
social, are displayed in art, music, drama, literature, political systems, and architecture around the world. They are like a meadow
dotted with a palette of colorful flowers. How can we say one experience is more authentic than another? How can we say one flower is
more beautiful than another? *De gustibus non est disputandum—*
About tastes there can be no dispute. Instead, a delight in the diversity of human experience is a necessary condition for "respecting"
life. Human life is a gift, yes, but it is an *experienced* gift. We interpret it. Respect for life means both respect for the givenness of life
and for the experience of life.

**3. Prudence.** Prudence is a virtue of practical perception. It helps
us, armed with a respect for diversity and tolerance, nonetheless, to
cut through a lot of detritus. We can learn from reflections of geron-
tologists who have listened to the aged very carefully. Alex Comfort,
renowned for his work as a physician on aging, wrote: "What may
increase with age in those susceptible to development is intolerance
of triviality."[39] Even though one develops a virtue of tolerance for
diversity, this does not mean we throw our sense of judgment to the
winds. We couple it with prudence, a sort of intolerance for trivial
questions, inconsequential arguments, overspecialized concerns,
tunnel vision, and misperception about the proper ends of human
life and a decent human society. Besides intolerance of trivia, then,
prudence requires an intolerance of any tendency to reduce complex realities to simplistic viewpoints. Watch out for those who
might say something like, "Well, it's all a question of economics."

**4. Unconstrained communication.** Unconstrained communication,
or openness between persons, is an international yet personal virtue

parallel to the right of free speech. The phrase " unconstrained communication" comes from the writings of Jürgen Habermas, who has grappled with a general theory of the ethical foundations for a pluralistic modern age.[40] I use it here to illustrate how we cannot avoid reductionistic tendencies, even in position A, if we are not listening to the full range of human experience. If we tune out some experiences we do not want to hear from others, or from our own secret chambers of the heart, then the conditions of respect for life have been artificially—and tragically, I might add—truncated.

Worse yet, without this virtue, we fall prey to a more narrow interpretation of the position A baseline—the irreducible value of *all* forms of human life. In other words, we would interpret "all forms" to mean "only those with which I am familiar" or "only those forms I pay attention to." By so doing, we simply perpetuate a kind of bigotry.

Earlier I mentioned a concern about position A, that it is easily expressed by zealots, magnets for some but repulsive to others. Here I would draw an important distinction between zealots and true leaders. The former do not listen to what they do not want to hear. Hitler's maniacal disregard for his generals' advice was legendary. The latter, the authentic leaders, seek out new experiences. Note that Jesus goes to the well to talk to a Samaritan woman, he hobnobs with such outcasts as prostitutes and tax collectors, and he avoids any attempt to reduce his mission to political and religious zealotry.

**5. Political patience.** This virtue is required while we try to resolve difficult issues of life. We cannot listen to others, we cannot establish conditions of unconstrained communication, if we are immediately tempted to legislate an answer to the problem. While we are discussing the respect due to battered children, to spare embryos, to blacks who are subjects of medical research mostly of benefit to whites, to working women, to the aged we store away from sight, to the dying, to defective newborns, to the possible victims of an international arms race, while we are discussing and negotiating these rights, it makes little sense to legislate one party's answer, an answer viewed coercive by another. No real resolution results. Note the difference between legislating an answer and "falling back" to position B. The first predetermines the outcome of our conduct; the second makes explicit on the front end of debates a commitment at least to respect human life, liberty, and opportunity to compete. While we wrangle about definitions, evidence, and criteria, and while we rush to resolve the problem with our best technological and human efforts, legislation seems inappropriately abrupt.

**6. Respecting all life.** A commitment to respect the inherent value of all human life must rest on a general base of respecting all life itself. As Hans Jonas has pointed out, a creationist belief (that God created the world and everything in it) leads rather directly to an ethic of care for the future of the earth.[41] Pierre Teilhard de Chardin held that a religious faith in Christ inexorably tied the physical world to the divine order with concomitant obligations.[42] These are but two respected, even revered, thinkers who have seen that the moral climate of human life affirmation depends also upon a broader sense of responsibility for all other life forms on earth.

This outlook demands an alteration in the way Westerners subject, dominate, and change our environment. In this subjugation, we have become accustomed to downplaying the value of nonhuman living things as well as the resources of the earth itself. Thus, in regard to a choice between personal self-affirmation and personal privacy versus a not-yet-personal fetus, it comes as little surprise that the Supreme Court chose the former. If nothing else, its decision was based on a cultural preference of one life form—viable human life—over other life forms. Current interest in the rights of animals and in ways in which we interlock with our environment can serve as a corrective foil to this presumption.[43] Is it always true that our lives and our interests should outweigh the survival of whales as a species ("His only enemy is man") and the undisturbed beauty of a mountain peak? The habit of thinking that it does is dangerous.

There is a deeper question raised by inter-species justice, just as by analogy there is about intergenerational justice. Does the fact that we belong to a single species make us morally superior to other species? Do we obtain rights as a consequence of such membership? These questions are hotly debated by animal rights scholars. Diana T. Meyers, for example, holds that one gains rights by reason of being an individual, not a member of a species.[44] Peter Singer holds that the morally significant aspect of a being is its suffering and that the effects of our actions on nonhuman species have a moral significance. He remarks, "If a being suffers, the fact that it is not a member of our own species cannot be a moral reason for failing to take its suffering into account."[45]

Despite this important viewpoint, it does seem that certain rights accrue to us as a species, especially those based on our ability to ratiocinate and choose. Rights such as free speech and assembly come to mind immediately.[46]

**7. Distributive justice.** This important virtue distributes goods and services in a society to citizens on the basis of some principle of equity. If each human life form is to be considered of equal inherent value, it would seem that we would have to adopt the libertarian view of equity: Each person would be entitled to an objectively equal share of the world's goods and services regardless of status. This appears to be Charles Fried's position, and that of the disembodied entity, LIBER. At first, it sounds attractive. When one person's "toke" runs out, however, he or she has no claims on any further goods and services.

I think this principle of equity is flawed. It fails to recognize that we belong to one another. It fails to provide for the fact that justice is a voice of charity. The principle of equity required by a commitment to the supreme value of each human life would not permit the libertarian consequence of abandonment after resources are used up. Instead, equity would be based on a notion that each of us would receive according to our need. Remember that this standard occurs in normal times.

In emergencies, respect for persons is not suspended, but the normal principle of equity is exchanged for an emergency principle. In a broadened perspective of equity according to need, incipient and burdensome forms of human life, refugees, the senile, the poor, the oppressed, the unborn, and those who are dying are treated with *even greater attention* because they are in greater need. They are more vulnerable. As Pellegrino and I have argued, vulnerability establishes at least two duties. First, we have the standard duty to care for the condition that makes that person or persons more vulnerable. But second, we have the duty to right the imbalance in the relationship between us that might diminish that person in any way.[47]

8. Political action. The final, though not exhaustive, condition for implementing position A is that our political and social structures must be capable of implementing our commitment to the value of human life. The common humanity through which we meet one another as persons establishes this need. That is why Aristotle and Thomas Aquinas both held that working out the common good was the highest virtue attainable by human beings in this life. Schillebeeckx calls this an "anthropological constant," a requirement of all human societies, and a pressing need of modern life—working out the good of all in society.[48] Some of the actions I have called for are:

A complete reduction of all arms, not just a freeze
Ability to adopt unwanted defective newborns
Transplant of fetuses and embryos to carriers and surrogate mothers
Absolutely open housing
Technological direction toward housing for all persons and keeping the unborn alive for eventual adoption by citizens

A change from an arrogant individualism to a sense that rights
engender duties we have to all forms of human life

These few virtues function as conditions under which an ethic of
discretion may apply in a society that affirms the value of human life.
As can be seen, establishing such affirmation only lays the groundwork for productive ethical dialogue and policy decisions. It does
not take that dialogue away. Within the context of these virtues or
conditions, the dialogue and solutions can be carried out as discretionary ethics rather than as one of rules.

The commitment to life lies at a deeper level of belief than ethical
and policy discussion. The commitment does not grow through arguments. It can grow only through dramatic new experiences, conversion experiences, if you will. That is why so much of the modern
debate about human rights and the right to life appears to many of
us as tired or, worse, strident. Arguments don't convince. Experiences do. Much of our energy has been spent in this century on
arguments rather than on changing the environment to allow a new
and different experience of care for individual worth to emerge.

In an atmosphere of poverty, ugliness, drug abuse, poor education, racism, and violence, how can we expect a teenager to want to
bring an unborn child into the world? There is little or no experience of life affirmation. In the middle class, the lack of life affirmation is equally real, although it takes a different shape. It is a rat
race, bills are just barely paid, drudgery and boredom exist at home
and on the job, there is insecurity about long-term availability of
work, and children have a lack of respect for the accomplishments of
adults—all of these add up to life-demeaning rather than life-enhancing experiences.

Care for individual worth then will require, as it always has, constant rededication. Within this rededication, adults must be able to
exercise discretionary ethical judgment about shifting needs, duties,
requirements, policies, and public action. The Indiana Supreme
Court, in its apparently landmark decision regarding the Infant Doe,
judged that the discretionary judgment of parents and the doctor is
the best way to resolve difficult moral problems regarding human
life. The fact is, hundreds and thousands of us make that kind of
judgment every day, and they are not contested. As I see it, the
tragedy of the Infant Doe case was that the child's life could have
been saved and the baby adopted by one of the six families who
volunteered to do so. Thus an ethics of discretion would be established, but the baseline life affirmation of society would have as the
ready alternative policies for protecting the vulnerable from harm
better than the one pursued in the Infant Doe case—allowing the
baby to die. All it would take would be some changes in the law to

provide for emergency adoptions. Once adopted, Infant Doe could have been saved by the new parents in a decision to correct surgically the esophageal blockage.

## Summary

Recall that my purpose in writing this volume has not been to formulate answers to difficult dilemmas. The most problematic along the way has been the conflict between individual choices and social policy. Why do we seem to impose our values on certain behaviors (like the brutal murders perpetrated by Charles Manson) but not on others (like injecting one unborn child in the heart in order to deliver the other)? I have invited the reader to reflect on these matters, realizing that considerably more philosophically and theologically rigorous efforts must be made to resolve these issues than are contained in this volume. Yet overriding that realization has been a stronger one. Affirming all forms of human life, regardless of personal status, requires a new kind of social action, not words. The issues cannot be resolved until we choose to resolve them by directing our technology toward affirmation of life and our political communities toward respect for the custody we have been given of life itself.

In addition to this social action realization, however, there are seven other arguments I offered that contribute to the moral debates of our age. These are summarized here, just as John Stuart Mill summarized his theories on liberty, without all the major applications of the theory spelled out. Reflection on the theories and choices of action and application is still required.

First, a belief in the intrinsic value of all forms of human life is an established credo of our culture. It is not capricious. One does not impose this value on others so much as insist on its merits by acting on its behalf. It undergirds, however, at least three possible positions (A, B, and C). To address the issue as if only one position is authentic and the others are not is therefore inadequate. Moreover, recognizing the diversity of positions permits one to acknowledge a shared belief in others without giving up one's convictions. In this way we may search for a thread, beneath the surface arguments, that could lead to life-affirming actions.

Yet no position that only acknowledges the extrinsically measured worth of individuals truly represents the thinking of our heritage. This is the second contribution. As I said in Chapters 5, 6, and 7, once one has pondered the ideas set forth herein, it would take many profound arguments or a catastrophic suspension of our beliefs to counteract the force of a cultural tradition like ours. To be sure, one can cite hundreds of lapses when human life was not respected. But these do not detract from the authentic belief that condemns those actions, either on humanistic grounds or through a recognition of the fallenness of human persons.

A third contribution is the argument that a new, technological ethic is needed, such that our concern be focused on directing our enormous complex toward human rather than machinelike ends. To argue the questions of human rights without paying attention to technology is to ignore the very air expelled by debates, the "ether" in which they arise. Additionally, the crucial question of gaining control over technology is different from the questions posed by past moral systems. Hence, to use these systems of thought uncritically in trying to resolve postindustrial problems is antiquated in the extreme. For this reason, I hold past ethical theories somewhat suspect.

In this regard, for example, the arguments about abortion have centered on whether or not the fetus is a human person. This debate arises from criteria of viability, and merit through that viability, as compared to the mother. As I have argued, however, the debate should be cast in terms of the equal intrinsic merit of both forms of human life (mother and unborn child), by condemnations from both pro-lifers and pro-choicers of the society that improperly spends its resources on death (weapons) instead of on options for life (artificial wombs, adequate housing, and the like). To adopt the view that one form of life has less intrinsic value than another is to think of living entities as if they were machines with externally imposed values based on their functions. This turnabout of good thinking is what Yablonsky meant by people becoming robopaths.[49]

Fourth, I have contributed to the debate by employing a historical argument based on fittingness. In this way, all who share the values and heritage of our culture can reflect on the possibilities for resolution rather than become bottled up in sectarian and political urns that appeal to one another only by clanging against one another. Thus I suggested a path for discussion that permits all of us to walk beyond the tired clichés of so many of these debates.

Fifth, I have pointed out that only position A seems to represent a view held by the major religious leaders of the West, particularly by Jesus, and that positions B and C are modifications introduced because, frankly, we live in a sinful situation. I further suggested that B is a platform for striving for A, and that C can be held consistently only during emergencies. Yet many thinkers put "a hedge" around our religious heritage by interpreting what I called the "fierce vision" to suit their own philosophical stance, implying two things thereby: first, that not valuing human life is all right after all, *as a consistent position;* and, second, that their position has the merit of revelation itself.

Thus the contribution I hope I make is to help persons see that a single, usually preindustrial, moral tradition needs to be drastically recast in the light of our religious and political heritage and the plurality of positions possible. Also I showed that adopting viewpoints found in position B does not permit one to continue to use position A arguments about one issue, like abortion, without adopting the rigors of the position itself. Hence to claim that abortion is wrong because it violates innocent human life is either (1) to adopt position B or C in which counterarguments that fetuses are not as "valuable" as fully functioning human beings are entirely consistent or (2) to adopt position A itself which rules out all killing of any form of human life.

Arguments about the personal status or social status of human life, which I suggested as a sixth contribution, are misplaced. It makes no difference what the status of human life might be. It must have inestimable value. To introduce any qualifiers, such as that one "lost" value by murdering someone else, is suddenly to rely on external measures of personal worth and to slip back from A to B, or even to C. Although I argued that these positions are consistent ways of affirming the intrinsic value of human life, I also argued that they cannot be adopted permanently if we are adequately to recognize our heritage, particularly our religious heritage.

Finally, I have proposed the reason why we must sometimes move to positions B and C. The reason is not based on American respect for pluralism, although this would be a valid political reason, but on a theological theory of human choice. According to this theory, it is better to encourage moral choices despite the consequences than to legislate moral activity too early in an issue. Even though there are pragmatic and even technical reasons for delaying legislation about moral issues until the debate has produced the best arguments on both sides of the issue, so we may discern what values are truly at stake, there is even a more profound reason. To protect human choice is to affirm the very core of human value required by all three positions.

The point of this book, of course, is to encourage a greater social commitment to the intrinsic value of human life, thus creating a more universal consensus regarding life and death issues.

## Conclusion

It is odd, is it not, that when confronted by an almost obvious truth, we tend to turn away in embarrassment? Of course, a confirmation of the value of human life would reap the wonders of peace, justice, and compassion in the world. We all long for it. It is a law "written in our hearts." And yet it seems so incredibly naïve to actually think that this confirmation could take place.

As I have written this book, I have struggled to overcome the embarrassment of my own idealism. Yet I kept bumping up against a conviction stronger than any pragmatic persuasion to the contrary, that unless we alter the vision we hope to accomplish, secondary gains will never be forthcoming. If our sights are set too low, we will become mired in trivia. But if they are set on a consistent commitment to the irreducible value of all forms of human life, sweeping social changes in our conduct and respect for others are made possible. The power of this conviction has been demonstrated in the collapse, during the 1990s, of "Cold War" geopolitical realities. People's convictions can tear down the Berlin Wall. They can also build up the democratic maturity of civilization.

Just as geopolitical realities change in our time, so too are the older methods of excoriating individuals regarding their beliefs and public positions on human life issues. Strong pro-life governor of Idaho Cecil D. Andrus vetoed an abortion bill because he considered it too restrictive. Andrus noted that the bill did not provide for women who were victims of incest or rape.[50] In the Midwest, only 7 percent of citizens polled describe themselves as "pro-life," while 39 percent describe themselves as pro-choice, and 31 percent say abortion should be permitted in cases of rape or when the mother's life is endangered. This means that politicians describing themselves as "pro-life" would have a difficult time getting elected in the Midwest, where attitudes are usually thought to be more conservative than on either coast.[51] Perhaps because of the growing realization that both positions, for life and for choice, contain seeds of ways in which individuals can respect life, walls between both groups are coming down. Thus Cardinal Bernardin does not support removing public officials from the church, even if they do not support the church's public teaching on human life issues.[52] And Archbishop Rembert Weakland, in a first for the Catholic hierarchy, opened a dialogue with those who oppose the church's teaching on abortion in which he simply listened to women express their views on the subject.[53]

These changes are occurring as individuals realize the inconsistency inherent in taking a strong human life position on one issue (e.g., opposing nuclear war) and neglecting other important issues (e.g., feeding the homeless, caring for the vulnerable, and providing for the poor and elderly in our society).[54] This awareness, along with discoveries in embryology, has prompted several major protestant denominations (including the Episcopalians and Presbyterians) in the past two years to add new limitations to their stands on abortion.[55]

Being committed to the value of human life, in every dimension and form, is what Cardinal Bernardin has called the "Consistent Ethic of Life," or what has been dubbed the "seamless garment." What do you think?

# Notes

## Introduction

1. John C. Gardner, *Grendel* (New York: Alfred A. Knopf, 1971).
2. Lewis Mumford, *The Myth of the Machine*, 2 vols. (New York: Harcourt Brace Jovanovich, 1967–1970).
3. Barbara Tuchman, *A Distant Mirror: The Calamitous Fourteenth Century* (New York: Ballantine Books, 1978).
4. James Fyfe, "Eventually the Crazies Will Kill Each Other Off," *USA Today*, Feb. 6, 1989.
5. K. Danner Clouser, *Teaching Bioethics: Strategies, Problems and Resources* (Hastings-on-Hudson, N.Y.: Hastings Center Institute, 1980).
6. The Society for the Right to Die has been the most active of these organizations.
7. Thomas Pynchon, *Gravity's Rainbow* (New York: Viking Press, 1973).
8. "Tainted Fish Killed Dolphins, Experts Say," *Chicago Tribune*, Feb. 2, 1989.
9. Peter Gorner, "Greenhouse Effect Worries May Be Blooming Too Soon," *Chicago Tribune*, Jan. 15, 1989.
10. David C. Thomasma, *An Apology for the Value of Human Life* (St. Louis: Catholic Health Association, 1983).
11. Persuasion about the value of human life is the most important tool that can be used in fostering it. Evidence exists that we have not been very persuasive to date: "Abortion Rate Found Same for Protestants, Catholics," *Chicago Tribune*, April 30, 1982.
12. Thomas Aquinas, *Summa Contra Gentiles*, tr. A. Pegis, 5 vols. (Garden City, N.Y.: Doubleday & Co., Image Books, 1955).
13. Larry R. Churchill and José Jorge Siman, "Abortion and the Rhetoric of Individual Rights," *Hastings Center Report* 12, no. 1 (Feb. 1982), 9–12.
14. John Henry Cardinal Newman, *Apologia pro vita sua* (London: J. M. Dent, 1949).
15. "Must Deal with Soviets on Arms, Clerics Say," *Chicago Tribune*, May 13, 1982.
16. "Sick, Elderly Rejected for Post-Nuclear 'Ark,'" *Chicago Tribune*, May 13, 1982.
17. Physicians for Social Responsibility, the American branch of an inter-

national organization, has dedicated its Nobel Prize-winning efforts to convincing people of the inherent stupidity of even the possibility of nuclear war. H. Jack Geiger, M.D., one of the leaders of this movement, has made this clear in his "Why Survival Plans Are Meaningless," *Hastings Center Report* 13, no. 2 (April 1983), 17–19.

18. So we gulp again when more nations are added to the nuclear arsenal family: "Book Says Israel, Taiwan, S. Africa Join on A-Arms," *Chicago Tribune*, May 13, 1982.

19. Victor Grassian, *Moral Reasoning: Ethical Theory and Some Contemporary Moral Problems* (Englewood Cliffs, N.J.: Prentice-Hall, 1981), p. 255.

20. Joseph B. Tybor, "Should Juvenile Killers Die?" *Chicago Tribune*, Jan. 22, 1989.

21. Jorge Casuso, "Crowd Cheers Bundy's Execution," *Chicago Tribune*, Jan. 25, 1989.

22. Saul Bellow, *Henderson, the Rain King* (New York: Viking Press, 1959). I quote here from Leon Kirchner's musical setting of the text in his *Lily*.

23. René Dubos "A Celebration of Life," *United* 26 (April 1982), 9.

24. Ibid.

## Chapter 1: The Meaning of "The Value of Human Life"

1. Ludwig Wittgenstein, *Philosophical Investigations*, ed. Kenneth Scott (New York: Macmillan Co., 1973).

2. Milton Crane, *The Roosevelt Era* (New York: Boni & Gaer, 1947).

3. Marvin Kohl, *The Morality of Killing: Euthanasia, Abortion and Transplants* (New York: Humanities Press, 1974).

4. Eric Cassell, "The Nature of Suffering and the Goals of Medicine," *New England Journal of Medicine* 306, no. 11 (1982), 639–645.

5. David C. Thomasma, "The Range of Euthanasia," *Bulletin of the American College of Surgeons* 73, no. 8 (Aug. 1988), 4–13.

6. David C. Thomasma, "Decision to Use the Respirator: Moral Policy," *Bioethics Quarterly* 2 (Winter 1980), 229–236.

7. Thomas A. Raffin, Joel N. Shurkin, and Wharton Sinkler III, *Intensive Care: Facing the Critical Choices* (New York: W. H. Freeman & Co., 1989).

8. Eric Cassell, "Life as a Work of Art," *Hastings Center Report* 14, no. 5 (Oct. 1984), 35–37.

9. Matt Clark, Mariana Gosnell, and Dan Shapiro, "When Doctors Play God," *Newsweek* (special issue), Aug. 31, 1981, 48–54.

10. David C. Thomasma and Glenn C. Graber, *Euthanasia: Toward an Ethical Social Policy* (New York: Continuum, 1990).

11. Alasdair MacIntyre, "Why Is the Search for the Foundations of Ethics So Frustrating?" *Hastings Center Report* 9, no. 4 (Aug. 1979), 16–22.

12. George Orwell, *1984*, ed. Irving Howe (New York: Harcourt, Brace & World, 1963).

13. George Orwell, *Animal Farm* (New York: Harcourt, Brace & Co., 1954).

14. "Illegal Aliens Win Education Rights," *Chicago Tribune*, June 16, 1982.

15. G. R. Paterson, "The Political Manipulation of Language," *Chicago Tribune*, June 1, 1982.

16. "Israelis Smash Into Lebanon," *Chicago Tribune*, June 7, 1982.

17. Maurice Merleau-Ponty, *Signs*, tr. Richard C. McCleary (Evanston, Ill.: Northwestern University Press, 1964).

18. Plato, *Gorgias* and *Theaetetus*, in *The Collected Dialogues of Plato*, ed. Edith Hamilton and Huntington Cairns (Princeton, N.J.: Princeton University Press, 1980), 454d, p. 238.

19. Plato, *Gorgias* 456b, p. 239.

20. Plato, *Theaetetus* 201a-b, p. 908.

21. Ibid., 202c, p. 909.

22. Karol Wojtyla, "The Task of Christian Philosophy Today," in *The Human Person*, Proceedings of the American Catholic Philosophical Association, vol. 53, ed. George F. McLean (Washington, D.C.: American Catholic Philosophical Association, 1979), pp. 3–4.

23. Hans Jonas, "Responsibility Today: The Ethics of an Endangered Future," *Social Research* 43 (Jan. 1975), 77–97.

24. Robert S. Hartman, *The Structure of Value: Foundations of Scientific Axiology* (Carbondale, Ill.: Southern Illinois University Press, 1967).

## Chapter 2: Pre-Persons and Post-Persons

1. Mary Peterson Kauffold, "Infertility: High Tech Breeds High Hopes," *Chicago Tribune*, Feb. 12, 1989.

2. This recollection belongs to Barbara De Camp Hammack, as quoted in Kauffold, "Infertility."

3. Kauffold, "Infertility."

4. Harris Brotman, "Battle Over Test-Tube Babies," *Chicago Tribune Magazine*, Oct. 3, 1982, i, 13–20.

5. "Test-Tube Baby Pioneer Is Criticized Over Tests," *Chicago Tribune*, Sept. 28, 1982.

6. Ibid.

7. Brotman, "Battle Over Test-Tube Babies." This law was struck down by Illinois courts as unconstitutional in May 1990.

8. Peter Singer and Deane Wells, *Making Babies: The New Science and Ethics of Conception* (New York: Charles Scribner's Sons, 1985).

9. David Ozar, "The Case Against Thawing Unused Frozen Embryos," *Hastings Center Report* 15, no. 4 (Aug. 1985), 7–12.

10. Clifford Grobstein, "The Moral Uses of 'Spare' Embryos," *Hastings Center Report* 12, no. 3 (June 1982), 5–6.

11. As quoted in James T. Burtchaell, "The Moral Defect in Human Fetal Tissue Research," *Chicago Tribune*, Feb. 3, 1989.

12. Ibid.

13. Patricia House, "A 'Gift'?" (letter to the editor), *Chicago Tribune*, Jan. 1, 1989.

14. Congregation for the Doctrine of the Faith, *Instruction on Respect for Human Life in Its Origin and on the Dignity of Procreation* (Vatican City: Polyglot Press, Mar. 1987). Articles both laudatory and critical of the document can be found in *Health Progress* 68, no. 6 (July–Aug. 1987), 45–65.

15. Kenneth L. Vaux, "Op-Ed," *Chicago Tribune*, March 20, 1987, as

quoted in Joseph Cardinal Bernardin, "Science and the Creation of Life," *Health Progress* 68, no. 6 (July–Aug.), 48.

16. It may be dangerous to identify reproductive powers with the holiness of God too closely. This is the concern of a group of 170 prominent Roman Catholic theologians in Western Europe who issued a statement warning that the teaching office of the church was being misused by making this identification. See "Professors Challenge Pope's Role," *Chicago Tribune*, Jan. 27, 1989.

17. Henlee H. Barnette, *Exploring Medical Ethics* (Macon, Ga.: Mercer University Press, 1982), pp. 81–90.

18. Congregation of the Faith, *Instruction*.

19. Hans Moravec, *Mind Children: The Future of Robot and Human Intelligence* (Cambridge, Mass.: Harvard University Press, 1988).

20. Andrew Jameton, "In the Borderlands of Autonomy: Responsibility in Long-Term Care Facilities," *Gerontologist* 28 (June 1988), 18–23 (supplementary issue).

21. E. Cohen, "The Elderly Mystique: Constraints on the Autonomy of the Elderly with Disabilities," *Gerontologist* 28 (June 1988), 24–31 (supplementary issue).

22. *In re Conroy*, 98 N.J. 321, 486 A.2d 1209 (1985).

23. H. Witt, "Don't Deny Past, Pope Tells Austria," *Chicago Tribune*, June 27, 1988.

24. M. A. Iris, "Guardianship and the Elderly: A Multi-Perspective View of the Decisionmaking Process," *Gerontologist* 28 (June 1988), 39–45 (supplementary issue); and Dallas High, "All in the Family: Extended Autonomy and Expectations in Surrogate Health Care Decisionmaking," *Gerontologist* 28 (June 1988), 46–52 (supplementary issue).

25. "Health Care for the Elderly: The Nightmare in Our Future" (Dallas, Tex.: National Center for Policy Analysis, 1988), as reported in *Hospitals*, May 5, 1988, 79.

26. Dennis O'Leary, "The Torturous Road to Realistic Solutions," in *Health Care for the Uninsured: Politics, Economics, and Social Justice: The Proceedings* (Omaha, Nebr.: Creighton University Center for Health Policy and Ethics, 1987), pp. 26–38.

27. "Insurance for Long-Term Care: What Patients Should Know," *Senior Medical Review* 2 (Feb. 1988), 7.

28. Hon. David Durenberger, "Health Care: Policy and Politics in the 100th Congress," in *Health Care for the Uninsured*, pp. 3–10.

29. Alan Otten, "Local Groups Attempt to Shape Policy on Ethics and Economics of Health Issues," *Wall Street Journal*, May 25, 1988; and Daniel Wikler, "Ought the Young Make Health Care Decisions for Their Aged Selves?" *Journal of Medicine and Philosophy* 13 (Feb. 1988), 57–72.

30. Harry R. Moody, "Generational Equity and Social Insurance," *Journal of Medicine and Philosophy* 13 (Feb. 1988), 31–56.

31. Helga Kuhse and Peter Singer, "Age and the Allocation of Medical Resources," *Journal of Medicine and Philosophy* 13 (Feb. 1988), 101–116.

32. Dan Brock, "Justice and the Severely Demented Elderly," *Journal of Medicine and Philosophy* 13 (Feb. 1988), 73–100.

33. Corrine Bayley, "Access to Health Care: A Case of National Schizophrenia," in *Health Care for the Uninsured*, pp. 12–25.

34. R. Hoopes, "When It's Time to Leave: Can Society Set an Age Limit for Health Care?" *Modern Maturity*, 31 (Aug.–Sept. 1988), 38–43.

35. Richard D. Lamm, *Megatraumas: America at the Year 2000* (Boston: Houghton Mifflin Co., 1985), pp. 35–50.

36. "Daniel Callahan, Ph.D.," *American Medical News*, Feb. 19, 1988, 41–46; quote from p. 42.

37. Daniel Callahan, *Setting Limits: Medical Goals in an Aging Society* (New York: Simon & Schuster, 1987).

38. Norman Daniels, *Just Health Care* (Cambridge: Cambridge University Press, 1985).

39. Norman Daniels, *Am I My Parents' Keeper?* (New York: Oxford University Press, 1988).

40. "U.S. in 21st Century: Population May Ebb," *Chicago Tribune*, Feb. 1, 1989.

41. "Abortion Rights Down the Drain?" *Hastings Center Report* 18, no. 6 (Dec. 1988), 4.

42. Charles M. Madigan, "Abortion on Trial: Supreme Court Review Sparks Adversarial Emotions," *Chicago Tribune*, Jan. 16, 1989.

43. Sarah L. Hoagland, "A Note on the Logic of Protection and Predation," *Newsletter on Feminism and Philosophy, American Philosophical Association* 88, no. 1 (Nov. 1988), 7.

44. Sherrill Cohen and Nadine Taub, eds., *Reproductive Laws for the 1990s* (Clifton, N.J.: Humana Press, 1989).

45. *People* 30, no. 14 (Dec. 3, 1988), front cover.

46. Ronald Kotulak, "New Proton Accelerator Draws Bead on Cancer Cells," *Chicago Tribune*, Jan. 15, 1989.

47. See the enormous letter mailed to homes in January 1989 by the National Committee to Preserve Social Security and Medicare.

48. E.g., Charles Richter, "Catastrophic" (letter to the editor), *Chicago Tribune*, Feb. 1, 1989.

49. H. Tristram Engelhardt, Jr., and Michael Rie, "Morality for the Medical-Industrial Complex: A Code of Ethics for the Mass Marketing of Health Care," *New England Journal of Medicine* 319, no. 16 (Oct. 20, 1988), 1086–1089.

50. Jack C. Siebe, "Are Health Providers Still Patients' Chief Advocates?" *Physician Executive* 13, no. 5 (Sept.–Oct. 1987), 23–25.

51. Edmund D. Pellegrino and David C. Thomasma, *For the Patient's Good: The Restoration of Beneficence in Health Care* (New York: Oxford University Press, 1988).

52. Ronald Kotulak, "Clinical Trials Provide Answers, but at a Risk," *Chicago Tribune*, Feb. 12, 1989.

53. "Drugs' Greatest Tragedy: Damaged Babies" (editorial), *Chicago Tribune*, Feb. 3, 1989.

## Chapter 3: The Value of Human Life in a Technological Age

1. Lewis Yablonsky, *Robopaths: People as Machines* (New York: Pelican Books, 1972).

2. Bertrand Russell, as quoted in "Medicine's Technical Feats Forcing New Emphasis on Study of Ethics," *American Medical News*, Dec. 2, 1974, 17.

3. Augustine, *City of God: Basic Writings of St. Augustine*, ed. J. Whitney Oates, 2 vols. (Grand Rapids: Baker Book House, 1981).

4. Malcolm Muggeridge, "Books," *Esquire*, Feb. 1975, 20.

5. Plato, *Apology* 38a, p. 23.

6. Albert Camus, *A Happy Death*, tr. Richard Howard (New York: Alfred A. Knopf, 1972), p. 74.

7. Bertrand Russell, *The Problems of Philosophy*, Home University Library of Modern Knowledge (Henry Holt & Co., 1912), p. 250.

8. Daniel Callahan, *The Tyranny of Survival and Other Pathologies of Civilized Life* (New York: Macmillan Co., 1973).

9. Daniel Callahan, "Shattuck Lecture: Contemporary Biomedical Ethics," *New England Journal of Medicine* 302 (May 29, 1980), 1228–1233.

10. Daniel Callahan, "Minimalist Ethics," *Hastings Center Report* 11, no. 5 (Oct. 1981), 19–25.

11. Daniel Callahan, *Setting Limits: Medical Goals in an Aging Society* (New York: Simon & Schuster, 1987).

12. Thomas Pynchon, *Gravity's Rainbow* (New York: Viking Press, 1973), p. 521.

13. Ibid., p. 566.

14. Ibid., p. 645.

15. John Mamana, "Ethics and Medical Technology—Crossroads in Decision-Making," *Hospital Medical Staff* 19 (Nov. 1981), 18–22.

16. Lewis Mumford, *The Myth of the Machine*, 2 vols. (New York: Harcourt Brace Jovanovich, 1967–1970); and Yablonsky, *Robopaths*.

17. Joshua Lederberg, "Foreword," in Joseph Fletcher, *The Ethics of Genetic Control* (Garden City, N.Y.: Doubleday & Co., Anchor Books, 1974), p. vi.

18. Milton Singer, "Culture and Religion," *Center Magazine* 7 (Nov.–Dec. 1974), 47–60.

19. John Stuart Mill, *Utilitarianism*, ed. George Sher (Indianapolis: Hackett Publishing Co., 1979).

20. Karl Marx, *The Communist Manifesto*, in Karl Marx and Friedrich Engels, *Basic Writings on Politics and Philosophy*, ed. Lewis S. Feuer (Garden City, N.Y.: Doubleday & Co., Anchor Books, 1959).

21. Callahan, *Tyranny of Survival*.

22. R. Buckminster Fuller, *Utopia or Oblivion: The Prospects for Mankind* (New York: Overlook Press, 1973); and idem, *Ideas and Integrities* (New York: Collier Books, 1963).

23. Muggeridge, "Books," 20.

24. Alasdair MacIntyre, "Why Is the Search for the Foundations of Ethics So Frustrating?" *Hastings Center Report* 9 (1979), 16–22.

25. Alasdair MacIntyre, *After Virtue: A Study in Moral Theology* (Notre Dame, Ind.: University of Notre Dame Press, 1981). The only basis for a shared vision in this work seems to be common practices, such as perhaps medicine might be, that incorporate standards to which all might give assent.

26. Jacques Ellul, *The Technological Society*, tr. John Wilkinson (New York: Alfred A. Knopf, 1964).

27. Paul Tillich, *The Protestant Era* (Chicago: University of Chicago Press, 1957).

28. I use the small "p" because this is not a mainstream Protestant view.

29. Albert Camus, *Resistance, Rebellion, and Death*, tr. Justin O'Brien (New York: Modern Library, 1963), p. 17.

30. See the perceptive sketch of this social paranoia in "Talk of the Town," *The New Yorker*, Jan. 16, 1989, 23–24.

31.. Thomas Aquinas, *Summa Theologiae* 2-2, q. 23, aa. 6–8, and q. 114, a.1.

32. Ibid.

33. Camus, *Resistance*, p. 17.

## Chapter 4: Technological Progress and Human Values

1. Anthony Burgess, *A Clockwork Orange* (London: William Heinemann, 1962).

2. Nikolaus Lobkowicz, *Theory and Practice: History of a Concept from Aristotle to Marx* (Notre Dame, Ind.: University of Notre Dame Press, 1967).

3. Glenn C. Graber and David C. Thomasma, *Theory and Practice in Medical Ethics* (New York: Continuum, 1989).

4. Hallett D. Smith, as quoted in Milton MacKaye, *Saturday Evening Post*, April 23, 1955, 40.

5. "The Humanist Manifesto," *The Humanist*, Sept.-Oct. 1973, 8.

6. David C. Thomasma, "Cultural Issues in Medical Research," in *Research in Philosophy and Technology* ed. Paul T. Durbin (Greenwich, Conn.: JAI Press, 1980), vol. 3, pp. 66–75.

7. Joan Beck, "It's Not Time to Sing the 'Greenhouse Blues' Yet—But Just Wait," *Chicago Tribune*, Jan. 30, 1989.

8. Van Rensselaer Potter, *Bioethics* (Englewood Cliffs, N.J.: Prentice-Hall, 1974).

9. Lewis Yablonsky, *Robopaths: People as Machines* (New York: Pelican Books, 1972).

10. "City Faltering on Public Health," *Chicago Tribune*, Jan. 30, 1989.

11. Karl Marx, *The Communist Manifesto*, in Karl Marx and Friedrich Engels, *Basic Writings on Politics and Philosophy*, ed. Lewis S. Feuer (Garden City, N.Y.: Doubleday & Co., Anchor Books, 1959).

12. "Awesome Secret Is His," *Memphis Commercial Appeal*, Mar. 1, 1975.

13. Jon Van, "Out of Chaos Comes a Revolutionary Theory of Exploring Nature's Mysteries," *Chicago Tribune*, Feb. 12, 1989.

14. Jurrit Bergsma with David C. Thomasma, *Health Care: Its Psychosocial Dimensions* (Pittsburgh: Duquesne University Press, 1982).

15. R. Buckminster Fuller, *Utopia or Oblivion: The Prospects for Mankind* (New York: Overlook Press, 1973).

16. "U.S. Veterans Aid Soviets: Afghan, Vietnam Ordeals Bring Shared Remembrances," *Chicago Tribune*, Jan. 30, 1989.

17. David C. Thomasma, "Decision to Use the Respirator: Moral Policy," *Bioethics Quarterly* 2 (Winter 1980), 229–236.

18. Kathleen Nolan, "Genug ist Genug: A Fetus Is Not a Kidney," *Hastings Center Report* 18, no. 6 (Dec. 1988), 13–19.

19. Richard Barnett and Ronald Muller, "Global Reach—I," *The New Yorker*, Dec. 2, 1974, 53–128.

20. Hans Jonas, *Philosophical Essays: From Ancient Creed to Technological Man* (Englewood Cliffs, N.J.: Prentice-Hall, 1974).

21. Martin Heidegger, *The Question Concerning Technology and Other Essays*, tr. William Lovitt (New York: Harper & Row, 1977), "Only a God Can Save Us."

22. Samuel Florman, *Blaming Technology: The Retreat from Responsibility* (New York: St. Martin's Press, 1981).

23. William Kuhns, *The Post-Industrial Prophets: Interpretations of Technology* (New York: Harper & Row, Colophon Books, 1973).

24. Florman, *Blaming Technology*.

25. Lewis Mumford, *The Myth of the Machine*, 2 vols. (New York: Harcourt Brace Jovanovich, 1967–1970).

26. Jeff Lyon, "The Doctor's Dilemma," *Chicago Tribune*, Aug. 15, 1982.

27. Erich H. Loewy, *Ethical Dilemmas in Modern Medicine: A Physician's Viewpoint* (Lewiston, Maine: Edwin Mellen Press, 1986), pp. 19–32.

28. Jacques Ellul, *The Technological Society*, tr. John Wilkinson (New York: Alfred A. Knopf, 1964).

29. Lynn Emmerman, "Live Births at Hospital Stir Abortion Ruckus," *Chicago Tribune*, June 6, 1982.

30. Ibid.

31. "Fetal Tissue Transplants Stir Controversy," *Christianity Today*, Mar. 18, 1988, 52–54; Roger Lewin, "Caution Continues Over Transplants," *Science* 242 (Dec. 9, 1988), 1379; "The Startling Font of Healing: Cures from Aborted Fetal Tissue," *U.S. News and World Report*, Nov. 3, 1986, 68–71; "NIH Approves Fetal Tissue Experiments," *Christianity Today*, Oct. 21, 1988, 42.

32. Daniel Callahan, *Setting Limits: Medical Goals in an Aging Society* (New York: Simon & Schuster, 1987).

33. Victor Marchetti and John D. Marks, *The CIA and the Cult of Intelligence* (New York: Alfred A. Knopf, 1974), pp. 5–6.

34. David C. Thomasma, "The Goals of Medicine and Society," in *The Culture of Biomedicine, Studies in Science and Culture*, ed. D. Heyward Brock and Ann Harward (Newark, Del.: University of Delaware Press, 1984), pp. 34–54.

## Chapter 5: Our Religious Heritage

1. "Mother Teresa Evacuates 37 Handicapped Children," *Chicago Tribune*, Aug. 15, 1982.

2. James V. Schall, S.J., "Surgical Death," *Linacre Quarterly* 49 (Nov. 1982), 307.

3. Most often this argument is made in defense of the rights of animals. It

is part of an argument that there is no special moral dignity conferred on an individual by reason of membership in a species. Since this argument will appear again in the final chapter, no further details are provided here.

4. Frank E. Reynolds, "History of Religions: Condition and Prospects," *The Council on the Study of Religion Bulletin* 13 (Dec. 1982), 130.

5. Michael Schmaus, *The Essence of Christianity*, tr. J. Holland Smith (Chicago: Scepter, 1961), p. 234.

6. Hans Urs von Balthasar, *Word and Revelation*, tr. A. V. Littledale and Alexander Dru (New York: Herder & Herder, 1964), "God Speaks as Man," p. 96.

7. Gabriel Moran, *Theology of Revelation* (New York: Herder & Herder, 1966), p. 129.

8. Bill Baskerville, "Life Goes On for Boy Born Without Brain," *Chicago Sun-Times*, July 16, 1989.

9. Karl Rahner, *Spirit in the World*, tr. William Dych (New York: Herder & Herder, 1968), pp. 393–408; and idem, *Hearers of the Word*, tr. Michael Richards (New York: Herder & Herder, 1969), esp. p. 158, n. 6.

10. Karl Rahner and Karl Lehmann, *Kerygma and Dogma* (New York: Herder & Herder, 1969).

11. Edward Schillebeeckx, *God, the Future of Man*, tr. N. D. Smith (New York: Sheed & Ward, 1968), p. 5.

12. Annemarie De Waal Malefijt, *Religion and Culture: An Introduction to Anthropology of Religion* (New York: Macmillan Co., 1968).

13. Bronislaw Malinowski, *Magic, Science and Religion, and Other Essays* (Garden City, N.Y.: Doubleday & Co., Anchor Books, 1954).

14. Mircea Eliade, *The Sacred and the Profane* (New York: Harper & Row, Harper Torchbook, 1961).

15. Emile Durkheim, *The Elementary Forms of the Religious Life*, tr. Joseph Ward Swain (New York: Collier Books, 1961, first published in English, 1915).

16. Robert Ranulph Marett, *The Threshold of Religion* (London: Methuen & Co., 1909).

17. John B. Noss, *Man's Religions*, 3rd ed. (New York: Macmillan Co., 1963).

18. Adolphus P. Elkin, *The Australian Aborigines* (New York: Longmans, 1961); and Clark Wissler, *The Social Life of the Blackfoot Indians* (New York: American Museum of Natural History, 1911), vol. 7.

19. William J. Goode, *Religion Among the Primitives* (Glencoe, Ill.: Free Press, 1951).

20. Mircea Eliade, *From Primitives to Zen: A Thematic Sourcebook of the History of Religions* (New York: Harper & Row, 1967).

21. Mircea Eliade, *Patterns in Comparative Religion* (Cleveland: World Publishing Co., 1963).

22. Robert Graves, *The White Goddess: A Historical Grammar of Poetic Myth* (London: Faber & Faber, 1948).

23. Claude Lévi-Strauss, *The Savage Mind* (Chicago, Ill.: University of Chicago Press, 1962).

24. Mircea Eliade, *The Sacred and the Profane: The Nature of Religion*, tr. Willard R. Trask (New York: Harper & Brothers, 1961).

25. Ralph Linton, *The Study of Man: An Introduction* (New York: D. Appleton-Century Co., 1936).

26. Max Weber, *The Sociology of Religion,* tr. Ephraim Fischoff (1922; Boston: Beacon Press, 1964).

27. Malefijt, *Religion and Culture.*

28. Mark R. Harrington, *Religion and Ceremonies of the Lenape* (New York: Museum of the American Indian, Heye Foundation, 1921 reprint), pp. 87–88, Indian Notes and Monographs.

29. Raymond Moody, *Life After Life* (New York: Bantam Books, 1976).

30. Harrington, *Religion and Ceremonies of the Lenape,* pp. 88–92.

31. Frank G. Speck, *Naskapi, the Savage Hunters of the Labrador Peninsula* (Norman, Okla.: University of Oklahoma Press, 1935).

32. Noss, *Man's Religions.*

33. H. H. Rowley, *The Growth of the Old Testament* (1950; New York: Harper & Row, Harper Torchbooks, 1963), p. 173.

34. Donald J. Selby and James King West, *Introduction to the Bible* (New York: Macmillan Co., 1971), pp. O.T. 3–5.

35. Ibid.

36. Herbert F. Hahn, *The Old Testament in Modern Research* (London: SCM Press, 1956), ch. 1; and Raymond E. Brown, Joseph Fitzmyer, and Roland E. Murphy, eds., *The Jerome Biblical Commentary,* 2 vols. in 1 (Englewood Cliffs, N.J.: Prentice-Hall, 1968).

37. Roland de Vaux, *Ancient Israel: Its Life and Institutions,* 2 vols. (New York: McGraw-Hill Book Co., 1961).

38. Hermann Gunkel, *The Legends of Genesis, the Biblical Saga and History,* tr. W. H. Carruth (New York: Schocken Books, 1964).

39. Selby and West, *Introduction to the Bible,* pp. O.T. 59–64.

40. John Bright, *A History of Israel,* 3rd ed. (Philadelphia: Westminster Press, 1959).

41. William F. Albright, *The Biblical Period from Abraham to Ezra* (New York: Harper & Row, Harper Torchbooks, 1963).

42. The Decalogue appears to have been adopted from the suzerainty treaty form. For a discussion of the origins and development of the Decalogue, see Erhard Gerstenberger, *Wesen und Herkunft des apodiktischen Rechts* (Neukirchen-Vluyn: Neukirchener Verlag, 1965); and Eduard Nielsen, *The Ten Commandments in New Perspective: A Traditiohistorical Approach,* tr. David Bourke (London: SCM Press, 1968), pp. 71–93.

43. Walter J. Harrelson, "Law in the Old Testament," *The Interpreter's Dictionary of the Bible* (New York: Abingdon Press, 1962), vol. 3, pp. 77–89.

44. Selby and West, *Introduction to the Bible,* pp. O.T. 171–175; and Walter J. Harrelson, *From Fertility Cult to Worship* (Garden City, N.Y.: Doubleday & Co., Anchor Books, 1970).

45. B. W. Anderson and Walter Harrelson, eds., *Israel's Prophetic Heritage* (New York: Harper & Brothers, 1962).

46. John Skinner, *Prophecy and Religion: Studies in the Life of Jeremiah* (Cambridge: Cambridge University Press, paperback, 1961).

47. Peter Ackroyd, *Exile and Restoration* (Philadelphia: Westminster Press, 1968).

48. Harvey H. Guthrie, *Israel's Sacred Songs: A Study of Dominant Themes* (New York: Seabury Press, 1966); and William McKane, *Prophets and Wise Men* (London: SCM Press, 1965).

49. Andre-Alphonse Viard and Pierre Grelot, "The Plan of God," in *Dictionary of Biblical Theology*, ed. Xavier Léon-Dufour (New York: Desclée & Co., 1961), pp. 382–385.

50. Richard Carlisle, ed., *The Illustrated Encyclopedia of Mankind* (New York: Marshall Cavendish, 1984), vol. 10, p. 1321; also see Carl Beckwith, ed., *Maasai* (New York: Harry N. Abrams, 1980), p. 29.

51. Eric C. Rust, *Towards a Theological Understanding of History* (New York: Oxford University Press, 1963).

52. Carroll Stuhlmueller, "Deutero-Isaiah," in *The Jerome Biblical Commentary*, vol. 1, pp. 366–386.

53. Walther Eichrodt, *Theology of the Old Testament* (Philadelphia: Westminster Press, 1961), vol. 1.

54. William F. Albright, *From the Stone Age to Christianity*, 2nd ed. (Baltimore, Md.: Johns Hopkins Press, 1946).

55. Aubrey R. Johnson, *The Vitality of the Individual in the Thought of Ancient Israel* (Cardiff, Wales: University of Wales Press, 1949).

56. Gerard A. Vanderhaar, *Enemies and How to Love Them* (Mystic, Conn.: Twenty-Third Publications, 1985).

57. David C. Thomasma, "The Basis of Medicine and Religion: Respect for Persons," *Hospital Progress* (now *Health Progress*) 60 (Sept. 1979), 54–57, 90.

58. "Declaration on Religious Freedom," in *The Documents of Vatican II*, ed. Walter M. Abbott, Jr. (New York: Herder & Herder, 1966), pars. 1–15, pp. 675–696.

59. "The Church in the Modern World," in Abbott, ed., *The Documents of Vatican II*, pars. 1–93, pp. 199–308.

60. Ibid., par. 26, pp. 225–226.

61. Ibid., par. 29, p. 228.

62. "Declaration on Religious Freedom," in Abbott, ed., *The Documents of Vatican II*, pars. 1, 2, pp. 675–680.

63. Louis Boyer, *Christian Humanism* (Westminster, Md.: Newman Press, 1959).

64. "Fiery Christians Burning Books to Banish Evil and Save the Kids," *Chicago Tribune*, June 16, 1982.

## Chapter 6: Our Philosophical Heritage

1. Aristotle, *Protrepticus* 39, reconstructed and tr. Anton-Hermann Chroust (Notre Dame, Ind.: University of Notre Dame Press, 1964), p. 16.

2. Peter Singer, "Moral Experts," *Analysis* 32 (1972), 115–117.

3. José Ortega y Gasset, *The Origin of Philosophy*, tr. T. Talbot (New York: W. W. Norton & Co., 1967), pp. 52–53.

4. Aristotle, *Protrepticus*, p. 11.

5. Martin Heidegger, "Aletheia," in *Vorträge und Aufsetze*, Teil III (Pfullingen: Neske Verlag, 1967), pp. 53–78.

6. H. Tristram Engelhardt, Jr., "Philosophy, Health Care, and Public Policy," *Möbius* 2 (July 1982), 17–22.

7. Albert Ellis, "Psychotherapy and Atheistic Values: A Response to A. E. Bergin's 'Psychotherapy and Religious Values,'" *Journal of Consulting and Clinical Psychology* 48 (1980), 635–639.

8. John B. Massen, "An Atheist's View of Nuclear War," *Chicago Tribune,* May 20, 1982.

9. Thomas Aquinas, *Summa Theologiae* 1, q.1.

10. Alasdair MacIntyre, "A Crisis in Moral Philosophy: Why Is the Search for the Foundations of Ethics So Frustrating?" in *Knowing and Valuing: The Search for Common Roots,* ed. Daniel Callahan and H. Tristram Engelhardt, Jr. (Hastings-on-Hudson, N.Y.: The Hastings Center, 1980), pp. 18–35.

11. Kai Nielsen, "On Being Skeptical About Applied Ethics," in *Clinical Medical Ethics: Exploration and Assessment,* ed. T. Ackerman, G. Graber, D. Thomasma, and C. Reynolds (Lanham, Md.: University Press of America, 1987), pp. 95–116.

12. Alasdair MacIntyre, "The Essential Contestability of Some Social Concepts," *Ethics* 84 (Oct. 1973), 1–9.

13. George Edgin Pugh, *The Biological Origin of Human Values* (New York: Basic Books, 1977), p. 4.

14. Massen, "Atheist's View."

15. John Locke, *Essay on Human Understanding,* 2 vols. (New York: Dover Books, 1959).

16. Albert R. Jonsen, "Can an Ethicist Be a Consultant?" in *Frontiers in Medical Ethics: Applications in a Medical Setting,* ed. Virginia Abernethy (Cambridge, Mass.: Ballinger Publishing Co., 1980). In addition to the work by Graber et al. cited in n. 11, other articles on this topic are being prepared for the Proceedings of the Second Annual Meeting of the Society for Bioethics Consultation, St. Louis, Sept. 1988. Also see David C. Thomasma, "The Role of the Clinical Medical Ethicist: The Problem of Applied Ethics and Medicine," *The Applied Turn in Contemporary Philosophy* in *Bowling Green Studies in Applied Philosophy,* vol. 5, eds. M. Gradie, T. Attig, and N. Rescher (Bowling Green, Ohio: Bowling Green State University Press, 1983), pp. 136–157; and Jacqueline Glover, David Ozar, and David Thomasma, "Teaching Ethics on Rounds: The Ethicist as Teacher, Consultant, and Decision Maker," *Theoretical Medicine* 7 (1986), 13–32.

17. John Harris, *Violence and Responsibility* (London: Routledge & Kegan Paul, 1980), pp. 136–141.

18. MacIntyre, "Essential Contestability"; and Daniel Callahan, "Shattuck Lecture: Contemporary Biomedical Ethics," *New England Journal of Medicine* 302 (May 29, 1980), 1228–1233.

19. See, on this point, Martin E. Marty and Kenneth L. Vaux, eds., *Health/ Medicine and the Faith Traditions: An Inquiry Into Religion and Medicine* (Philadelphia: Fortress Press, 1982). This summary of a project undertaken by the Park Ridge Center of Lutheran General Hospital has led to a series of books on medicine and ethics from the perspectives of many faith traditions. Similarly, Robert Veatch edited an issue of the *Journal of Medicine and Philosophy* ("Comparative Medical Ethics," vol. 13, no. 3, Aug. 1988) on alternative professional ethics codes (other than the Hippocratic one), a topic

that has interested him for some years. He published a book on this topic as well: *Medical Ethics* (Boston: Jones and Bartlett, 1989).

20. Carla Carwile, "Reclaiming Rightful Power: Conference Confirms Meaning and Momentum of Grassroots Bioethics Movement," *Frontlines* 5, no. 3 (Dec. 1988), 1–3. Colorado's "Colorado Speaks Out on Health," and California's similar program, "California Health Decisions," are just two state coalitions that have begun initiatives on getting large numbers of citizens involved in health care policy analysis and lobbying. Other states are New Jersey and Oregon.

21. Alexander Capron, "Autonomy and Community," *Frontlines* 5, no. 3 (Dec. 1988), 7, 10.

22. H. Tristram Englehardt, Jr., *The Foundations of Bioethics* (New York: Oxford University Press, 1987).

23. A typical example of this is the book, edited by James J. Bopp, Jr., *Human Life and Health Care Ethics* (Westport, Conn.: Greenwood Press, 1985). All the authors, except one or two, appeal to arguments that the audience will not dispute, start with premises that are, for prolifers, indisputable but are precisely the points at issue in the abortion debate.

24. Aristotle, *The Nicomachean Ethics: A Commentary*, ed. Harold Joachim (Oxford: Clarendon Press, 1951).

25. John Rawls, *A Theory of Justice* (Cambridge, Mass.: Harvard University Press, 1971).

26. Thomas Aquinas, *Summa Theologiae* 1, qq. 50–64.

27. Locke, *Human Understanding.*

28. Richard B. Brandt, *Ethical Theory* (Englewood Cliffs, N.J.: Prentice-Hall, 1973).

29. Rawls, *Theory of Justice.* Also see Norman Daniels, *Reading Rawls* (New York: Basic Books, 1975). In his *Just Health Care* (Cambridge: Cambridge University Press, 1985), Daniels applies Rawls's thinking to the problems of access to health care, an issue only indirectly found in Rawls's book. More recently, Daniels has amplified his own thinking on this thorny topic in his *Am I My Parents' Keeper?* (New York: Oxford University Press, 1988).

30. Kai Nielsen and Roger Shiner, eds., *New Essays on Contract Theory* (Guelph, Ont.: Canadian Association for Publishing Philosophy, 1977).

31. Aristotle, *Nicomachean Ethics*, in *The Basic Works of Aristotle*, ed. R. McKeon (New York: Random House, 1941), 5, c1–7, 1129a–1135a, pp. 1002–1014.

32. H. H. Joachim, *Aristotle: The Nicomachean Ethics, A Commentary*, ed. D. A. Rees (Oxford: Clarendon Press, 1955); also see Thomas Aquinas' development of the virtue of justice, and the ways that influence his own political thinking, in *The Political Ideas of St. Thomas Aquinas*, tr. The Fathers of the English Dominican Province (New York: Hafner Publishing Co., 1953).

33. Immanuel Kant, *Metaphysical Foundations of Morals*, ed. C. G. Friedrich (New York: Modern Library, 1965), pp. 140–187.

34. R. S. Downie and Elizabeth Telfer, *Respect for Persons* (New York: Schocken Books, 1970).

35. Charles Fried, *Right and Wrong* (Cambridge, Mass.: Harvard University Press, 1979).

36. John Arthur and William H. Shaw, eds., *Justice and Economic Distribution* (Englewood Cliffs, N.J.: Prentice-Hall, 1978).

37. Robert Veatch, *The Foundations of Justice: Why the Retarded and the Rest of Us Have Claims to Equality* (New York: Oxford University Press, 1986). Veatch is an egalitarian who grapples with the problem of treating the retarded and others from a philosophical point of view.

38. Engelhardt, e.g., holds that autonomy is the condition of possibility of ethics in his *Foundations of Bioethics* pp. 66–103. But what is surely wrong about this principle is the tendency to miss how all human beings are social, a point that Alasdair MacIntyre makes repeatedly in his writings (see his excellent book, *After Virtue* [Notre Dame, Ind.: University of Notre Dame Press, 1981]). The same insight infuses Erich Loewy's critique of Engelhardt, "Communities, Obligations, and Health Care," *Social Science and Medicine* 25/7 (1987): 783–791.

39. Jeremy Bentham, *An Introduction to the Principles of Morals and Legislation* (New York: Hafner Publishing Co., 1948). A good example of how Bentham's concerns about social justice and public health required utilitarian thinking can be found in Henk ten Have, *Jeremy Bentham: Een Quantum theorie Van de Ethiek* (Kampen: Kok Agora, 1986).

40. John Stuart Mill, *On Utility*, ed. Mary Warnock (Cleveland: World Publishing Co., 1962).

41. John Stuart Mill, *On Liberty*, ed. C. V. Shields (Indianapolis: Bobbs-Merrill Co., 1956).

42. A good sketch of the contrasting theories can be found in almost every introductory book in ethics and medical ethics. One of the best is Glenn C. Graber's in his "Basic Theories in Medical Ethics," in *Medical Ethics: A Guide for Health Professionals*, ed. John F. Monagle and David C. Thomasma (Rockville, Md.: Aspen Systems, 1988), pp. 462–475.

43. Glenn C. Graber, "In Defense of a Divine Command Theory of Ethics," *Journal of the American Academy of Religion* 43 (March 1975), 62–69.

44. Lawrence A. Blum, *Friendship, Altruism, and Morality* (London: Chapman & Hall, 1982).

45. Aristotle, *Nicomachean Ethics* 1136b30–1137b32.

46. Thomas Aquinas, *Summa Theologiae* 2-2, qq. 23 and 114.

47. Edmund D. Pellegrino and David C. Thomasma, *For the Patient's Good: The Restoration of Beneficence in Health Care* (New York: Oxford University Press, 1988).

48. Leo Tolstoy, *Anna Karenina*, tr. Rosemary Edmonds, rev. ed. (London: Penguin Books, 1978).

49. Stephen Toulmin, "The Tyranny of Principles," *Hastings Center Report* 11 (Dec. 1981), 31–39.

50. Albert R. Jonsen and Stephen Toulmin, *The Abuse of Casuistry: A History of Moral Reasoning* (San Francisco: University of California Press, 1988).

51. David C. Thomasma, "A Contextual Grid for Medical Ethics," *AAR Abstracts* (Minnesota: Scholars Press, 1979), pp. 117–118; Glenn C. Graber and David C. Thomasma, *Theory and Practice in Medical Ethics* (New York: Continuum, 1989), pp. 125–150.

52. Aristotle, *Nicomachean Ethics*, pp. 1136b30–1137b32.

53. Leo Strauss, *Natural Right and History* (Chicago: University of Chicago Press, 1953).

## Chapter 7: Our Political Heritage

1. R. W. Carlyle and A. J. Carlyle, *A History of Medieval Political Theory in the West*, 6 vols.; reprint (Darby, Pa.: Arden Library, 1979).
2. Richard Sherlock, "Public Policy and the Life Not Worth Living: The Case Against Euthanasia," *Linacre Quarterly* 47 (May 1980), 121–132.
3. Plato, *Republic: The Forms of Government* (New York: Basic Books, 1968).
4. Aristotle, *Politics*, bk. 1, ch. 5, 20–25, p. 1132.
5. Marcus Aurelius, *Meditations*, tr. Maxwell Stanforth (London: Penguin Books, 1964).
6. Thomas Hobbes, *Leviathan*, ch. 8, reproduced in *Social and Political Philosophy, Readings from Plato to Gandhi*, ed. John Somerville and Ronald E. Santoni (New York: Doubleday & Co., Anchor Books, 1963), p. 152.
7. John Locke, *Two Treatises on Government*, ch. IX, ff. 123, in Somerville and Santoni, eds., *Social and Political Philosophy*, p. 184.
8. Jean Jacques Rousseau, *The Social Contract*, tr. W. Kendall (Chicago: H. Regnery and Co., 1954), Book 1, ch. 1, p. 2.
9. Garry Wills, *Inventing America: Jefferson's Declaration of Independence* (Garden City, N.Y.: Doubleday & Co., 1978), pp. 167–180.
10. Ibid., p. 180.
11. Edward C. Stewart, *American Cultural Patterns: A Cross-Cultural Perspective* (LaGrange Park, Ill.: Intercultural Network, 1972), p. 50.
12. Mulford Q. Sibley, "The Traditional American Doctrine of Freedom of Thought and Speech," in *The American Culture: Approaches to the Study of the United States*, ed. Hennig Cohen (Boston: Houghton Mifflin Co., 1968), pp. 168–178.
13. Karl Marx, *The Communist Manifesto*, tr. Samuel Moore (Baltimore: Penguin Books, 1967).
14. Karl Marx and Friedrich Engels, *Das Kapital* (New York: Modern Library, 1936).
15. Dante L. Germino, *Modern Western Political Thought: Machiavelli to Marx* (Chicago: Rand McNally & Co., 1972).
16. Marx, *The Communist Manifesto*, p. 29.
17. Leonard Dinnerstein and Kenneth T. Jackson, eds., *American Vistas*, 2 vols. (New York: Oxford University Press, 1971).
18. Charles Madigan contrasted the Norman Rockwell America that Ronald Reagan believed in with the real, violent America that is part and parcel of reality in his reflections on the inauguration of George Bush as president of the United States: "America: 1989: Bush Takes Over a Lovely Country . . . and an Ugly One," *Chicago Tribune*, Jan. 22, 1989. Bush himself, in part of his inaugural address quoted in that article, noted that the "deeper success" of a nation consists in "better hearts and finer souls."
19. Dislike of capitalism seems to go hand in hand with a mistrust of parliamentary democracy precisely because of the fear of rapacious greed

that seems built into human beings. George Bernard Shaw is just one of many major personages, like Jack London, who embraced either fascism or communism for this reason: *Bernard Shaw: Collected Letters 1926–1950*, ed. Dan H. Laurence, vol. 4 (New York: Viking Press, 1988). Contrast this political commitment to ostensibly repressive structures with Shaw's view of the individual character building of art: "Art should refine our sense of character and conduct, of justice and sympathy, greatly heightening our self-knowledge, self-control, precision of action, and considerateness, and making us intolerant of baseness, cruelty, injustice and intellectual superficiality or vulgarity" (as quoted in "George Bernard Shaw," *The New Yorker*, Jan. 2, 1989, p. 65). It seems clear from this contrast that the worth of the individual is not abandoned in a socialist vision.

20. Mary C. Segers, "Can Congress Settle the Abortion Issue?" *Hastings Center Report* 12, no. 3 (June 1982), 20–28.

21. Ibid.

22. Phillip Heymann and Sarah Hotz, "The Severely Defective Newborn: The Dilemma and the Decision Process," in *Decision Making and the Defective Newborn*, ed. Chester A. Swinyard (Springfield, Ill.: Charles C. Thomas, 1978), p. 428.

23. David C. Thomasma, "An Apology for the Value of Human Life: A Response to Paul T. Menzel's 'Pricing Life,' " *Hospital Progress* (now *Health Progress*) 63 (April 1982), 49–52, 68.

24. Peter Singer, *Animal Liberation* (New York: Avon Books, 1977).

25. Note that H. Tristram Engelhardt, Jr., tends toward this species confusion in his article on abortion, in which he expresses greater concern for the rights of animals than of fetuses ("The Ontology of Abortion," *Ethics* 84 [April 1974], 217–234).

26. Abraham Lincoln, "Speech at Columbus, Ohio, 1859," in *In the Name of the People*, ed. Robert W. Johannsen and Harry V. Jaffa (Columbus, Ohio: Ohio State University Press, 1959), pp. 267–268.

27. Eugene Diamond, " 'Quality' vs. 'Sanctity' of Life in the Nursery," *America*, Dec. 4, 1976, 396–398.

28. Robert M. Veatch, *Death, Dying, and the Biological Revolution: Our Last Quest for Responsibility* (New Haven, Conn.: Yale University Press, 1976).

29. David C. Thomasma, "Professional and Ethical Obligations Toward the Aged," *Linacre Quarterly* 48 (Feb. 1981), 73–80.

30. Susan Braithwaite and David C. Thomasma, "New Guidelines on Foregoing Life-sustaining Treatment in Incompetent Patients: An Anti-Cruelty Policy," *Annals of Internal Medicine* 104 (1986), 711–715.

31. Joseph B. Tybor, "Rights in Conflict: Who Lives, Who Dies, and Who Decides?" *Chicago Tribune*, May 2, 1982.

32. Gilbert Meilaender, "If This Baby Could Choose . . . ," *Linacre Quarterly* 49 (Nov. 1982), 313–314.

33. Renate Justin, "The Value History: A Necessary Family Document," *Theoretical Medicine* 8, no. 3 (Oct. 1987), 275–282.

34. "In Coma Since '79, Cop Regains Consciousness," *Chicago Tribune*, April 26, 1982.

35. "I Am Not What You See," Canadian Broadcasting System television

program. After that experience, the woman went on to get a Ph.D. degree in psychology, all the time with great ambivalence about the quality of her own life. As her cerebral palsy progressed, she became more despondent. After the television program was taped, she committed suicide.

## Chapter 8: The Complexity of Human Life Issues

1. John Hersey, *Hiroshima* (New York: Alfred A. Knopf, 1949).

2. Ruth Adams and Sue Cullen, eds., *The Final Epidemic: Physicians and Scientists on Nuclear War* (Chicago: Educational Foundation for Nuclear Science, 1982).

3. "New Pentagon Plan Is Based on Protracted Nuclear War," *Chicago Tribune*, May 30, 1982.

4. Ruth L. Sivard, *World Military and Social Expenditures 1980* (Leesburg, Va.: World Priorities, 1980), chart 11.

5. Rogers Worthington, "A-Bomb Still Burns in Minister's Mind," *Chicago Tribune*, Oct. 11, 1982.

6. Gerard A. Vanderhaar, *Christians and Nonviolence in the Nuclear Age: Scripture, the Arms Race and You* (Mystic, Conn.: Twenty-Third Publications, 1982).

7. "Will START Ever Finish?" *The Economist* 310 (Jan. 14, 1989), 28–30.

8. A survey in summer 1982 conducted by Rep. John Erlenborn of his 14th district in Illinois showed almost 63 percent in favor of unilateral reductions. Opinion survey results: "The U.S. should move toward nuclear disarmament only if the Soviets agree to reduce their arms"—37 percent; "The U.S. and Soviets should freeze their supplies of nuclear arms at existing levels and then pursue reductions"—45 percent, a combined reduction sentiment totaling 82 percent, plus another 4 percent for unilateral reduction. Sentiment would be even higher now, after the summit of June 1990.

9. Vitaly A. Korotich, "A Soviet View of the Inauguration: Let Us Shape the Future Together," *Chicago Tribune*, Jan. 22, 1989.

10. "Why War?" Letters of Einstein and Freud, displayed in the Chicago Public Library Cultural Center, May 21–June 14, 1982.

11. "Bishops, U.S. Aides Debate Nuclear War," *Chicago Tribune*, Oct. 5, 1982.

12. Bruce Buursma, "Pacifist Archbishop Makes New Appeal," *Chicago Tribune*, Oct. 9, 1982.

13. Vanderhaar, *Christians and Nonviolence*, p. 9.

14. Charles M. Madigan, "Abortion on Trial: Supreme Court Review Sparks Adversarial Emotions," *Chicago Tribune*, Jan. 16, 1989.

15. Joan Beck, "Parents, Teens, Sex and Trouble," *Chicago Tribune*, Oct. 11, 1982.

16. Charles Curran, "Abortion: Contemporary Debate in Philosophical and Religious Ethics," in *Encyclopedia of Bioethics*, ed. Warren T. Reich, 4 vols. (New York: Free Press, 1978), vol. 1, p. 23.

17. Timothy J. McNulty, "Quayle Gets Role in Abortion Fight," *Chicago Tribune*, Jan. 24, 1989.

18. Suzanne Brenner, "Grabbing Hold" (letter to the editor), *Chicago Tribune*, Jan. 30, 1989.

19. Glen Elsasser, "High Court Will Hear Key Abortion Case," *Chicago Tribune,* Jan. 10, 1989.

20. Michael Tackett, "Long Battle Returned Abortion to High Court," *Chicago Tribune,* Jan. 15, 1989.

21. Glen Elsasser, "High Court Lineup Changed Since Roe," *Chicago Tribune,* Jan. 15, 1989.

22. The annual "March for Life" in Washington was held on January 23, to mark the date of the *Roe v. Wade* decision. Under the headline "Pro-Lifers See Hope in Court Decision, Disappointed by Koop Letter," Samuel Lee is quoted as saying, "The right to life of the unborn was first lost in the courts: I believe that right will be finally gained back in the courts" (*New Catholic Explorer* 29, no. 2 [Jan. 27, 1989], 1 and 28).

23. George Bush's choice for Secretary of Health and Human Services was a black physician, Dr. Louis W. Sullivan, who was from Morehouse School of Medicine. His confirmation was held up for a while because of his stand in favor of the right of women to have abortions, although not at public expense. One strategy to preserve this nomination, since it regarded the only black person in the cabinet, was to "surround Dr. Sullivan with top aides opposed to legalized abortion" (Janet Caly and Elaine S. Povich, "Abortion View Unlikely to Derail Nominee," *Chicago Tribune,* Jan. 25, 1989).

24. John Lipsis, "The Challenge to Be 'Pro-Life'" (Santa Barbara, Calif.: Santa Barbara Pro-life Education, 1978), p. 1.

25. Valerie Vance Dillon, *Life in Our Hands* (Baltimore: Family Life Bureau, United States Catholic Conference, 1973).

26. George F. Dietz, "Curious Euphemisms, *Primum non nocere,*" *Newsletter of the World Federation of Doctors Who Respect Human Life, American Section* 3 (Summer 1982), 8.

27. M. Finnis, "Abortion: Legal Aspects," in Reich, ed., *Encyclopedia of Bioethics,* vol. 1, pp. 26–32.

28. "Girl, 12, Denied Abortion, Faces Neglect Charges," *Chicago Tribune,* June 11, 1982.

29. Nancy E. Degnan, "Shallow Attitude?" (letter to the editor), *Chicago Tribune,* Jan. 30, 1989.

30. See *The Choice* 14 (Winter 1989), 1.

31. Ibid., 3.

32. Bruce Buursma, "Theologian Prods the Right," *Chicago Tribune,* May 22, 1982.

33. Mary C. Segers, "Can Congress Settle the Abortion Issue?" *Hastings Center Report* 12, no. 3 (June 1982), 20–28.

34. Karl Binding and Alfred A. Hoche, *Die Freigabe der Vernichtung lebensunwerten Lebens* (Leipzig, 1920), as quoted in H. Lauter and J. E. Meyer, "Active Euthanasia Without Consent: Historical Comments on a Current Debate," *Death Education* 8 (1984), 89–98.

35. George Will, "Retarded Gain Rights," *Chicago Sun-Times,* June 27, 1982.

36. Pat Allen, "Life Said No to Jeff, but Boy, Family Didn't Listen," *Suburban Life,* Sept. 4, 1982.

37. Heymann and Hotz, "The Severely Defective Newborn," in *Decision Making,* ed. A. Swinyard.

38. Norman Fost, "Putting Hospitals on Notice," *Hastings Center Report* 12, no. 4 (Aug. 1982), 5–8.

39. The classic article in this regard is R. W. Duff and A. G. M. Campbell, "Moral and Ethical Dilemmas in the Special Care Nursery," *New England Journal of Medicine* 289 (1973), 890–894.

40. "Bill Seeks Ban on Allowing Babies to Die," *Chicago Sun-Times*, May 27, 1982.

41. Beverly Draper, "A Boy Who Will Never Be" (letter to the editor), *Chicago Sun-Times*, April 25, 1982.

42. Susan Benes, "Success with Down's Syndrome Babies" (letter to the editor), *Chicago Tribune*, April 25, 1982.

43. "Illinois May Seek Custody of Baby Denied Surgery," *St. Louis Post-Dispatch*, May 20, 1982.

44. This process is one that ought to be condoned. See "Adoptive Family Found for Baby with Birth Defect," *Chicago Tribune*, June 11, 1982.

45. Rep. John Erlenborn, Summer 1982 Opinion Survey Results: "Do You Favor Enactment of the Handicapped Infants Protection Act?" 54 percent Yes; 46 percent No.

46. Fost, "Putting Hospitals on Notice."

47. "First Person: Chicago Surgeon David McLone Describes His Fight Against 'The Worst Birth Defect,'" *Chicago Tribune Magazine*, May 9, 1982, 9, 29–30.

48. Department of Health and Human Services, "Child Abuse and Neglect Prevention Treatment Programs," *Federal Register* 50, no. 72 (April 15, 1985), 14878–15101.

49. See the CBS videotape of this argument, "Face the Nation: Baby Jane Doe/Dr. C. Everett Koop," 11/6/83.

50. Eugene Diamond, " 'Quality' vs. 'Sanctity' of Life in the Nursery," *America*, Dec. 4, 1976, 396–398.

51. Effie A. Quay, *And Now Infanticide*, 2nd ed. (Thaxton, Va.: Sun Life, 1980).

52. Gilbert Meilaender, "If This Baby Could Choose . . . ," *Linacre Quarterly* 49 (Nov. 1982), 313–314.

53. Living will legislation, "Right to Die Backgrounder," *News from the Society for the Right to Die*, Jan. 1989.

54. *In re Quinlan*, 70 N.J. 10, 44; 355 A. 2d 647; cert. den., 429 U.S. 922; 50 L. Ed. 2d 289 (N.J. 1976).

55. *Superintendent of Belchertown State School v. Saikewicz*, 373 Mass. 738; 370 NE 2d 417, 424 (Mass. 1977).

56. "Doctors Debate Right to Stop 'Heroic' Effort to Keep Elderly Alive," *Wall Street Journal*, Sept. 2, 1982.

57. "MD's Charged with Murder," *American Medical News*, Sept. 3, 1982.

58. See Eugene Diamond's review of David C. Thomasma, *An Apology for the Value of Human Life*, *Linacre Quarterly* 56, no. 1 (Feb. 1984), 89–91.

59. William May and Richard Westley, *Catholic Perspective: The Right to Die* (Chicago: Thomas More Press, 1980).

Chapter 9: Taking Responsibility for Our Technology

1. "Presbyterians Revise Nuclear War Statement," *Chicago Tribune*, June 13, 1988.

2. Jon Van, "International Plea Made on AIDS Bias," *Chicago Tribune*, June 13, 1988.

3. Deborah Dawson, "AIDS Knowledge and Attitudes: August 1988," *NCHS Advanced Data*, n. 163 (Dec. 15, 1988). Available as Department of Health and Human Services Publication No. 89–1250.

4. James D. Watkins, "Tracking AIDS: Let's Take Off the Gloves and Fight," *CUA* (Catholic University of America) *Magazine* 1, no. 1 (Winter 1989), 12–15; quote from p. 13.

5. Michael Hirsley, "Episcopalians Debate New Teaching on Sex," *Chicago Tribune*, June 12, 1988.

6. For the kinds of issues that must be covered in the future, see issues of the journal *Science, Technology, and Human Values* (Newbury Park, Calif.: Sage Publications).

7. As quoted by Timothy M. Samorajaski, "Fetus Burial" (letter to the editor), *Chicago Tribune*, Aug. 18, 1988.

8. Robert L. Johnston, "An Important Voice for Justice," *Chicago Tribune*, Dec. 5, 1988.

9. Renate Justin, "The Value History: A Necessary Family Document," *Theoretical Medicine* 8, no. 3 (Oct. 1987), 275–282.

10. Tony Mauro, "Blackmun Sees Switch on Abortion," *USA Today*, Sept. 14, 1988.

11. Sherry Roberts, "The Womb Is a Crowded Place," *USA Today*, Feb. 6, 1989.

12. Peter B. Gemma, Jr., "Protect the Unborn by Jailing Mothers," *USA Today*, Feb. 6, 1989.

13. "Hospital Study Finds Care Disparity," *Chicago Tribune*, Mar. 10, 1986. The federally funded study showed that among 13 hospitals and 5,000 patients some intensive care units saved three times as many lives as others and that the staff's attitude was more important than the technology in saving lives.

14. *Canterbury v. Spence*, 464 F. 2d 772 (D.C. Cir.), cert. den., 409 U.S. 1064, 93 S. ct. 560, 43 L. Ed. 2d 518 (1972).

15. Russell L. McIntyre, "Comment: Perspective on Medical Ethics," *Info Trends: Medicine, Law & Ethics* 4, no. 1 (Nov. 1988), 5–6. The case upon which he comments is called the Largey case, *Largey v. Rothman*, 110 N.J. 204.

16. See "Another Decision in the *Bouvia* Case," *Ethical Currents*, no. 7 (May 1986), 1–2, 7.

17. "Right-to-Die Backgrounder," *News from the Society for the Right to Die*, Jan. 1989.

18. Ibid., p. 2.

19. " 'Right-to-Die' Movement Takes Turn Toward Hard Times," *Medical Ethics Advisor* 5, no. 1 (Jan. 1989), 1–5.

20. David C. Thomasma, "Ethical Considerations in the Care of the Dying Patient and the Hospice Concept," *Linacre Quarterly* 49 (Nov. 1983), 341–345.

21. "Woman in Coma Has Abortion," *Chicago Tribune*, Feb. 12, 1989.

22. " 'Right-to-Die' Movement Takes Turn Toward Hard Times," 1–5.

23. Barbara Coleman, "Defining Life: New Issues Sidetrack Living Wills," *NRTA* (National Retired Teachers' Association) *News Bulletin* 30, no. 2 (Feb. 1989), 1, 8.

24. "Right-to-Die Backgrounder," Jan. 1989.

25. "O'Connor Case Highlights Problem of Incompetent Patient with No Living Will," *Medical Ethics Advisor* 5, no. 1 (Jan. 1989), 13–16.

26. Ibid., 15.

27. As quoted in ibid., 15–16.

28. See the chapter on family decision making for incompetent patients in Edmund D. Pellegrino and David C. Thomasma, *For the Patient's Good: The Restoration of Beneficence in Health Care* (New York: Oxford University Press, 1988), pp. 162–171.

29. The Joint Commission for the Accreditation of Hospitals mandates that each hospital have a policy for Do Not Resuscitate orders. These control cardiopulmonary resuscitation technology.

30. Fidel Davila, Eugene Boisaubin, and David Sears, "Patient Care Categories: An Approach to Do-Not-Resuscitate Decisions in a Public Teaching Hospital," *Critical Care Medicine* 14, no. 12 (1986), 1066–1067.

31. Thomas Shannon and James Walter, "The PVS Patient and the Forgoing/Withdrawing of Medical Nutrition and Hydration," *Theological Studies* 49 (1988), 623–647; and Joanne Lynn, ed., *By No Extraordinary Means: The Choice to Forgo Life-Sustaining Food and Water* (Bloomington, Ind.: Indiana University Press, 1986).

32. Kenneth Micetich, Patricia Steinecker, and David C. Thomasma, "Are Intravenous Fluids Morally Required For a Dying Patient?" *Archives of Internal Medicine* 143 (May 1983), 975–978. A good example of policy governing the dying process called "permanent vegetative state" can be found in Executive Board, American Academy of Neurology, April 21, 1988, Cincinnati, Ohio, "Position of the American Academy of Neurology on Certain Aspects of the Care and Management of the Persistent Vegetative State Patient," *Neurology* 39 (1989), 125–126. Also see Maynard Cohen, Elena Cohen, and David C. Thomasma, "Making Treatment Decisions for Permanently Unconscious Patients," in *Medical Ethics: A Guide for Health Professionals*, ed. John Monagle and David C. Thomasma (Rockville, Md.: Aspen Publications, 1988), pp. 186–192; and Joel Brumlik and David C. Thomasma, "Ethical Issues in the Treatment of Patients with a Remitting Vegetative State," *American Journal of Medicine* 77 (Aug. 1984), 373–377.

33. Pope Pius XII, "The Prolongation of Life," *The Pope Speaks* 4 (1958), 393–398.

34. This is the distinction used in court cases like *Bartling, Bouvia, Jobes, Conroy*, and others already cited in this book. For further information, see Micetich, Steinecker, and Thomasma, "Are Intravenous Fluids and Nutrition Morally Required for a Dying Patient?" pp. 975–978.

35. Edmund D. Pellegrino, "The Clinical Ethics of Pain Management in the Terminally Ill," *Hospital Formulary* 17, no. 11 (Nov. 1982), 1493–1496.

36. William M. Lamers, Jr., "Hospice Care in North America," in *Cancer,*

*Stress, and Death,* ed. Stacey B. Day, 2nd ed. (New York: Plenum Publishing Co., 1986), pp. 133–148.

37. David Himmelstein et al., "A National Health Program for the United States: A Physician's Proposal," *New England Journal of Medicine* 320, no. 2 (Jan. 1989), 102–108.

38. Victor Cohn, "Kinder, Gentler Nation? Begin with Health Care," *Chicago Sun-Times,* Feb. 12, 1989.

39. Michael Millenson, "Poll: 90% Want Key Health Care Changes," *Chicago Tribune,* Feb. 15, 1989.

40. R. C. Longworth, "Britain Offers Health Care Reform," *Chicago Tribune,* Feb. 1, 1989.

41. Marjorie Hope and James Young, "Resuscitating U.S. Health Care," *Chicago Tribune,* April 28, 1988.

42. "Group Urges Tax Aid for Long-Term Care," *Chicago Tribune,* Jan. 10, 1989.

43. "Will the Public Support Health Care Rationing?" *Hospitals* 62 (May 5, 1988), 79; and Michael Weinstein, "Pros and Cons of National Health Insurance," *American College of Physicians Observer* 8, no. 5 (May 1988), 18.

44. Cory Franklin, M.D., "A Safety Net in Need of Repair," *Chicago Tribune,* Sept. 15, 1988.

45. Joan Beck, "Patients Could Gain from These Tools of Cost Containment," *Chicago Tribune,* Feb. 2, 1989.

46. John La Puma, Christine Cassel, and Holly Humphrey, "Ethics, Economics, and Endocarditis," *Archives of Internal Medicine* 148 (Aug. 1988), 1809–1811.

47. Carola Eisenberg, "It Is Still a Privilege to Be a Doctor," *New England Journal of Medicine* 314 (Apr. 24, 1986), 1113–1114.

48. Tim Friend, "Group Seeks $13B Revamp of Medicaid," *USA Today,* Feb. 17, 1989.

49. David C. Thomasma, "Advance Directives and Health Care for the Elderly," *Advance Directives in Medicine,* ed. C. Hackler, R. Moseley, and D. Vawter (New York: Praeger Publishers, 1989), pp. 93–109.

50. Edmund D. Pellegrino and David C. Thomasma, *A Philosophical Basis of Medical Practice: Toward a Philosophy and Ethic of the Healing Professions* (New York: Oxford University Press, 1981), pp. 155–169.

51. Ibid., p. 278.

52. H. Tristram Engelhardt, Jr., and Michael Rie.

53. H. Tristram Engelhardt, Jr., *The Foundations of Bioethics* (New York: Oxford University Press, 1987).

54. See Erich Loewy, review of *For the Patient's Good,* by Edmund D. Pellegrino and David C. Thomasma, "Beneficence-in-Trust," *Hastings Center Report* 19, no. 1 (Feb. 1989), 42–43.

55. Pellegrino and Thomasma, *For the Patient's Good.*

56. Robert M. Veatch, *A Theory of Medical Ethics* (New York: Basic Books, 1982).

57. David Ozar, "The Social Obligations of Health Care Practitioners," in Monagle and Thomasma, eds., *Medical Ethics,* pp. 271–283.

58. David C. Thomasma, "Ethical and Moral Issues in Access to Cancer

Care," *Cancer Cure and Cost: DRG'S and Beyond*, ed. Richard M. Scheffler and Neil C. Andrews (Ann Arbor, Mich.: Health Administration Press Perspectives, 1989), pp. 211–223.

59. David C. Thomasma, "The Quest for Organ Donations: A Theological Response," *Health Progress* 69, no. 7 (Sept. 1988), 22–24, 28.

60. Erich H. Loewy, "Personhood and Moral Worth: A Tentative Approach," *Ethics in Situ: Clinical and Situational Ethics in Honor of Joseph Fletcher* (Champaign, Ill.: University of Illinois Press, forthcoming).

61. See Edmund D. Pellegrino and David C. Thomasma, *Medicine, Religion, and Moral Pluralism* (New York: Continuum, forthcoming).

62. Laurence O'Connell, "The Preferential Option for the Poor and Health Care in the United States," Monagle and Thomasma, *Medical Ethics*, pp. 306–313.

63. Stephen Miles, "When Medical Technology Replaces Caregiving," *Chicago Tribune*, Feb. 17, 1989. Miles was a consultant for the family of Sidney Greenspan, who had suffered a stroke, was unresponsive, and had given advance directives to his family that he would not have wanted to live in this condition. The family was defending their right to speak about his wishes and have them honored before the Illinois Supreme Court in January and February of 1989.

64. Carla Carwile, "Reclaiming Rightful Power," *Frontlines* 5, no. 3 (Dec. 1988), 1, 3.

65. See, in this regard, "Enhancing Personal Autonomy of Elderly Individuals in Long Term Care," *Phase II Report* (Park Ridge, Ill.: Retirement Research Foundation, 1989).

66. Eugene Stead, Jr., "Unsolved Issues in Medicine: Geriatrics as a Case in Point" *Journal of the American Geriatrics Society* 30 (1982), 231.

67. Fenella Rouse, "Legal and Ethical Guidelines for Physicians in Geriatric Terminal Care," *Geriatrics* 43, no. 8 (Aug. 1988), 69–75.

68. Hastings Center Staff, *Guidelines on the Termination of Life-Sustaining Treatment and the Care of the Dying* (Bloomington, Ind.: Indiana University Press, 1988).

69. Office of Technology Assessment, *Life-Sustaining Technologies and the Elderly* (Washington, D.C.: U.S. Government Printing Office, July 1987).

70. A. R. Somers, "Long-Term Care for the Elderly and Disabled," *New England Journal of Medicine* 307 (1982), 221–226.

71. David C. Thomasma, "Freedom, Dependency, and the Care of the Very Old," *Journal of the American Geriatrics Society* 32 (1984), 906–914.

72. M. Komrad, "A Defence of Medical Paternalism: Maximising Patient's Autonomy," *Journal of Medical Ethics* 9 (1983), 8–11.

73. David C. Thomasma, "Geriatric Ethics," *Journal of the American Geriatrics Society* 36, no. 10 (Oct. 1988), 959–960.

74. William May, "Who Cares for the Elderly?" *Hastings Center Report* 12, no. 6 (Dec. 1982), 31–37.

75. Thomasma, "Freedom, Dependency, and the Care of the Very Old," 906–914.

76. David C. Thomasma, "Keeping Faith with Incompetent Patients," unpublished manuscript.

77. James Birren and Candice Stacey, "Paradigms of Aging: Growth Ver-

sus Decline," in *Ethics and Aging*, ed. James E. Thornton and Earl R. Winkler (Vancouver: University of British Columbia Press, 1988), pp. 54–72.

78. Peggy Eastman, "New Role for Older Workers," *NRTA News Bulletin*, 30, no. 1 (Jan. 1989), 1, 12.

79. J. A. Barondess, et al., "Clinical Decision-Making in Catastrophic Situations: The Relevance of Age," *Journal of the American Geriatrics Society* 36, no. 10 (1988), 919–937.

80. John C. Bennett, "Ethical Aspects of Aging: Justice, Freedom, and Responsibility," in Thornton and Winkler, eds., *Ethics and Aging*, pp. 41–53.

81. Muriel Gillick, "Is the Care of the Chronically Ill a Medical Prerogative?" *New England Journal of Medicine* 310, no. 3 (Jan. 19, 1984), 190–193.

82. An example of the role of nurses acting as consultants to caregivers of the aged is Journeywell, a consultation and training program in Minnesota. As the program brochure explains: "Providing care for individuals who are very frail, seriously ill or dying, is very demanding. The extent of those demands is finally being recognized as a major concern—not only by caregivers and their families but by health care administrators, legislators, and corporate employers."

83. See the entire issue of *Generations* 12, no. 5 (Fall 1988), for a thorough investigation of this need.

84. Birren and Stacey, "Paradigms," p. 67.

85. Somers, "Long-Term Care," 221–226.

86. Joseph Fletcher, "Ethics and Old Age," *Update* 4, no. 1 (1988), 2–5.

87. Ronald Cranford and Evelyn Van Allen, "The Implications and Applications of Institutional Ethics Committees," *American College of Surgeons Bulletin* 70, no. 6 (June 1985), 19–24.

88. Michael Weinstein, "Ethics Committees Changing Medical Habits," *American College of Physicians Observer* 8, no. 11 (Dec. 1988), 1, 14.

89. "Nursing Homes Join Ethics Committee Bandwagon," *Hospital Ethics* 4, no. 5 (Sept.-Oct. 1988), 5–7.

90. David C. Thomasma, "The Range of Euthanasia," *Bulletin of the American Academy of Surgeons* 73 (Aug. 1988), 3–13.

91. Daniel Callahan, "Terminating Treatment: Age as a Standard," *Hastings Center Report* 17, no. 5 (Oct.–Nov. 1987), 21–25.

92. Fletcher, "Ethics and Old Age," 4.

93. Joseph Fletcher, "Medical Resistance to the Right to Die."

94. Ibid., 679.

95. Ibid., 679–680.

96. Howard Brody, "Ethics in Family Medicine: Patient Autonomy and the Family Unit, *Journal of Family Practice* 17 (1983), 975.

97. Jack Siebe, "Are Health Providers Still Patients' Chief Advocates?" *Physician Executive* 13 (Sept.-Oct. 1987), 23–25.

98. Gene H. Stollerman, "Decisions to Leave Home," *Journal of the American Geriatric Society* 36 (1988), 375–376.

99. David C. Thomasma, "Quality-of-Life Judgments, Treatment Decisions, and Medical Ethics," *Clinics in Geriatric Medicine* 2 (1986), 17–27.

100. Sophie Kramer, "The Gap Between Ethical Principle and Practice," *American College of Physicians Observer* 8 (April 1988), 20–21.

101. American College of Physicians, "Comprehensive Functional Assessment for Elderly Patients," *Annals of Internal Medicine*, Feb. 1988, as reported in *Senior Medical Review* 2, no. 2 (April 1988), 1.

102. See *Senior Medical Review* 2, no. 2 (April 1988), 1.

103. Lynn, *By No Extraordinary Means.*

104. D. Radcliffe, "Expanding the Armamentarium: Why Most Primary-care MDs Don't Screen for Hearing Loss—and Why They Should," *Hearing Journal*, July 1987, 7–12.

105. National Institutes of Health Consensus Development Conference Statement, "Differential Diagnosis of Dementing Diseases" (Washington D.C.: U.S. Department of Health and Human Services, Public Health Service, National Institutes of Health, 6; July 6–8, 1987), 1–7; C. H. Winograd and L. F. Jarvik, "Physician Management of the Demented Patient," *Journal of the American Geriatrics Society* 34 (1986), 295–308; and G. Warshaw, "Management of Cognitive Impairment in the Elderly," *New Developments in Medicine* 1 (Sept. 1986), 40–53.

106. James Childress and Mark Siegler, "Metaphors and Models of Doctor-Patient Relationships," *Theoretical Medicine* 6 (1984), 17–29; and "Living Will Invites Patient-Physician Dialogue," *Frontlines* 2 (1985), 1.

107. David C. Thomasma, "The Range of Euthanasia," *Bulletin of the American College of Surgeons* 73, no. 8 (Aug. 1988), 4–13.

108. Dr. Stein Husebo explicitly asks himself this question, examines some of the most powerful cases with which he has been associated, and concludes, "I emphasize, however, that in a very few situations, active euthanasia will be a caring thing for doctors to do" ("Is Euthanasia a Caring Thing to Do?" *Journal of Palliative Care* 4, nos. 1 and 2 [1988], 111–114; quote from 113–114). By contrast, Kenneth MacKinnon considers active euthanasia a copout ("Active Euthanasia: A 'Cop-out'?" *Journal of Palliative Care* 4, nos. 1 and 2 [1988], 110).

109. Robert Jay Lifton, *The Nazi Doctors: Medical Killing and the Psychology of Genocide* (New York: Basic Books, 1986).

110. Joseph Cardinal Bernardin, "Euthanasia: Ethical and Legal Challenge," address to the center for Clinical Medical Ethics, University of Chicago Hospital, May 26, 1988, 16.

111. Bernardin, "Euthanasia," 14.

112. Anonymous, "It's Over, Debbie," *Journal of the American Medical Association* 259 (1988), 272.

113. Marcia Angell, "Euthanasia," *New England Journal of Medicine* 319, no. 20 (Nov. 17, 1988), 1348–1350.

114. Eric Cassell, "The Nature of Suffering and the Goals of Medicine," *New England Journal of Medicine* 306, no. 11 (Mar. 18, 1982), 639–645.

115. Marion Dolan, "Controlling Pain in a Personal Way," *Thanatos* 5 (Winter 1982), 5.

116. Marcia Angell, "The Quality of Mercy," *New England Journal of Medicine* 306, no. 2 (Jan. 14, 1982), 98–99; "Who Should Teach Pain to Medical Students?" *Pain Management* 4, no. 2 (Sept. 1988), 2, 4; and E. A.

Mohide, J. A. Royle, M. Montemuro, et al., "Assessing the Quality of Cancer Pain," *Journal of Palliative Care* 4, no. 3 (1988), 9–15.

117. John C. Liebeskind and Ronald Melzack, "The International Pain Foundation: Meeting a Need for Education in Pain Management," *Journal of Pain and Symptom Management* 3, no. 3 (Summer 1988), 131–132.

118. Cassell, "The Nature of Suffering."

119. Eric Cassell, "Life as a Work of Art," *Hastings Center Report* 14 (Oct. 1984), 35–37.

120. Cicely M. Saunders, "Spiritual Pain," *Journal of Palliative Care* 4, no. 3 (1988), 29–32.

121. Health and Public Policy Committee, American College of Physicians, "Drug Therapy for Severe, Chronic Pain in Terminal Illness," *Annals of Internal Medicine* 99 (1983), 870–873; Daniel Goleman, "Physicians Said to Persist in Undertreating Pain and Ignoring the Evidence," *New York Times*, Dec. 31, 1987; and "Judge Urges Allowing Medicinal Use of Marijuana," *New York Times*, Sept. 7, 1988.

122. James Walter, "The Meaning of Quality of Life Judgments in Contemporary Roman Catholic Medical Ethics," *Louvain Studies* 13 (1988), 195–208.

123. Cicely M. Saunders, "The Evolution of the Hospices," in *The History of the Management of Pain*, ed. R. Mann (Park Ridge, N.J.: Parthenon Publishing Co., 1988), pp. 167–178.

124. Ibid., p. 167.

125. Erich Loewy, "Communities, Self-Causation and the Natural Lottery," *Social Science in Medicine* 26, no. 11 (1988), 1133–1139.

126. National Institutes of Health, "The Integrated Approach to the Management of Pain," 6, no. 3.

127. Arthur Dyck, *On Human Care* (Nashville, Tenn.: Abingdon, 1977).

Chapter 10: A Life-Affirming Society

1. Robert Hudson, "How Real Is Our Reverence for Life?" *Prism*, June 1975, 19–21, 58–59.

2. Melody Beattie, *Co-Dependent No More* (Center City, Minn.: Hazelden Foundation, 1987).

3. Bruce Buursma, "Mentally Impaired Receive New Ministry," *Chicago Tribune*, Oct. 16, 1982.

4. Ibid.

5. "Lebanon Seeks Pullout," *Chicago Tribune*, Oct. 19, 1982.

6. "Hospitals Put New Limits on Late Abortions," *Chicago Tribune*, Oct. 19, 1982.

7. Curtis Bill Pepper, "Denton Cooley: Success Runs in His Veins," *Chicago Tribune*, Oct. 19, 1982.

8. Søren Kierkegaard, *Either/Or*, tr. Walter Lowrie, 2 vols. (Princeton, N.J.: Princeton University Press, 1944).

9. Richard Westley, *What a Modern Catholic Believes About the Right to Life* (Chicago: Thomas More Press, 1973), pp. 73–103.

10. Erich Maria Remarque, *All Quiet on the Western Front*, tr. A. W. Wheen (Boston: Little, Brown, & Co., 1929).

11. Studs Terkel, *The Good War: An Oral History of World War Two* (New York: Pantheon Books, 1984).

12. Andrew Griffin and David C. Thomasma, "Triage and Critical Care of Children," *Theoretical Medicine* 4 (1983), 136–137.

13. Jürgen Habermas, *Knowledge and Human Interests,* tr. Jeremy J. Shapiro (Boston: Beacon Press, 1981).

14. Hans Jürgen Schulz, *Jesus in His Time* (Philadelphia: Fortress Press, 1971).

15. In this, I criticize myself in "A Contextual Grid for Medical Ethics," *Journal of Medical Ethics.* See *American Academy of Religion Abstracts* (Minneapolis: Scholar's Press, 1979), pp. 117–118.

16. Albert R. Jonsen and Stephen Toulmin, *The Abuse of Casuistry: A History of Moral Reasoning* (San Francisco: University of California Press, 1988).

17. Congregation for the Doctrine of the Faith, *Instruction, on Respect for Human Life in Its Origin and on the Dignity of Procreation* (Vatican City: Polyglot Press, 1987).

18. In this regard, see Mary Williams's response to the charge that prolifers are single-issue persons. She cites the large number of persons who do get involved in hospice, day care, against abuse, war, and other human life issues (Mary Williams, "Child Abuse" [letter to the editor], *Chicago Tribune,* Feb. 13, 1989).

19. Pope Pius XII, "The Prolongation of Life," *The Pope Speaks* 4 (1958), 393–398.

20. Paul Ramsey, *Ethics at the Edges of Life: Medical and Legal Intersections* (New Haven, Conn.: Yale University Press, 1978).

21. Robert M. Veatch, *A Theory of Medical Ethics* (New York: Basic Books, 1982).

22. Paul Ramsey, *The Patient as Person: Exploration in Medical Ethics* (New Haven, Conn.: Yale University Press, 1970).

23. Oscar Cullmann, *Jesus and the Revolutionaries* (New York: Harper & Row, 1970).

24. David C. Thomasma, "Ethical and Legal Issues in the Care of the Elderly Cancer Patient," *Clinics in Geriatric Medicine* 3 (August 1987), 541–547.

25. Kenneth Micetich and David C. Thomasma, "Avoiding Quality of Life Judgments: Medical Indications," in draft.

26. Gilbert Meilaender, "If This Baby Could Choose . . . ," *Linacre Quarterly* 49 (Nov. 1982), 313–314.

27. Ramsey, *Ethics at the Edges of Life.*

28. Benedict M. Ashley, O.P., and Kevin D. O'Rourke, O.P., *Health Care Ethics: A Theological Analysis,* 2nd ed. (St. Louis: Catholic Health Association, 1982).

29. Alexander Capron, "Autonomy and Community," *Frontlines* 5, no. 3 (Dec. 1988), 7, 10.

30. David C. Thomasma, "Commitment and Tolerance," *Health Progress* 69, no. 9 (Nov. 1988), 56, 59.

31. Sidney Callahan, "Persuasion and Change," *Health Progress* 69, no. 9 (Nov. 1988), 57–59.

32. Charles Fried, *Right and Wrong*, (Cambridge, Mass.: Harvard University Press, 1979).

33. John Stuart Mill, *On Liberty*, ed. C. V. Shields (Indianapolis: Bobbs-Merrill Co., 1956).

34. Stephen Toulmin, "The Tyranny of Principles," *Hastings Center Report* 11, no. 6 (Dec. 1981), 31–39.

35. John Dewey and James Tufts, *Ethics* (New York: Henry Holt & Co., 1908).

36. Nicholas Rescher, *Unpopular Essays on Technological Progress* (Pittsburgh: University of Pittsburgh Press, 1980).

37. Westley, *What a Modern Catholic Believes*.

38. Ibid.

39. Alex Comfort, *What Is a Doctor?* (Philadelphia: George F. Stickley Co., 1980), ch. 6.

40. Habermas, *Knowledge and Human Interests*.

41. Hans Jonas, "Commentary: Response to James Gustafson," in *Knowing and Valuing: The Search for Common Roots*, ed. H. Tristram Engelhardt, Jr., and Daniel Callahan (Hastings-on-Hudson, N.Y.: Hastings Center, 1980), pp. 203–217.

42. Pierre Teilhard de Chardin, *The Phenomenon of Man* (New York: Harper & Row, 1965).

43. Peter Singer, *Animal Liberation* (New York: Avon Books, 1977).

44. Diana T. Meyers, *Inalienable Rights: A Defense* (New York: Columbia University Press, 1985), p. 116.

45. Peter Singer, "Not for Humans Only: The Place of Nonhumans in Environmental Issues," in *Ethics, Theory and Practice*, ed. Manuel Velasquez and Cynthia Rostankowski (Englewood Cliffs, N.J.: Prentice-Hall, 1985), p. 479.

46. Morton Winston, "Species Membership and Moral Standing," *Contemporary Philosophy* 12, nos. 5 and 6 (Winter 1988), 20–23.

47. David C. Thomasma and Edmund D. Pellegrino, "Philosophy of Medicine as Source for Medical Ethics," *Metamedicine* (now *Theoretical Medicine*) 2 (1981), 5–11.

48. Edward Schillebeeckx, *God, the Future of Man*, tr. N. D. Smith (New York: Sheed & Ward, 1968).

49. Lewis Yablonsky, *Robopaths: People as Machines* (New York: Pelican Books, 1972).

50. "Idaho Abortion Bill is Vetoed," *Chicago Tribune*, March 31, 1990.

51. Charles M. Madigan, "Poll Finds Surprises on Economy, Abortion," *Chicago Tribune*, Mar. 30, 1990.

52. Daniel J. Lehmann, "Bernardin on Abortion, Pols," *Chicago Sun-Times*, Mar. 21, 1990.

53. Barbara Brotman, "Milwaukee Archbishop Opens Abortion Dialogue," *Chicago Tribune*, Mar. 30, 1990.

54. "Priests Arrested at Anti-Nuclear, Pro-Life Protests on Same Day," *Joliet Catholic*, Feb. 2, 1990.

55. "Churches Shift on Abortion," *Chicago Tribune*, Aug. 4, 1989.

# Index